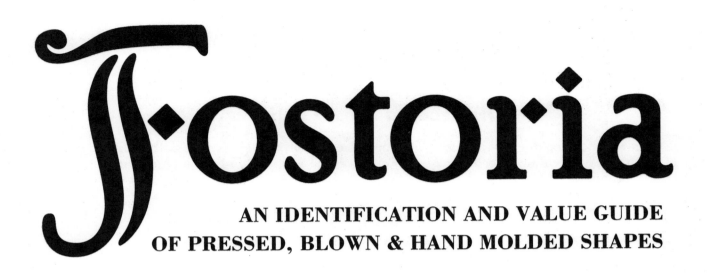

AN IDENTIFICATION AND VALUE GUIDE
OF PRESSED, BLOWN & HAND MOLDED SHAPES

Ann Kerr

COLLECTOR BOOKS
A Division of Schroeder Publishing Co., Inc.

Searching For A Publisher?

We are always looking for knowledgeable people considered to be experts within their fields. If you feel that there is a real need for a book on your collectible subject and have a large comprehensive collection, contact us.

COLLECTOR BOOKS
P.O. Box 3009
Paducah, Kentucky 42002-3009

Cover design by Beth Summers
Book design by Beth Ray and Terri Stalions
Copy editing by Rose Volkholz

Additional copies of this book may be ordered from:

COLLECTOR BOOKS
P.O. Box 3009
Paducah, Kentucky 42002-3009

or

Ann Kerr
P.O. Box 437
Sidney, OH 45365

@$24.95. Add $2.00 for postage and handling.

Table of Contents

⋖⟹ Acknowledgments ⟸⋗

My study and writing on Fostoria Glass has been supported and encouraged by many friends, all students of glass and most more experienced than I. We shared common interests.

In the late 1970's I met a fellow collector who was a buyer in the china and glass department of what was then the Rike-Kumler Company in Dayton, Ohio. Recognizing my need for documentation, he gave me back-dated catalogs, old advertising material and loaned me his loose-leaf up-to-date catalog which Fostoria furnished its retailers. With that information, I wrote a series of articles on Fostoria Glass for *The Glaze* and for the *Glass Review*, collector periodicals of the 1970's. I had asked The Fostoria Glass Company's permission to use this material and to write the articles as proposed. Permission to do so had been readily given me by marketing director David Young and by David Dalzell, president of the company. That information and that support, important then, has been extended to this work.

Writer-friends encouraged me as my involvement with my writing continued. Gail Krause, recognized as a glass expert, told me early and late that I had "a book or two" in my materials. Roserita Ziegler and Gwen Shumpert, already established writers on glass, were early supporters as I studied. They remain great teachers and friends.

As the concept of this book took shape, no one was more involved and supportive than Mike Baker, past president of the Fostoria Glass Society, glass student, enthusiast, conservator, friend. Calls early and late to Mike always brought good counsel and he shared his files as quickly as his friendship.

Blanche Younger, a life-long friend of Fostoria glass and one of my first Moundsville friends, has been willing to help where she could. She threw open her cupboards for items to picture and gave me coffee with good conversation, something I look forward to when I plan a trip to West Virginia. All Fostoria collectors are indebted to Blanche, for she has been active in the Fostoria Glass Society from the beginning, helping where she is needed, as is her way.

Of Moundsville, West Virginia, natives, no one is more expert on the Fostoria animals and figurals than are Bob and Angelana Clark. They shared information generously and allowed me to picture things from their extensive and varied collection.

Their pricing information was very important for they are well acquainted with the local Moundsville price/rarity relationship, but I also see them at many major eastern shows and sales. They are in a position to see pricing from several viewpoints.

Jerry Gallagher and Randy Supplee, glass researchers and students of handmade glass, have extensive files, and they were generous in opening them to me, sharing photos and pricing which I would not have otherwise obtained. The catalogs shown in this book are complete, loaned to me by them, and show information not before presented. Such original material adds much to our recognition and understanding of Fostoria's early production.

Gary Schneider's extensive files and ready offerings were equally important. His pricing is reflected, especially where older pressed glass items are shown. Hands-on experience augmented by extensive records offered by Gary has been important to this work. His quick recognition that Fostoria glass enthusiasts needed a broad base-line format with all inclusive line information has reflected collectors' desire for complete and up-to-date information.

Those who helped with pricing for this book did not always agree on values, but they readily agreed to participate in the process of evaluation. No one to whom I turned refused. Each made an important, sometimes unique contribution which I appreciate. Mike Baker, Beverley Hanson, Angelana and Bob Clark, Michael

Krumme, Helen and Jim Gallaher, Jerry Gallagher, Gary Schneider, Gene Loveland: all these I am able to name for you, but many others also contributed. I drew heavily from advertising pricing found in antique periodicals, allowing a broader sampling than would have been possible otherwise.

I join with many others who are indebted to the Schroeder family for the interest and insight they have shown repeatedly as they make research available to the collecting world.

David Dalzell and David Gerlach, President of Lancaster Colony, were generous with their support. Without that no such study could have been made.

Ann Kerr
1993

⊷⇒ Dedication ⇐⊶

This book is dedicated to those friends of Fostoria who met and formed the Fostoria Glass Society of America in June of 1980. At that time, I had been writing articles on Fostoria glass and fellow writers had encouraged me to find what interest existed in forming a national Fostoria Glass collectors' group. I placed advertisements in the antique trade papers as well as the Moundsville, West Virginia, paper, drew up a tentative constitution and by-laws and *waited*.

On June 24 glass enthusiasts from across the country joined local Moundsville people to meet for three days, wording, rewording, writing and rewriting until all were satisfied that we had recorded a constitution and by-laws which would serve a national organization. We elected officers and directors. None of us could lay claim to being "experts on Fostoria Glass," but we all shared common enthusiasm and goals: we hoped to found a museum of Fostoria Glass, and we dedicated our efforts to disseminating information about Fostoria Glass so that we and others could learn more about it.

Company officials and glass-knowledgeable townspeople joined us as we made our beginning and each of us, as we were able, assumed what responsibility we could to support this new national organization, The Fostoria Glass Society of America. I was very proud to be named the first coordinator and president, serving later as a member of the board of directors.

All of the founding members have cause to be proud of the beginning we made. They remain special to the organization, special to me. Their friendships have enriched my life. I dedicate this to their efforts.

Mike Baker, Jerry Barnett, Georgiana L. Beach, Hugh R. Buzzard, Hugh Buzzard Sr., Ed Cheesman, David B. Dalzell, Dallas E. Duer, Nancy and Troy Gedden, Austin and Shirley Hartsock, Georgann and Jim Hemry, Gail Krause, William S. Litman, Frank and Milbra Long, Betty and Bill Losch, Eugene and Margaret McPeek, Patrick McGrain, Joanne D. Parker, Alfred and Elsa Philcrantz, Charles Shaw, Bernice Shoemaker, Gwen and Billy Shumpert, Ruth Suter Stanley, B.N. Suter, Del Templin, Charles and Zeta Todd, Bill Tumblin, David Young, Blanche Younger, Roserita and Henry Ziegler.

Introduction

This Volume I of *Fostoria: an Identification and Value Guide* covers the pressed, hand blown and hand molded production of the Fostoria Glass Company as it applies to the Formal Dinnerware lines, the less complete Casual Dinnerware lines and the Giftware lines which fall into those descriptions. Items with self detail or the adaptation of banding are included with only a few exceptions. Information on older pressed lines has not been fully documented and the etched, carved, and cut lines are outside the scope of this study. We expect to cover those in a second volume.

These listings are presented in as nearly an alphabetical order as possible. That has been a difficult position to assume and maintain since the Fostoria Company did not always use alphabetical listings in their records and sales materials, sometimes using a format more meaningful to marketing requirements. The intent of this study is to show each pattern, line and decoration, with item listings presented in entirety. Each line, pattern, as well as design and decoration, is presented as an entire unit with dates, colors, and cross referencing information noted. This approach is taken in order to present a quick research tool, a broad background upon which further study may be based.

Numbers are primary to line, decoration, and pattern identification and those are included here along with corresponding names. Measurements follow each item and item number and they remain correct with only small fractional differences allowed for mold changes, minor manufacturing changes or variances which collectors may make in considering handles, footed items and the like. Blown ware measurements are as true as hand work allowed. In handmade glass exactness is desirable and Fostoria achieved that exactness with few exceptions. Every effort has been made to achieve accuracy and completeness in transcribing numbers in these listings and errors found are probably the fault of the writer, in spite of good intentions. Proofreading a docu-

ment with such number detail is very difficult. The reference value of these numbers is important and a personal experience underscores that. Recently I came upon a small ashtray; "Mayfair," I told myself at once. "Camphor Glass," the seller identified it. To myself I asked if it could be Silver Mist treatment on a piece of Mayfair. The price was right and, at home, with numbers before me, I was able to check the Mayfair ashtray number by description, turn to the Silver Mist listings and the pieces quickly fell together. The ashtray from the Mayfair line had been lifted out, treated with Silver Mist and listed as a giftware item. Without the Mayfair number, my guess would have been a guess.

Fostoria's numbering system is a complicated study but collectors will agree that numbers are important, especially when we consider that 100 or so of their etchings, carvings, and cuttings appear on Baroque, Century, Fairfax, Mayfair and Lafayette, all self detailed plain patterns.

Try not to be overwhelmed by the numbers here. They will guide your search in many ways. Some duplication will be found in the names of lines, patterns, designs, and decorations. Over such an extended production time, a name, found to be popular, was often used again after the original line was discontinued, resulting in some confusion for today's collectors. Numbers are even more important in those instances. Few of these troublesome names exist but readers should be aware of them.

It has been difficult to separate dinnerware, casual dinnerware and gift lines. Very generally, we have included a line with stems into the dinnerware section. That has been an arbitrary position taken solely for the point of separating gifts from dinnerware. If you cannot locate an item in the dinnerware section, turn to the gift section of this book. Crossovers between these groups were intentional marketing duplications, with items frequently listed in more than one position in company materials, presenting an item as both a dinnerware item and a gift suggestion. In this book such duplication has been limited, but there remain important items used in one or more listings. We have attempted to cross reference in those cases.

Every effort has been made to assign uniform item prices to items which may be found in the dinnerware sections as well as the giftware section. That has not been possible in every case. A reissue with only slight variation, a different color — these and other factors alter pricing.

Another word on numbers must be included. Prices listed here do not represent absolute values and neither the writer nor the publisher intends them to do so. Collectors and dealers across the country have generously contributed their experience in pricing each item, a mountain of work. Each readily agreed to help with this project. Their pricings have been averaged after casting out the highest and the lowest price for each item. You may or may not find them to be realistic in your area, or for your collection. Pricing here is meant to be general, not specific.

Some contributor points of interest not reflected in the pricing are significant to our study. Most had little experience with older pattern glass lines and the figures presented here represent a smaller number of contributors than do the figures in the greater body of the work. Milk glass, most agreed, was not as popular today as it has been in the past and lower prices reflect that trend. Smoking items, less useful with fewer smokers, are not as valued as they have been in the past. Wine glasses in older lines were smaller than later wines and today's larger glasses are more popular today than the older wines were in their day, even doing double duty holding chilled desserts. America's habits have changed. Several contributors pointed out that plain blown stemware, with a sameness that makes it difficult to recognize, often goes unidentified as Fostoria glass. In those cases, value is low. Most felt that those values can only increase as the plain lines become recognized as the quality glass it is. Your "box-lot" of today may be tomorrow's treasure.

Prices given here are for crystal unless otherwise noted. As a general rule, color will add to

value. Where specifics are not indicated, add 25% for pastel colors, 50% for Dark Blue, Green, Ebony, Ruby and the like. Wisteria should be double the price.

Information on the older pressed glass lines has been less complete than we would like, but all information which the writer has been able to confirm is presented here. A significant addition has come our way late in the research for this writing, however. From the source files of Jerry Gallagher and Randy Supplee we have obtained three complete and very early catalogs which we show in their entirety. New information not before available to many collectors is a bonus for us all. Within our time constraints, comparative across-the-country pricing could not be completed but it seemed wise to include it here since the information adds so much to our understanding of Fostoria's early work. Included here are: Catalog #3 "Decorated Lamps" dated 1915 – 1916, #6 "By Ye Candlelight" 1909, and #5 "Silver Deposit" which appears to be part of the same series. These catalogs open up a new world of older Fostoria production.

General information important to our understanding of Fostoria glass is presented in the following section rather than in text in our encyclopedic listings. That information remains open ended and your experience as well as your findings may be additional. Your information will be welcomed, noted as updated material in the next edition.

All information presented here is taken from company advertising material and sales manuals. Line information has been drawn from catalogs, which were ever-changing. Yearly catalogs were issued, supplemental material was sent to retailers. Eastern and Western supplements were issued with regularity. Permission to use this material was given by David Dalzell, former president of Fostoria Glass, an early supporter of collector's interests. David Gerlach of Lancaster Colony Corporation also understood the collector's need to know. The interest and aid received from both have been central to this writing. The extensive research material owned by the Fostoria Glass Society of America was not available to the general membership or to me at the time of this writing.

A few remarks to those who are new collectors: In Fostoria production ground or polished bottoms are the general rule, as it is in other handmade glass. There are exceptions, however, and the absence of that quality, while meaningful, is not always an absolute in identification. However, it often narrows our search. Water clear color and brilliance are the marks of good quality handmade crystal. Placing a piece against a white background should show the absence of color. Inferior grades will show a dull or cloudy tinge. The "tinkle" sound of inferior crystal differs from the "tone" of good lead crystal.

In colored glass, richness and sparkle are to be considered. Good quality glass will show these properties and will have a luster from repeated fire polishings. Balance and symmetry of design should be considered. Shoddy, "off center" items are often of second quality and of much less value. Examine the glass for defects. Streaks and bubbles as well as overly prominent mold marks are manufacturing flaws and items with these properties are not desirable. More discrimiting collectors will reject such items. Be careful as you examine all glass. Even elegant glass may have imperfections.

The recognition of stem, handle, finial design is important as we identify glass. A pressed stem is formed separately in a mold and attached after the bowl is formed. Such a stem can add pattern, detail and other beautiful effects. Pulled stems are completely hand processed. Bowl and stem are actually pulled out of a piece of molten glass with the foot added later. Pulled stem decoration is unusual but interesting effects were sometimes achieved by the use of color. Stems used with various decorations are often the signature of the manufacturer and our recognition of them will direct our study to a special glass house, a particular line. Handles, cup handles or handles on a serving item are also research indicators.

I wish you luck as you look, rewards as you study, pleasure in your findings and the challenge of the chase as you go. The possibility of a wonderful Fostoria Glass collection remains an expectancy for us and the joy of it is a rewarding adventure.

General Information

Trade journals on August 4, 1887 brought news that the Fostoria Glass Company of Fostoria, Ohio, would break ground no later than January 1st, 1888. The townspeople, grateful for the new industry, had granted the glass company free land and had promised free gas for the furnaces. Machinery had been purchased and men were at work on molds. Experienced workers at every level of production, management, and sales were quickly employed and the enterprise seemed destined for success.

Within six months after that opening, glass bottles, shakers, utility items of all sorts were produced. At the same time, an announcement was made that one of the prettiest things in the glass world was a six light candelabra with pink holders being shown at the company's showroom in New York City. The elegance of the line did not end there, readers were told. A Princess lamp with cut foot and colored peg was also on display.

With such a beginning, it seemed unlikely that misfortune would strike, but it did, and at once. The natural gas, so vital for production, had unexpectedly run out and work could not continue on the scale which had been outlined by the officers of the company. The glass company responded almost at once with the announcement in the trade paper *China, Glass and Lamps* that the Fostoria Glass Company had been re-established in Moundsville, West Virginia, and had new lines for buyers in their showrooms. Without missing a step, or seeming to, the company had opened a new chapter in the handmade glass industry. A diverse selection of candelabra, perfume items, vanity boxes and jars, as well as cologne bottles, paperweights and sundry everyday items were soon in production. Oil lamps, many of which were hand painted, were offered. Needle etchings and blown ware followed. Pressed ware production met the highest standards for clarity, quality and good design. An important beginning had been made.

Throughout its life span, the Fostoria Glass Company enjoyed the good fortune of having the Dalzell glass family as guides. W. A. B. Dalzell, William F. Dalzell, David B. Dalzell, David Dalzell Jr., and Kenneth Dalzell all steered the company toward the highest standards of quality with diversity and excellence the primary goals. Each member of the Dalzell family added a unique contribution. Each showed resiliency, seizing every opportunity to enlarge the lines, to add variety, to add to the efficiency of the operation, to achieve excellence.

When hard times turned into the Great Depression, the Dalzells believed that a worker with part-time hours would be better off and more willing to return when times improved. This concept retained skilled workers, necessary to the production of quality hand work. Loyalty to the company was achieved and workers believed "We are in this together." A bond, a family relationship was established at the worst financial time in the century. The company stepped ahead of the industry and extended their labor practices to incorporate benefit programs for workers. The Fostoria company was the first in the industry to establish motion management as a production standard. Turning out elegant lines was made possible by experienced workers skilled beyond those of other glass houses. The size and intricacy of Fostoria's production also set the lines apart from those of other firms.

Changing with the times with attention to the needs and wishes of customers, rather than change for the sake of change, required vigilance and willingness to alter production frequently. When older pressed patterns and needle etchings fell from favor, plate etchings and master etchings were offered. When color became popular, Fostoria quickly adapted. True and extensive, Fostoria color offerings excelled those of its competition. Always in step with the day, the company made the transition from pattern to plain when the designers told us that "Less is more." When pattern once more found favor, "Nostalgia," a reissue of old intricate etchings, was offered. When social changes were made, Fostoria met the style of the day. Teas and luncheons gave way to brunches and cocktail parties and Fostoria anticipated the changes with new items added to existing lines, reflecting the needs of the times. While full dinnerware lines — Baroque, Fairfax, Mayfair and the like — were still produced, Casual lines, informal dinnerware lines filled the needs of those who would use less formal glass accessory items. Fostoria set America's tables with grace.

"Assortments" and "Collections" were established as giftware listings. Parts of old pattern glass lines were incorporated into vase assortments, smoking assortments, as many assortments as the marketing department could conceive. This practice served the company long and well.

Sales and marketing pratices were those which retailers continue to consider as standards in home furnishings. A sales force was organized to penetrate the better quality retailers across the country. Large department store accounts with tested marketing programs became the models for boutiques, small retail accounts, jewelry stores and the like.

Salesmen employed by the company sold Fostoria glass only and were supported by a barrage of national advertising. The results were, again, text-book. Fostoria retailers, arbiters of good form and usage, guided the consumer through the use of each item. A personal relationship was established between the company, the retail "advisor" and the customer. While courting the buying public as a whole, the sales program was directed specifically to the brides of the day. Each bride chose her patterns locally and those choices were kept on file, providing suggestions for pleasing gifts. Such marketing combined new sales strategy and good form. Penetration of marketing was so deep that, in many cases, there was no competition. The glass was so well placed, so personally sold, that many buyers were not aware that other handmade glass existed. Buyers were told to "buy the pattern you love" and it was suggested that delicate blown patterns complemented fine china, silver and linens while smart casual patterns were durable and practically priced for Monday through Saturday use. Perhaps, it was suggested, you needed more than one pattern. Stores were given sales manuals which featured reasons for selecting this fine product:

good taste reflected on the hostess and her family, better service than lesser quality glass, handier to use, beauty, fineness, durability, suitability, ease of care, coordination of theme in decoration, and more. Retailers kept purchasers advised on changes and alterations in their selected lines. Buyers, so alerted, could be confident that registration would apprise them of new items, discontinued items, even ominous "Matching Service Only" warnings. No other part of Fostoria's business practices was more important than this concentration on personal contact with buyers. The company used national advertising to a great extent but also issued its own magazine, called *Creating with Crystal*. Table settings and crystal arrangements in the home were suggested, colored and thematically grouped. Patterns, of course, were named.

In 1965 the Morgantown Glass Company of Morgantown, West Virginia, announced that it had been sold to the Fostoria Glass Company who would operate it as a subsidiary at the Morgantown location. Having obtained the rights to Morgantown's colors and molds, Fostoria produced Morgantown lines at that site for a time, but in 1971 the situation changed when the Morgantown site was closed permanently. After that, some items remained in Fostoria's catalog but other lines, less fortunate, were closed out at Fostoria factory outlet stores. Morgantown's legacy had added new colors and high-styled designs of undisputed quality. Neither Morgantown nor Fostoria, however, was able to make lead crystal as popular with buyers as each had hoped.

Through it all, of course, ran the threat of foreign imports. It became increasingly certain that the quality of handmade American glass could not be achieved with the competition of lower priced labor from abroad. In the end, the company was forced to sell its operation to those who could compete. In 1983 the company was sold to the Lancaster Colony Corporation who operated it at the Moundsville site, combining their own lines with limited Fostoria production. In just three years the Moundsville operation was closed and Fostoria Glass, as it had existed, came to an end. Fostoria's warehouses were thrown open and buyers raced for the remains. In addition to stock, trials, experimental items, morgue items and sales literature, many one or few of a kind items were sold at bargain sale prices. It was a hard good-bye.

In House Designers

Edgar Bottome Mold Maker/Designer
Marvin Yutzey First Design Director 1936
Robert Cecanhouger
Fernando Alvarez
Robert Grove
Fred Yehl
John Saffel
Greg Pettit
William Hoffer
William Bradford

Contract Designers
Incomplete listing

Raymond Loewy — Radiance #2700
Ben Seibel — Pebble Beach, Corsage Plum, Facet
Helen Tynell — Serendipity
George Sakier — Jamestown, Coin, Crown Collection, Candleholder #2767, Selected Colony items
James Carpenter — Art Glass items

Early Undocumented Lines
May be an incomplete listing

#500	Atlanta, 1895 Said to be similar to #956, dated 1901
#640	Cameo, 1898
#150	Captain Kid
#575	Carmen, 1897
#112	Cascade
#677	Colorado
#444	Czarina
#602	Ermine, 1898
#301	Flat Diamond Box
#501	Hartford
	Marguerite, Line number not available
#235	Olive
#576	Persian
#233	Ruth
#234	Roco
#195	Swirl, 1890
#225	Vendome
#403	Vigilant
#1225	Heavy Jewel

Marks

The earliest known labels, dating from 1901 to 1927, spelled out the word *Fostoria* in plain block lettering. In 1909 a circular label incorporating the initials *F* and *G* and *CO* in a logo style duplicated on each side of the circle was used.

In an overlapping time span with the approximate dates of 1911 – 1920 labels were white circles with black lettering showing the Fostoria initials along with a stemmed sherbet and the words *Fostoria Product*. There followed a brown oval label with the Fostoria name in white lettering. This label, used from 1924 to 1957, was followed by the familiar rectangular label with the company name written in white lettering on a red ground, bands of white and two shades of blue following. This late label has been in use since 1957 but in 1951 stems were signed with the Fostoria name etched on the base.

1920

1920 to 1957

   **1957**

Fostoria Colors

* Amber (warm, autumnal gold), 1924 – 1941
* Azure (subtle, soft blue), 1928 – 1943
  Azure Tint (light blue with suggestion of green)
  Bitter Green, Late Color
* Blue (true blue), 1924 – 1928
* Regal Blue (rich, cobalt, luxurious), 1933 – 1943
  Burgundy (deep mulberry), 1935 – 1042
* Canary (palest yellow), 1924 – 1927
  Chartreuse (bright yellow/green), Late Color
  Cinnamon (delicate brown), Late Color
* Dawn (early rose 1928), Used again in 1970 – 1980
* Ebony (lustrous black), 1924 – 1943
  Gold Tint (topaz),1938 – 1943
* Empire Green (emerald green), 1933 – 1943
  Green (soft tint), 1924 – 1941
  Honey (warm yellow), Late Color
  Iridescence (delicate shadings of mother of pearl, Spanish luster, autumn glow), Open ended dating
  Lime, Late Color
  Moss Green (soft muted green), Late Color
* Orchid (an early lavender), 1927 – 1929
  Rose (delicate pink), 1928 – 1941
  Ruby (glowing red), 1935 – 1941
  Smoke (warm grey), Late Color
  Spruce Green (black/green shade), Late Color
  Teal (blue-green), Late Color
  Topaz (earlier gold tint), 1929 – 1938
  Wisteria (delicate lavender), 1931 – 1938

*Original Colors

Additional late colors were used less frequently and, in most cases, were identifiable by names given them. Some of these were old colors or slight variations of them renamed to update lines. Many of them date from about 1951 when colored glass enjoyed renewed popularity. They may include:

Amberina	Bittersweet
Black Pearl	Crystal Ice
Dusk	Dawn
Flaming Orange	Grey
Harvest Yellow	Lemon Twist
Marine	Nutmeg

Onyx	Pink Lady
Sky Blue	Sunrise
Lilac	Taupe

Enamel Decorations

Blue Border #19
Black Border #20
Enamel and Gold #21
Blue and Gold #22
Black and Gold #23
Encrusted Gold #35
Encrusted Gold #37
Encrusted Gold—Royal #39
Encrusted Gold—Riviera #44
Tinted Band of Green, Amber, Canary, Blue with Encrusted Gold #45
Imperial Decoration—Blue and Gold #47
DuBarry—Orange and Black #48
Ebony with Orange Band #53
Antique—Crystal with various colored bands: Yellow and Black, Black and Red, Blue and Red #56
Criterion—Amber, Green #65
Hammered Silver #66
Poinsettia—Ebony glass used in gift or accessory lines #67
Saturn—Amber, Green, Blue #68
Arlington—Amber, Blue, Green #69

RARE DECORATIONS

Apple Blossom—White enamel on Regal Blue #516
Butterfly—Topaz with Black Enamel #508
Cockatoo—Ebony with gold decoration #505 7
Grape—White enamel on Regal Blue #517
Nugget—Ebony with encrusted gold #507
Polka Dot—Ebony Base, Crystal Bowl #607
Richelieu—Etched and Gold filled #515
St. Regis—Cut with Gold encrusted edging #616
Viennese—Ebony with Gold Decoration #506

These seldom seen decorations may be found on blanks from the 1930's and 1940's. The numbers shown here indicate that more decorations are still to be identified.

Centennial II Collection

The name suggests the ambiance of this collection. It was produced in 1970 to be Fostoria's contribution to our centennial celebration. Reproductions of older pressed glass were made in Ruby, Cobalt Blue or Crystal. In some instances, new numbers were assigned to the items which had been part of the original production. These new numbers apply to those items made in the Centennial Collection colors. Generally, they are the 26- 27- 28-numbers, but there are a few exceptions. Values on these new production items vary from values on original items in many cases.

Henry Ford Museum Collection

This group was introduced in 1963 for The Henry Ford Museum and was popular with those who had earlier collected Fostoria's Coin pattern and older fine pressed styles. A spirit of renewal and patriotism was afoot in America and many glass collectors expressed their interest with these period pieces. All items which you will find listed in the Gift section will be marked HFM, seldom on the bottom of the item, but at a juncture a bit higher.

President's House

This line, an Old Morgantown Guild pattern, was Jacqueline Kennedy's choice for the crystal used in the White House during John Kennedy's administration. She chose it in 1961 and it soon became the choice of many other Americans. As it was first conceived and produced, it was of clear, simple crystal, gracefully styled, drawing upon its shape for elegance. Hand crafted, mouth blown, it was made in 21 items, all crystal. Those who would choose color found it later with a clear bowl

and colored disc foot, a light touch, a delicate treatment. When Fostoria bought the Old Morgantown Guild they retained President's House as part of their production. Prestige accrued to Fostoria, as it had to Morgantown. The listing here is the line as Morgantown produced it. It is uncertain whether Fostoria continued to produce all of the items listed, but they sold the complete line at the time of purchase.

The American Pattern

No Fostoria study would be complete without underscoring the importance of Fostoria's American pattern. Its position in the annals of glass production is singular. It is, by far, the most commercially successful pattern ever produced. It remains the most sought after by collectors. To many, the American pattern is synonymous with the company name. Its practicality has put it to daily use in many homes. Its faceted beauty reflects morning sunlight as beautifully as candle light. It dresses a table for a formal occasion, and greets one at breakfast with equal propriety. Its classic qualities have made it a favorite for many years and it has set a standard by which other glass patterns could be measured.

Reproductions

The following listings were obtained from company outlet stores and may be incomplete at this writing. They will certainly be incomplete when you read them, as Lancaster Colony can be expected to enlarge their production. Purists should be aware that some of the new production is of very high quality, easily confused with original production. If age is important to you, you will need to watch retailer's listings with regularity. No values can be given to reproduced items.

American

All excellent quality, said to have been made from original molds:

Small Boat
Large Boat
Divided Boat
Salad Bowl 8"
Salad Bowl 10"
Cake Plate, Handled
Cake Plate, Footed 10"
Candle 3"
Candle 7"
Candy and Cover, Footed
Celery 10"
Centerpiece 11½"
Child's Bowl
Cookie Jar, Covered
Cups and Saucers
Hat/Topper 4"
Jelly
Jug, Quart
Muffin Tray, Handled
Mug
Nappy 4½" regular
Nappy 8" Regular
Picture Frame
Pitcher, Quart
Plate, Salad 8½"
Plate, Dinner 9½"
Punch Bowl, Small, Footed
Rose Bowl
Serving Dish Handled 9"
Torte Plate 14"
Utility Tray, Handled
Vase, Footed, Flared 6"
Vase, Bud, Both Footed and Flared 8"
Vase 10"
Vase, Sweetpea

Ruby American

Bowl 6"
Nappy 8"
Salad Bowl 10"
Torte Plate 14"
Small Punch Bowl with Low Foot
Cracker Jar

Whitehall

American molds with variations — these are of lesser quality.

Basket with Reed Handle
Sugar and Cream
Oval Bowl 10"
Divided Vegetable 10"
Bon Bon, 3 Toed
Butter and Cover, Oblong
Salt and Pepper Shakers
Pitcher 51 oz.
Candy Box and Cover
Buffet Server
Votive Candle
Centerpiece, 3 Toed Bowl

Argus

Goblet
Ice Tea
Sherbet

Bennington

Double Old Fashioned

Coin

Coins are rougher than on older items. Reproduced in Crystal, Empire Green, Blue and Ruby.

Bowl, Round 8"
Bowl, Footed 8½"
Bowl, Oval 9"
Cream
Candlesticks 4"
Candy Jar and Cover
Comport, Footed
Sugar
Urn with Lid
Wedding Bowl, Covered

Heritage

Reproduced in Crystal, Pink, Blue.

Bowl 5"
Bowl 9"
Cake Plate, Footed
Goblet
Ice Tea
Plate, Dinner 10"
Wine

Monet

Goblet

Moonstone

Goblet
Ice Tea
Wine

Stowe

Double Old Fashioned

Stratton

Double Old Fashioned

Virginia

Reproduced in Crystal, Pink, Blue, Amber.

Candlesticks
Goblet
Ice Tea
Vase
Wine

Figural

Madonna and Saint Francis in Silver Mist
Duck family in green and crystal
Sleds, medium and large sizes in crystal, green, ruby and blue
Owls, Elephants, Horse bookends in crystal and perhaps in ebony
Colts produced in the 1970's in blue and sold privately under the Fostoria label
Henry Ford Museum Candlesticks in crystal, ruby, blue

The American Bottle/ Fostoria Light Bulb Mystery

Before you, as collectors, find what seems certain to be an American Pattern Coca-Cola® bottle, examine the facts. Recently an old style Coca-Cola bottle as we have come to recognize it has been found in a pattern much like Fostoria's American pattern. The faceted pattern is at the bottom and top of the bottle, with a plain banner band in the center. A paper label may have been used in that banner space. Bottles have been found with the Coca-Cola embossed signature and with either the "Sistersville & Wheeling" bottle mark or "Greensburg, Pa. Glass Co." Not deterred, American collectors were excited and took these bottles to their hearts and collections. Bottles were said to have been sold for as much as $1000 and as little as $50. When you find one, you will have to make the determination on pricing. Bottle collectors may actually value these more than American collectors will, after reflection. At best they are look-alikes, but they do look like American.

A Mazda® light bulb has been found with an oval brown label similar to Fostoria's own brown label. The word Fostoria is written in white and surely is suggestive of the Fostoria Glass label. Its finding is recent and no research has been done but those who have seen it agree that it is interesting to consider.

Fostoria Glass Society of America

The Fostoria Glass Society of America, with membership open to all glass collectors, has now established a museum in Moundsville, West Virginia. The museum is open to the public as well as to the membership. The newsletter, *Facets of Fostoria*, is published regularly and shares detailed product information as well as society news. Quarterly meetings as well as an annual convention are held. Exhibits, auctions, and sales are featured. Collectors meet and study with others of the same interest. When social times bring collectors together, their common interests are enriched. Glass friendships develop with Fostoria once more the subject of exchanged collecting accounts.

Local study groups or chapters are organized in several other states and membership in them is open to those who join the national organization. You are invited to join the society by writing to:

Fostoria Glass Society of America
Box 826
Moundsville, WV 26041

Introducing Fostoria's
Wonderful Colors

One of the early objectives of this writing was to acquaint collectors with the beauty of the Fostoria color spectrum. Many collectors have felt comfortable with their knowledge of original colors, but there has been confusion over colors which were added over the long period of production.

In the following section and for the first time, these many colors are shown as they actually appeared on a great many lines, a presentation which could only be accomplished through the use of original sales material previously available to only a few. That material is rich with illustrations and we have included as much as has been possible given the constraints of space. Also included are photographs of glass loaned by collectors. These illustrate rarity as well as color, another need readers have expressed. Some of the company's earliest and latest work is shown in these photographs. All photographs shown have been cross referenced for your convenience. Those who collect Fostoria glass have felt that its colors are unsurpassed. All will agree that it is a "sight to behold."

From the research files of Gary Schneider and used here in dedication to the Southern California Chapter of The Fostoria Glass Society of America.

Animals and Figurals:
Polar Bear, Serendipity
Paperweight, Goldfish,
Mermaid, Goldfish, and
Cardinal.

Animals and Figurals:
Horse Bookend, Seal,
Seahorse, Sitting Deer,
Standing Deer, and Elephant.

Animals and Figurals:
Owl, Standing Colt,
Chanticleer, Sitting
Colt, Eagle Bookend.

Animals and Figurals: Pelican, Turtle (Olive), Small Rabbit (Silver Mist), Large Rabbit (Amber), #2083 Salad Dressing Bottle, Standing Squirrel, and Running Squirrel.

#4095 Loop Optic Vase, Owl, Frog, Whale, Stork, Cat, and #2496 Baroque Vase.

#2404 6" Vase, Amber Duck Family, and #4101 5½" Flower Vase.

#2510 Sun-Ray Vase, #444 Vase, #2592 Myriad Vase, #1372 Essex Violet Bouquet Holder, and #1578 Tuxedo Spooner.

#37½ Paperweight, #1118 York Berry Bowl, #2106 Vogue Finger Bowl, #112 Large Early Cascade Inkwell (undocumented line), #306 Inkwell, #112 Small Early Cascade Inkwell, #511 Celery Dip.

Victoria #183 Creamer, #1300 Drape Comport, #2700 Radiance Creamer, #1372 Essex Punch Bowl, #CO13 Colonial Prism Bowl.

#2412 Queen Anne 14"
Candle Holders and
Footed Bowl.

#1704 Rosby Punch
Bowl.

Red Bubble Ball, Santa
Claus, #1229 Frisco
Toothpick, and Mardi
Gras Cigarette Box.

Art Glass: #724 Images, #501 Impressions, unidentified item, and #727 Images.

Art Glass: #302 Interpretations, #101 Images, #313 Impressions, and #727 Images.

Art Glass: #304 Interpretations, #731 Images, #711 Impressions, and unidentified item.

American Stemware

Goblet

Low Goblet

Claret

Wine

Luncheon Goblet/ Ice Tea

Footed Tumbler

High Sherbet Regular

High Sherbet Flared

Footed Dessert

Low Sherbet Flared

Low Sherbet Regular

Sundae

Ice Tea Regular

Ice Tea Flared

Tumbler Regular

Table Tumbler

Tankard

York Double Old Fashioned

York High Ball

211-286-567-987

620

241

300

306

129

128

047

386

447

762

798

799

763

347

448

505

222

363

15

554
552
550
549
661
704
360
649
650
502
499
501
540
421
495
307
536
492

521
548
517
331
319
866
314
673-674
512
506
632
680
584
16
648
396-397
311
836

631

639

630

686
687
688
697

622

567

979

600

456

458

602

388

707

614

137

377

17

American: Fostoria's all-time popular handmolded design that gives you every glass and every accessory imaginable —including punch bowls! Crystal only.

In back: American dresser tray and two cologne bottles. In front: sugar, pin box, pin tray, puff box or hair receiver (cover missing), and glove box.

CASUAL STEMWARE

ARGUS PATTERN

Color Key:
Crystal AR 01
Cobalt Blue AR 02
Grey AR 03
Olive Green AR 04
Ruby AR 05

002   002   002   002

The original of this elegant flint glass pattern is on display in the priceless collection of Americana at the Henry Ford Museum.

073   064   089   421   550   026   002   007   063

Argus

By Special Arrangement with The Henry Ford Museum

Made in
Green
Cobalt Blue
Crystal
Ruby

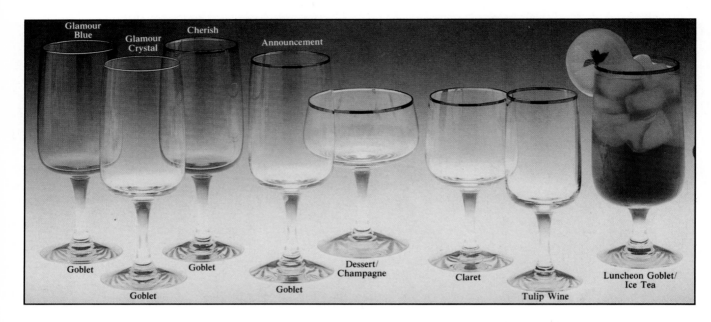

Cherish and Announcement Designs are derived from Glamour Pattern.

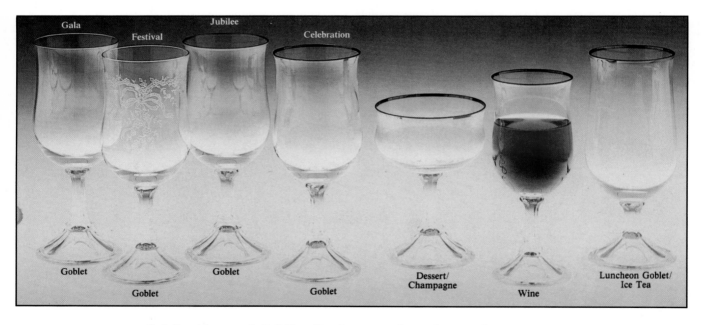

Celebration and Jubilee Designs are based on Gala Pattern.

Century Stemware and Giftware

550

549

Goblet

Sherbet

Wine

Ice Tea

350
351

211

836

540

567

707

300

316

204

650

649

512

396-397

499

622

620

306

18

Coin Glass

COIN PATTERN

Color Key:
Amber CO 02

829   326   199   326   162   799

499   448   354   673   680   652

119   114   123   179

347   453   316   189   316   381

Colonial Prism Giftware

212
568
297
649
506
620
687
688

Debutante

Goblet

Dessert/Champagne

Tulip Wine

Claret

Luncheon Goblet/
Ice Tea

Debutante

Distinction

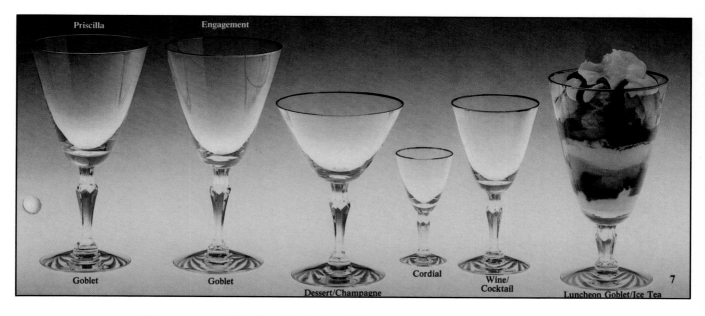

Engagement Design is derived from #6092 Priscilla Pattern.

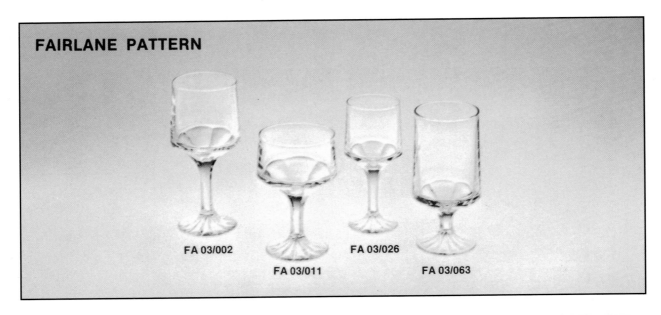

FAIRLANE PATTERN

FA 03/002

FA 03/011

FA 03/026

FA 03/063

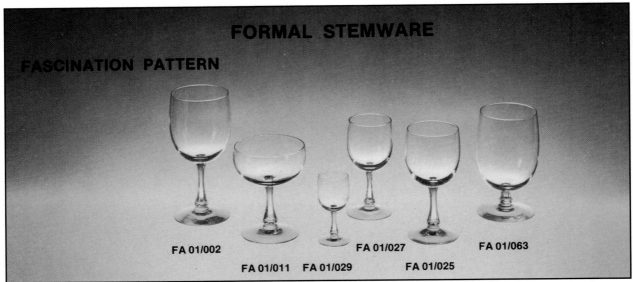

FORMAL STEMWARE

FASCINATION PATTERN

FA 01/002

FA 01/011   FA 01/029

FA 01/027

FA 01/025

FA 01/063

FESTIVE PATTERN

Color Key:
   Crystal FE 01
   Blue FE 03
   Yellow FE 02

002

002

002

063

011

025

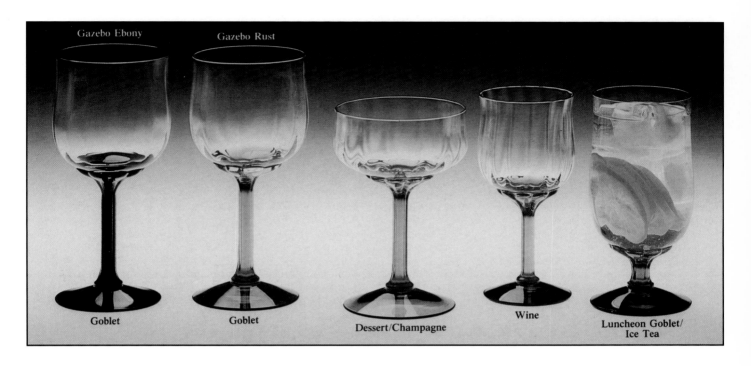

Gazebo

GLAMOUR PATTERN

Color Key:
  Grey Mist GL 04
  Blue GL 02
  Crystal GL 01
  Green Mist GL 05

Harvest (labels: Goblet, Dessert/Champagne, Magnum, Claret, Luncheon Goblet/Ice Tea)

Harvest. See also Sheraton.

Holly and Ruby Giftware

(item numbers: 312, 762, 682, 315, 567, 211, 506, 549, 584)

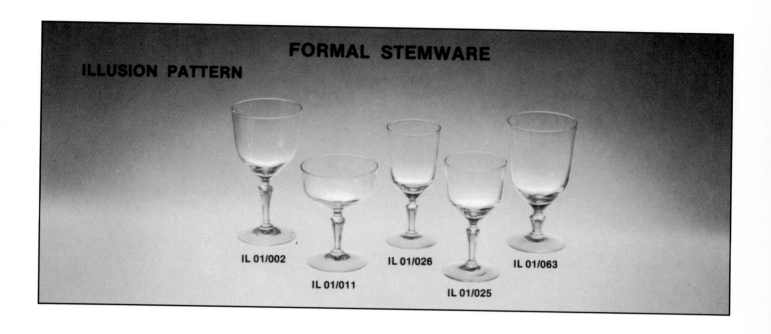

FORMAL STEMWARE

ILLUSION PATTERN

IL 01/002

IL 01/011

IL 01/026

IL 01/025

IL 01/063

Silhouette

Invitation

Goblet

Goblet

Dessert/
Champagne

11 oz. Wine

Tulip Wine

Claret

Brandy

Luncheon Goblet/
Ice Tea

Invitation Design is based on Silhouette Pattern.

Jamestown

JAMESTOWN PATTERN
No. 2719 Line
Made in Blue, Green, Amber, Pink,
Brown and Ruby as shown below.

				Retail Price Ea.
2719/2	9½ oz. Goblet	All Colors Except Ruby		$ 4.50
			Ruby	4.75
	Height 5¾ in.			
2719/7	6½ oz. Sherbet	All Colors Except Ruby		4.50
			Ruby	4.75
	Height 4¼ in.			
2719/26	4 oz. Wine	All Colors Except Ruby		4.50
			Ruby	4.75
	Height 4⅜ in.			
2719/63	11 oz. Luncheon Goblet/Ice Tea			
		All Colors Except Ruby		4.50
			Ruby	4.75
	Height 6 in.			
2719/64	12 oz. Tumbler	All Colors Except Ruby		4.25
			Ruby	4.50
	Height 5⅛ in.			
2719/88	5 oz. Footed Juice	All Colors Except Ruby		4.50
			Ruby	4.75
	Height 4¾ in.			
2719/211	10 in. Salad Bowl	Crystal		9.50
	Height 3¾ in.			
2719/286	10 in. 4-Pc. Salad Set	Crystal		22.00
	Height 4½ in.			
2719/550	8 in. Plate	All Colors Except Ruby		4.75
			Ruby	5.00
2719/567	14 in. Torte Plate	Crystal		10.75
2719/653	Shaker & Chrome Top "A"	Crystal		3.00
		Blue, Green, Amber, Pink, or Brown		3.25
	Height 3½ in.			
2719/679	Footed Sugar	Crystal		4.50
		Blue, Green, Amber, Pink, or Brown		4.75
	Height 3½ in.			
2719/681	Footed Cream	Crystal		4.50
		Blue, Green, Amber, Pink, or Brown		4.75
	Height 4 in.			

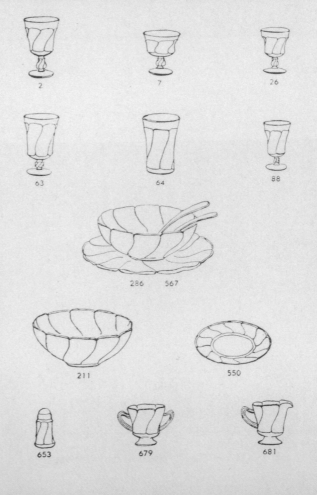

2   7   26

63   64   88

286   567

211   550

653   679   681

Jamestown
Made in
Green
Blue
Brown
Ruby
Amber
Pink

Jamestown Pink

Goblet

Sherbet

Footed
Juice

Wine

Luncheon Goblet/
Ice Tea

Ruby
Goblet

Amber
Goblet

Blue
Goblet

Brown
Goblet

Jamestown: Fostoria's sturdy hand-molded traditional design. In crystal and the high-style colors: amethyst, blue, pink, green, amber, brown, ruby.

Kimberly with coordinating Monarch barware.

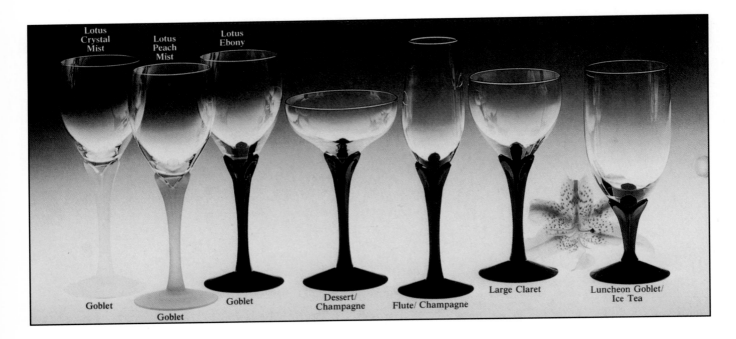

Lotus

42

New Classics
Lotus Crystal Mist

*Luncheon Goblet/Ice Tea,
Large Claret,   Goblet,
Dessert/Champagne*

Lotus Ebony

Goblet

*Dessert /
Champagne*

Large Claret

*Luncheon
Goblet /
Ice Tea*

Lotus

Maypole Light Blue
Maypole Peach
Maypole Yellow

Goblet   Goblet   Goblet   Dessert/Champagne   Wine   Luncheon Goblet/Ice Tea

Maypole

Maypole Giftware

Color Key:
MAO8/Light Blue
MAO9/Yellow
MA1O/Peach

764

314

319

319

319

195

567

44

Mesa

MESA PATTERN
No. 4186 Line
Made in Olive Green, Amber and Blue

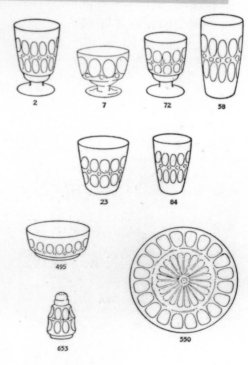

				Retail Price Ea.
4186/2	13	oz. Goblet ....Olive Green, Amber or Blue Height 5⅛ in.		$ 4.25
4186/7	8	oz. Sherbet ..Olive Green, Amber or Blue Height 3⅜ in.		4.25
4186/72	9	oz. On the Rocks/Wine.............. Olive Green, Amber or Blue Height 4¼ in		4.25
4186/58	15	oz. Ice Tea ..Olive Green, Amber or Blue Height 5⅝ in.		3.75
4186/23	12	oz. Double Old Fashioned Cocktail........... Ol've Green, Amber or Blue Height 3¾ in.		3.75
4186/84	7	oz. Juice .....Olive Green, Amber or Blue Height 4¼ in.		3.25
4186/495	4¾	in. Dessert ..Olive Green, Amber or Blue Height 2¾ in.		3.75
4186/550	8	in. Plate ....Olive Green, Amber or Blue		4.50
4186/653		Shaker & Chrome Top "A".....Crystal Olive Green, Amber or Blue Height 3½ in.		2.75
				3.00

Mesa: Fostoria's colorful new sculptured glass design*. A complete drinkware line . . . plus sherbets, desserts, plates and pitchers and other accessories. In Olive, Blue, Amber, Brown, Crystal. *Patents pending.

Come a-glow with casual Fostoria

Mesa

Misty

Moonstone

Goblet *Sherbet* *Wine* *Luncheon Goblet/Ice Tea*

Moonstone Dark Blue

Goblet   Sherbet   Wine   Luncheon Goblet/
Ice Tea   Light Blue
Goblet   Taupe
Goblet   Yellow
Goblet   Green
Goblet   Pink
Goblet

47

Needlepoint

Pavilion

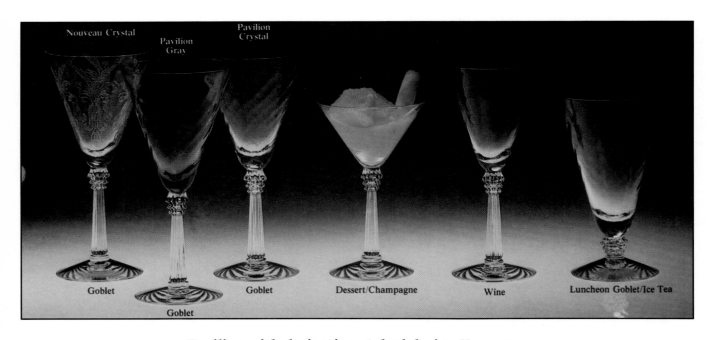

Pavilion with derivative etched design Nouveau.

Pebble Beach

PEBBLE BEACH PATTERN

No. 2806 Line

Made in Black Pearl, Lemon Twist and Flaming Orange

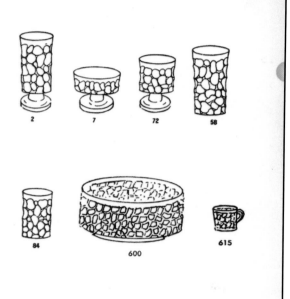

				Retail Price Ea.
2806/2	10	oz. Goblet	Black Pearl, Lemon Twist	$4.25
			Flaming Orange	5.00
		Height 6 in.		
2806/7	7	oz. Sherbet	Black Pearl, Lemon Twist	4.25
			Flaming Orange	5.00
		Height 2¾ in		
2806/72	8	oz. On the Rocks/Wine		
			Black Pearl, Lemon Twist	4.25
			Flaming Orange	5.00
		Height 4⅛ in.		
2806/58	14	oz. Ice Tea	Black Pearl, Lemon Twist	4.00
			Flaming Orange	4.75
		Height 5¾ in.		
2806/84	7	oz. Juice	Black Pearl, Lemon Twist	4.00
			Flaming Orange	4.75
		Height 4 in.		
2806/600	9	qt. Punch Bowl	Crystal	29.75
		Height 7¾ in. — Diam. 11½ in.		
2806/615	6½	oz. Punch Cup	Crystal	3.75
		Height 3⅜ in.		

Pebble Beach

Made in
Lemon Twist
Flaming Orange
Black Pearl

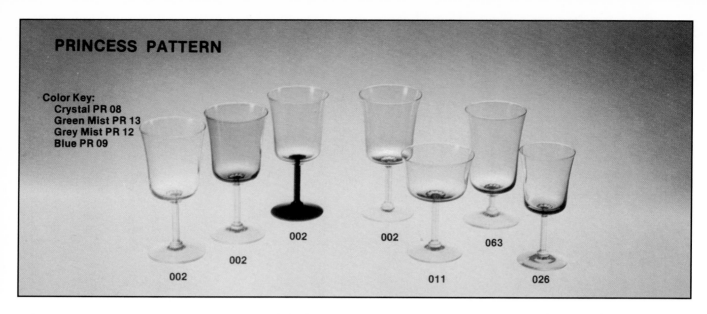

PRINCESS PATTERN

Color Key:
Crystal PR 08
Green Mist PR 13
Grey Mist PR 12
Blue PR 09

002

002

002

002

011

063

026

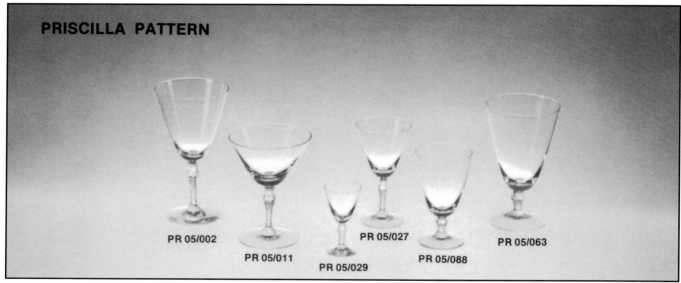

PRISCILLA PATTERN

PR 05/002

PR 05/011

PR 05/029

PR 05/027

PR 05/088

PR 05/063

Radiance

Coordinating
Lead Crystal
Heritage Barware

Goblet

Dessert/Champagne

Wine

Luncheon Goblet/
Ice Tea

Double Old Fashioned

High
Ball

Radiance with coordinating Heritage barware.

50

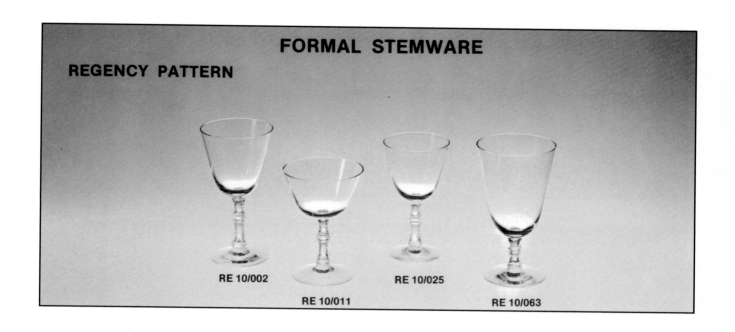

FORMAL STEMWARE

REGENCY PATTERN

RE 10/002

RE 10/011

RE 10/025

RE 10/063

Wilma Crystal   Victoria   Regis

Goblet   Goblet   Goblet   High Dessert/Champagne   Large Claret   Luncheon Goblet/Ice Tea

Regis and Victoria Designs are derived from Wilma Pattern.

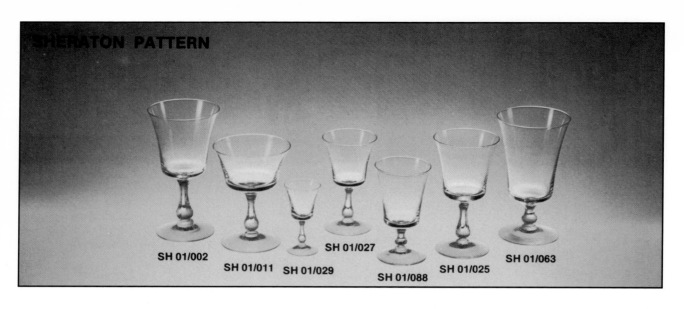

SHERATON PATTERN

SH 01/002

SH 01/011   SH 01/029

SH 01/027

SH 01/088

SH 01/025

SH 01/063

Sheraton   Richmond   Georgian   Sheffield

Goblet

Goblet

Goblet

Goblet

Dessert/
Champagne

Wine/
Cocktail

Claret

Magnum

Luncheon Goblet/
Ice Tea

Bell

Cordial

Footed
Juice

9

Sheffield with derivative designs Sheraton, Richmond and Georgian. See also Harvest.

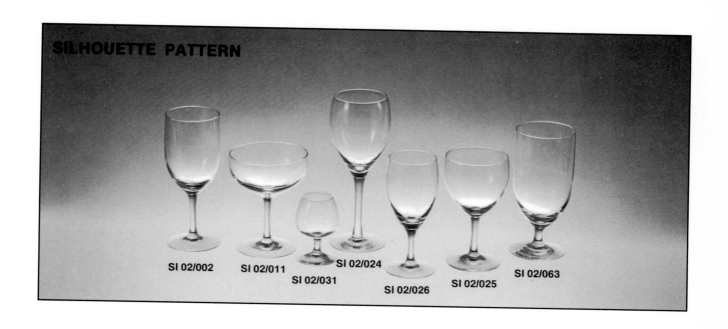

SILHOUETTE PATTERN

SI 02/002   SI 02/011   SI 02/024   SI 02/026   SI 02/025   SI 02/063
                         SI 02/031

Silhouette
Classics
Ebony

Silhoutte
Classics
Blue

Goblet   Goblet   Dessert/   Large Claret   Luncheon Goblet/
                                Champagne   Ice Tea

Silhouette

Sorrento

SORRENTO PATTERN
No. 2832 Line
Made in Blue, Green, Brown, Plum and Pink

			Retail Price Ea.
2832/2	9	oz. Goblet .... Height 6 in.	$ 4.00
2832/7	6½	oz. Sherbet .... Height 3⅝ in.	4.00
2832/23	10	oz. Double Old Fashioned .... Height 4 in.	4.00
2832/26	6½	oz. Wine .... Height 5 in.	4.00
2832/63	13	oz. Luncheon Goblet/Ice Tea .... Height 6¾ in.	4.00
2832/64	11	oz. Tumbler/Highball .... Height 5⅝ in.	4.00
2832/550	8	in. Plate	4.00

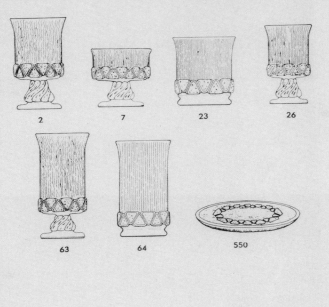

2 7 23 26

63 64 550

Fostoria Casual Stemware

Sorrento
Made in
Green
Blue
Brown

Splendor

Lead Crystal
Transition Barware and Accessories

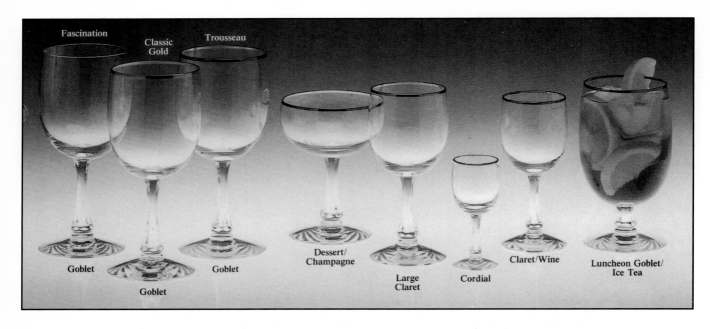

Trousseau and Classic Gold Designs are based on Fascination Pattern.

Virginia

Goblet, Wine, Sherbet
Luncheon Goblet/Ice Tea

FORMAL STEMWARE

WILMA PATTERN

Color Key:
Blue WI 03
Pink WI 04
Crystal WI 01

002   002   088   002   011   008   027   084   029   063   025   035

WIMBLEDON PATTERN

WI 02/002   WI 02/011   WI 02/026   WI 02/063

Westchester

Woodland

Goblet   Sherbet   Wine   Luncheon Goblet/Ice Tea

WOODLAND PATTERN

Gift Items

Color Key:
Crystal WO 01
Blue WO 02
Brown WO 03
Green WO 04

505   653   448   506

317   554   517   506   448   653   505

Stemware

Distinction Plum   Distinction Blue   Distinction Cobalt   Precedence Onyx   Eloquence Onyx   Princess Gray

Princess Green   Princess Blue   Glamour Green   Glamour Onyx   Glamour Gray   Glamour Blue

Debutante Gray   Silhouette Pink   Navarre Blue   Navarre Pink   Corsage   Firelight

Stemware

Princess Gray   Distinction Blue   Distinction Plum   Sphere Terra   Eloquence Onyx   Precedence Onyx

Princess Green   Princess Blue   Glamour Green   Glamour Onyx   Glamour Gray   Glamour Blue

Debutante Gray   Silhouette Pink   Biscayne Nutmeg   Biscayne Gold   Biscayne Blue   Biscayne Snow   Biscayne Onyx

Marquis   Glamour Onyx   Glamour Blue   Glamour Green   Wedding Ring

Engagement   Aurora   Andover   Biscayne Blue   Debutante Gray

Precedence Onyx   Biscayne Snow   Eloquence Onyx   Biscayne Nutmeg   Invitation

61

Misty Blue   Misty Yellow   Misty Brown   Classic Gold   Trousseau

Splendor Blue   Splendor Rust   Georgian   Bracelet   Greenfield

Exeter (also in Amethyst)

Golden Triumph
Silver Triumph

Precedence (no decoration)
Precedence Gray (gray mist bowl)
Precedence Onyx (black bowl)

Andover (encrusted gold band)

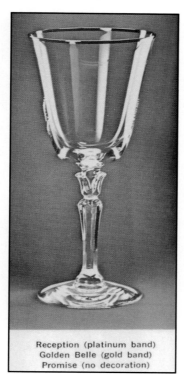

Reception (platinum band)
Golden Belle (gold band)
Promise (no decoration)

Wedding Ring (platinum band)
Courtship (no decoration)

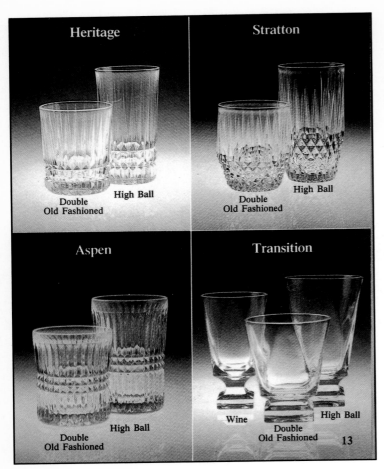

Heritage

Double
Old Fashioned High Ball

Stratton

Double
Old Fashioned High Ball

Aspen

Double
Old Fashioned High Ball

Transition

Wine Double
Old Fashioned High Ball

13

Monarch

High Ball Double
Old Fashioned

York

High Ball Double
Old Fashioned

Standish

Double
Old Fashioned High Ball
Old Fashioned

Fairlane

High Ball Double
Old Fashioned

ALEXIS Pattern #1630

Crystal Pressed Glass Pattern
1909 – 1925

Almond, Individual 10.00
Bowl, High, Foot 4½" 16.00
Butter, Covered 55.00
Catsup with Drop Stopper 42.00
Catsup with Ground Stopper 50.00
Celery, Tall 28.00
Celery Tray 16.00
Champagne, Tall 6 oz. 10.00
Claret 5 oz. 10.00
Cocktail 3 oz. 10.00
Cordial 1 oz. 10.00
Creme de Menthe 2½ oz. 10.00
Cream 20.00
Cream, Hotel 24.00
Crushed Ice and Plate 30.00
Custard (2 styles) 10.00
Decanter with Ground Stopper 70.00
Egg Cup 9.00
Finger Bowl 12.00
Goblet 10 oz. 10.00
Horseradish Jar with Spoon 40.00
Ice Cream, High, Foot 14.00
Ice Tea, Footed 10 oz. 10.00
Ice Tea Plate 8.00
Ice Tea Tumbler...10.00
Jug, ½ gallon...65.00
Jug, Ice, 3 pint..60.00
Jug, ½ quart...37.50
Mayonnaise Bowl 26.00
Mayonnaise Plate 10.00
Molasses Can, Nickel or Britannia or
    Silver Plate Top.....................................35.00
Molasses Can and Plate............................65.00
Mustard, Covered 35.00
Nappy 4½" 8.00
Nappy 5" 9.00
Nappy 7" 12.00
Nappy 8" 13.00
Nappy 9" 15.00
Nasturtium Vase 25.00
Nut Bowl 12.00

No. 1630 6 oz. Oil.

Olive Tray...14.00
Oil, Drop Stopper 2 oz. 20.00
Oil, Drop Stopper 4 oz. 26.00
Oil, Drop Stopper 6 oz. 28.00
Oil, Ground Stopper 2 oz. 22.00
Oil, Ground Stopper 4 oz. 28.00
Oil, Ground Stopper 6 oz. 30.00
Pickle Tray 14.00
Pitcher, Tall, ½ gallon 70.00
Pousse Café ¾ oz. 12.00
Salt, Flat, Table..10.00
Salt, Flat, Individual.................................10.00
Salt Footed, Individual 12.00
Shaker, Nickel or Silver Plate or Glass or
    Noncorrosive Top...................................15.00
Sherbet, Low, Footed (2 styles) 10.00
Sherbet, High, Footed...............................10.00
Spoon..22.00
Sugar, Covered..25.00
Sugar Sifter, Silver Plate Top 30.00
Sugar, Hotel..60.00
Sweet Pea Vase...40.00
Toothpick..18.00
Tumbler, Table, Footed 8½ oz. 30.00
Tumbler, Table (2 styles) 12.00
Vase 9"...38.00
Water Bottle 65.00
Whiskey Tumbler 10.00
Wine 2 oz. 13.00
Wine 3 oz. 12.00
Wine Tumbler..10.00

⟶ ALLEGRO Design #672 ⟵

Crystal with Gold Band on Bowl
See Inspiration Pattern and Betrothal Design
1966, Matching service only in 1971
Discontinued in 1972

#2 Goblet 11 oz. 8¼".................................14.00
#11 Sherbet 9 oz. 5⁷⁄₁₆"...........................12.00
#25 Claret 7½ oz. 5⅞"..............................15.00

#25 Tulip Wine 6½ oz. 6⅝".......................14.00
#29 Liqueur 2 oz. 4¼"...............................10.00
#63 Luncheon Goblet/Ice Tea 14 oz. 7½"..14.00
#549 Plate 7" (Narrow Rib Optic) 8.00

⟶ AMBASSADOR Design #637 ⟵

Crystal with Gold Band on Bowl and Foot
See Symphony Pattern
1956 – 1971
Matchings only in 1971
Discontinued in 1972

#2 Goblet 11 oz. 6⅛".................................15.00
#7 Sherbet, 7½ oz. 4¾" 12.00
#21 Wine/Cocktail 4 oz. 4⅝".....................14.00

#29 Cordial 1 oz. 3⅛"...............................16.00
#63 Luncheon Goblet/Ice Tea 12 oz. 6⅜"....15.00
#88 Juice, Footed 6 oz. 4⅝" 10.00
#495 Dessert/Finger Bowl..........................8.00
#549 Plate 7"..8.00
#550 Plate 8"..8.00

⟶ AMERICAN Pattern #2056 ⟵

Crystal Pressed Glass Pattern
See pages 23 to 27 for color photos
Early production of some items in Amber,
Blue, Canary, Green, Red, as well as an
Ebony ashtray. Limited amount of Milk
Glass, Aqua and Peach opaque sampled in
the 1950's. Viking and Lancaster Colony
have reproduced items, as has Fostoria (see
Reproductions, page 13).
1915 – 1985
Add 100% for Red, 300% for Amber, Blue and
Canary. These percentages do not apply in
very rare items where that factor becomes
the important pricing factor.
* Amber, Blue, Canary items
** Green   *** Red

Almond, Oval 2¾" 15.00
Almond, Oval 3¾" 18.00
Almond, Oval 4½" 17.50
Appetizer Tray, square.............................27.50
Appetizer Tray, 6 Inserts.........................235.00
Ashtray, oval 5½".....................................27.50
Ashtray, square 5".....................................48.00
Ashtray, with match stand 17.00

Ashtray, square 2⅞" 8.00
Banana Split 350.00
Basket with Reed Handle.........................115.00
Bell 300.00
**Boat, 8½" 18.50
**Boat, 12" 30.00
Boat, Sauce and Underplate 70.00
*Bon Bon, 3 toed 7" (red also) 17.50
Bottle, Bitters with Tube..........................70.00
Bottle, Catsup with Stopper.....................110.00
Bottle, Condiment with Stopper 6¾" 140.00
Bottle, Cordial with Stopper.....................100.00
Bottle, Water 375.00
Bowl, Baby 4½" (2 styles) 50.00
Bowl, Cupped 7"...62.50
Bowl, Finger with Underplate 70.00
Bowl, Footed Fruit (Tom and Jerry) 12"...225.00
Bowl, Footed Fruit 16"...............................200.00
Bowl, Footed, 2 Handled (Trophy) 8" 130.00
Bowl, Footed square 7" 100.00
Bowl, Handled 8½" 82.00
Bowl, Punch, High Foot 14" 200.00
Bowl, Punch, Low Foot 18" 300.00
Bowl, Rolled Edge 11½".............................55.00

Bowl, Rose, 3½" 23.00
Bowl, Rose 5" 33.00
***Bowl, Salad 10" 55.00
Bowl, Shallow, Fruit 13" 75.00
Bowl, Footed and Covered, square 7" 215.00
Bowl, 3 toed, 10½" 48.00
Bowl, 2 Part Vegetable 10" 50.00
Bowl, Watercress 33.00
Bowl, Wedding 6½" 55.00
Bowl, Wedding with Cover 6½" 90.00
Box, Candy 3 part divided with cover........82.00
*Box, Cigarette with Cover 35.00
Box, Oblong Flower with Cover 35.00
*Box, Glove with Cover 350.00
Box, Hairpin or Match with Cover..........525.00
*Box, Hair Receiver with Cover 535.00
*Box, Handkerchief with Cover 250.00
Box, Jewel with Cover 465.00
Box, Pomade or Rouge...........................275.00
*Box, Puff with Cover, square 148.00
Box, Puff with Cover, round....................165.00
Butter, oblong with cover........................35.00
Butter, round with cover 130.00
Cake Stand, Footed 12" 60.00
Cake Plate 2 Handle 35.00
Can, Molasses small...............................265.00
Can, Molasses large 285.00
Candelabra, 2 light................................130.00
Candle, Chamber ....pair 60.00
Candle, 3" ....pair 25.00
Candle, 6" ....pair 60.00
Candle, 7" 65.00
Candle, Duo 150.00
Candle, Twin 45.00
***Candy, Footed with cover, 7" 48.00
Celery Tray, 10".....................................25.00
Celery Tall, 6" 45.00
Centerpiece, 9½"....................................58.00
Centerpiece, 3 cornered 11" 68.00
Centerpiece, 15" 150.00
Cheese, Footed 30.00
Cheese and Cracker 55.00
Chiffonier (Jar and Tray Assortment) ...1,900.00
Coaster, cube bottom 9.00
Coaster, ray bottom................................9.00
Cocktail, Footed 3 oz. 15.00
Cocktail, Old Fashioned 6 oz. 18.50
Cocktail, Oyster 4½" 15.00
Comport with cover 5" 40.00
Comport 8½" 45.00
Comport 9½" 50.00
*Cologne, 6 oz. 75.00
Cologne, 8 oz. 100.00
Cookie Jar with Cover 8⅞" 250.00
Cracker Jar with Cover............................250.00
Cream, Individual 4¾" 10.00
Cream, 9½"..18.00

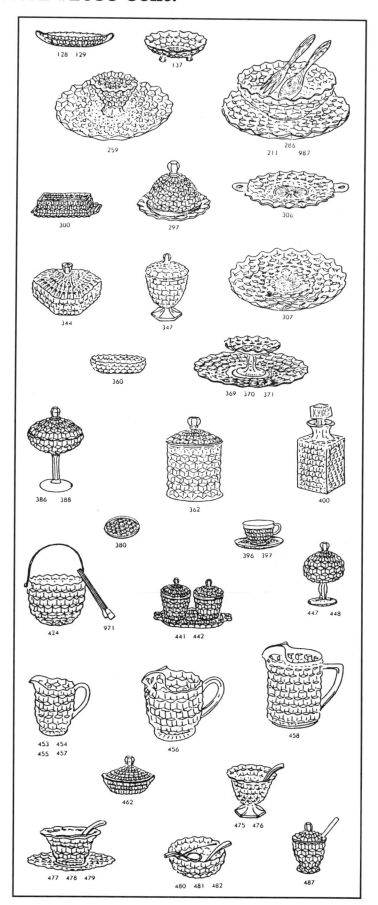

Cream, Tea 3 oz. 12.00
Cream Soup and Underplate 60.00
Crushed Fruit with Cover 1,600.00
Crushed Fruit Spoon 350.00
Cup, Footed 7.00
Cup, Custard or Punch, Flared................10.00
Cup, Custard or Punch, Regular..............10.00
Decanter with Stopper 24 oz..................115.00
Fruit Cocktail with Liner 33.00
Floating Garden,10" 65.00
Floating Garden 11½" 70.00
Goblet, Low 9 oz. 11.00
Goblet, Hexagonal Foot 10 oz. 15.00
Goblet, Claret 7 oz. 42.00
Goblet, Cordial 1 oz. 55.00
Hat/Topper, 2½"..20.00
Hat/Topper, 3" 28.00
Hat/Topper, 4" 45.00
Hat/Topper, Ashtray 18.00
Ice, Hotel Cracked 3,500.00
Ice Bucket with metal handle 60.00
Ice Cream, 5½" 55.00
Ice Cream, square 3½"...............................35.00
Ice Tea 12 oz. 15.00
Ice Tea Flared 12 oz. 18.00
Ice Tea Footed, Flared 12 oz. 18.00
Ice Tea, Flared with Plate 35.00
Ice Tea Handled......................................175.00
Ice Tub with Underplate 6½".....................95.00
Ice Tub with Underplate 5⅝" 100.00
Ice Tub with Liners 18.00
Jar, Jam with Cover 52.50
Jar, Pretzel 250.00
Jar, Pickle with Cover 300.00
Jar, Straw with Cover 250.00
Jelly, Footed...25.00
Jelly, Footed, Flared 35.00
Jelly, Footed with Cover 40.00
Jelly, Deep 40.00
Jug, Ice Lip 3 pint 6½"..............................65.00
Jug, Ice Lip 2 quart 110.00
Jug, quart 7¼"...50.00
Jug, 3 pint 8" 75.00
Jug, 2 quart 8" 85.00
Ladle 16.00
Lamp, Candle 3 pieces 175.00
Lamp, Hurricane 180.00
Lemon Dish...40.00
Lemon Dish with Cover 45.00
Lemonade, Footed with Handle..............175.00
Lily Pond 75.00
Marmalade with Cover and Spoon 65.00
Mayonnaise, Divided, with 2 Spoons 6¼" ..50.00
Mayonnaise, with Plate and Spoon 40.00
Mayonnaise, Footed with Plate
and Spoon 4⅝" 55.00
Mug, Beer 4½" 40.00
Mug, Tom and Jerry (Youth) 25.00
Mustard, Cover and Spoon 38.00
Napkin Ring 2" 7.00
Nappy, Regular 4¼" 11.00
Nappy, Fruit 3¾" 18.50
Nappy, Regular 5" 15.00
**Nappy, Regular 4½" 13.00
Nappy, Handled 5" 15.00
Nappy with Cover 5" 33.00
Nappy, Regular 6" 17.00
Nappy, Regular 7" 28.00
Nappy, Regular 8" 30.00
**Nappy, Deep 8"..53.00
Nappy, Deep 10"..43.00
Nappy, 2 Handles 8"..................................55.00
Nappy, Tab Handles 9" 43.00
Nappy, Flared 4½" 15.00
Nappy, Flared 6¼" 28.00
Nappy, Cupped 7¼" 45.00
Nappy, Flared 7"..40.00
Nappy, Regular or Flared 8¼" 45.00
Nappy, Deep Flared 8½"............................65.00
Nappy, Flared 9½" 57.00
Nappy, Flared 10"......................................53.00
Nappy, Shallow 7" 32.00
Nappy, Shallow 8" 36.00
Nappy, Shallow 10" 53.00
Nappy, Round, Handled 4½"......................12.00
Nappy, Square, Handled 4½" 15.00
Nappy, 3 Cornered 5" 15.00
Oil with Drop Stopper 5 oz. or 7 oz. 48.00
Oil with Ground Stopper 5 oz. or 7 oz. 50.00
Olive 6" 15.00
Party Server, Divided with Spoons 45.00
Pickle 8" 15.00
Picture Frame...15.00
Pitcher 1 pint 30.00
Pitcher Single serving 5⅗"........................35.00
Plate Bread and Butter 6"............................8.00
Plate, Crescent Salad..................................50.00
Plate, Salad 7" 12.00
Plate, Salad 8½"..15.00
Plate, Dinner 9½"..20.00
Plate, 3 Footed Dessert 23.00
Plate, Sandwich 9".......................................15.00
Plate, Sandwich 10½" 28.00
Plate, Sandwich 11½" 42.00
Plate, Syrup 6" 9.00
Plate, Torte oval 13½" 50.00
***Plate, Torte 14"...35.00
Plate, Torte 18"...105.00
Plate, Torte 20"...115.00
Plate, Torte 24"...300.00
Plate, Youth 6" 68.00
Plate, Watercress 8".....................................33.00
Platter, oval 10½"...45.00
Platter, oval 12" 55.00

Pot, Flower and Cover	1,175.00	Tray, oblong 5"	100.00
Preserve, Handled with Cover	68.00	Tray, oblong 10½"	90.00
Relish, 2 Part	35.00	Tray, oval 10½"	65.00
Relish, 3 Part	50.00	Tray, oval 12x8½"	75.00
Relish, 4 Part oval	65.00	Tray, round 12"	175.00
Relish, 4 Part square	165.00	Tray, Sugar and Cream Holder	15.00
Ring Holder	20.00	Tray, square	125.00
Salt, Individual	12.00	Tray, Utility with Handle	40.00
Salver, Round Cake	75.00	Tumbler, Baby 3"	300.00
Salver, Square Cake	90.00	Tumbler, Footed 5 oz.	18.00
Saucer	5.00	Tumbler, Juice 5 oz.	12.00
Shakers, Salt and Pepper 3½"	22.00	Tumbler, Old Fashioned 6 oz.	14.00
Shakers, Salt and Pepper,		Tumbler, Water, Flared 8 oz.	15.00
Individual with Tray 2"	35.00	**Tumbler, Water, Plain 8 oz.	12.00
Shaker, Sugar or Cheese	58.00	Tumbler, Whiskey 2 oz.	12.00
Sherbet 4½ oz.	10.00	Tumbler, Footed 9 oz. 4⅜"	15.00
Sherbet, Footed and Handled 4½ oz.	95.00	Urn, square 6"	42.00
Sherbet, High, Flared or Plain 4½ oz.	15.00	Urn, square 7½"	50.00
Sherbet, Low, Flared or Plain 5 oz.	11.00	Vase, Bagged	1,100.00
Shrimp Bowl 12¼"	300.00	Vase, Footed, Bud Cupped top 6"	32.50
Spoon	35.00	Vase, Footed, Bud Flared 6"	25.00
Sugar with Cover 6¼"	48.00	Vase, Footed, Bud Cupped or Flared 8½"	35.00
Sugar Handled with Cover 5¼"	22.00	Vase, Flared 6"	35.00
Sugar, Individual 2½"	12.50	Vase, Straight, Footed	38.00
Sugar, Tea 2¼"	25.00	Vase, Straight	35.00
Sundae, 6 oz.	13.00	Vase, Flared (Base for Tall Punch	
Syrup, Metal Screw Top 6 oz.	250.00	Bowl) 7"	85.00
Syrup, Glass Top and Underplate	175.00	Vase, Flared (Base for Tall Punch	
Syrup, Dripcut 6½ oz.	60.00	Bowl) 9"	65.00
Syrup, Sani-Server	80.00	Vase, Flared or Straight 8"	45.00
Tankard	50.00	Vase, Footed, square 9"	55.00
Tidbit, 3 Toed	25.00	Vase, Flared, 9½"	65.00
Tidbit with Metal Handle	45.00	Vase, Cupped 10"	110.00
Toothpick	25.00	Vase, Flared 10"	100.00
Toothpick, Ruby FGSA 1982	75.00	Vase, Straight 10"	85.00
Tray, Cake with Metal Handle	40.00	Vase, Straight 12"	125.00
Tray, Candy 7x5"	250.00	Vase, Porch, Small	2,150.00
Tray, Cloverleaf Condiment	165.00	Vase, Porch, Large	2,500.00
Tray, Ice Cream 13⅝"	200.00	Vase, Sweet Pea 4½"	65.00
Tray, Ice Cream 10⅝"	55.00	Vase, Swung 9" to 12"	100.00
Tray, Lunch with Handle	42.00	Vase, Swung 14" to 16"	165.00
Tray, Muffin with Handle	35.00	Vase, Swung 18" to 20"	250.00
*Tray, Pin oval 5¼"	125.00	Vase, Swung 23" to 26"	350.00
Tray, oval 6"	65.00	Wine, 2½ oz.	15.00

ANNIVERSARY Design #634

Crystal with Gold Rim Decoration
See Rhapsody Pattern
Matching Service only in 1971
1954 – 1975

		#27 Claret/Wine 4¼ oz. 4⅝"	15.00
		#20 Cocktail 3½ oz. 3⅞"	10.00
		#29 Cordial 1¼ oz. 3⁵⁄₁₆"	16.00
		#549 Plate 7"	8.00
		#550 Plate 8"	8.00
#2 Goblet 10 oz. 6⅛"	15.00	#60 Luncheon Goblet/Ice Tea 12¼ oz. 6⅛"	13.00
#7 Sherbet 6 oz. 4½"	12.00	#88 Juice, Footed 5½ oz. 4⅞"	14.00
#33 Oyster Cocktail 4¾ oz. 4"	10.00		

➣═ AMERICAN LADY Pattern #5056 ═⬿

Blown Lead Glass Stemware
Crystal, Crystal Base with Regal Blue Bowl,
  Crystal Base with Burgundy Bowl, Crystal
  Base with Empire Green Bowl
1933 – 1973
Line matchings only 1972
Add 100% for Burgundy, Green; 200% for
  Blue

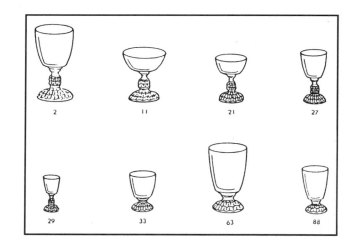

#2 Goblet 10 oz. 6⅛"...............................12.00
#63 Luncheon Goblet/Ice Tea 12 oz. 5½"..13.00
#11 Sherbet 5½ oz. 4⅛" 10.00
#21 Cocktail 3½ oz. 4" 10.00
#27 Claret/Wine 3½ oz. 4⅝".....................12.00
#29 Cordial 1 oz. 3⅛"...............................18.00
#495 Dessert/Finger Bowl.........................8.00
#33 Oyster Cocktail 4 oz. 3½" 10.00
#549 Plate 7"..8.00

#550 Plate 8"...8.00
#88 Tumbler, Juice, footed 5 oz. 4⅛" 10.00

➣═ ANDOVER Design #665 ═⬿

Crystal with Encrusted Gold Band on Bowl
See Sheraton Pattern
Discontinued late 1970s
1961 – 1978

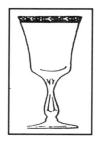

#2 Goblet 10 oz. 6⅝".................................15.00
#11 Sherbet 7 oz. 5³⁄₁₆".............................12.00
#27 Wine/Cocktail 3½ oz. 5".....................15.00
#29 Cordial 1 oz. 3⁹⁄₁₆"..............................16.00
#63 Luncheon Goblet/Ice Tea 12 oz. 6⁷⁄₁₆".18.00
#88 Juice, Footed 5 oz. 4¹¹⁄₁₆" 15.00
#495 Dessert/Finger bowl 8.00

#549 Plate 7"..8.00
#550 Plate 8"...8.00

➣═ ANNOUNCEMENT Design #666 ═⬿

Crystal with Platinum band on bowl
See page 30 for color photo
See Glamour Pattern for stems
1964 – 1984

#224 Bowl, Footed 10"..............................27.50
#31 Brandy 3½ oz. 3⅞" 15.00
#25 Claret 7½ oz. 5¾" 15.00
#681 Cream, Footed 10.00
#495 Dessert/Finger Bowl 8.00
#2 Goblet 12 oz. 7¼"................................16.00
#63 Luncheon Goblet/Ice Tea 14 oz. 6⅝"..14.00

#549 Plate 7"..8.00
#550 Plate 8"...8.00
#620 Relish 2 part 13.00
#643 Relish 4 part....................................16.00
#644 Relish 5 part 18.00
#679 Sugar, Footed 12.50
#11 Sherbet 8 oz. 15.00
#26 Tulip Wine 7 oz..................................16.00

~⇒ ARGUS Pattern #2770 ⇐~

Hand pressed giftware line made by special arrangement with the Henry Ford Museum. Stem added later.
See pages 28 and 29 for color photos
Crystal, Olive Green, Cobalt Blue, and Ruby. Grey was added in 1972
Early 1960's – 1985

Cream 6" 15.00
#2 Goblet 10½ oz. 6½" 15.00
#7 Sherbet, 8 oz. 5" 10.00
#26 Wine 4 oz. 4¾" 15.00
#63 Luncheon Goblet/Ice Tea 13 oz. 6¾"..15.00
#64 Tumbler/Highball 12 oz. 5¼" 14.00
#73 Tumbler/Old Fashioned 10 oz. 3⅞"....13.00
#89 Tumbler/Juice/Cocktail 4½ oz. 2⅞"...10.00
#386 Compote and Cover 8" 35.00
#421 Dessert 5".......................................8.00
#330 Dessert Plate 8" 8.00
#682 Sugar and Cream Set 8½ oz. 6"........18.00
Covered Sugar 6⅛" 18.00

~⇒ ASTRID Pattern #6030 ⇐~

Crystal blown stemware
1942 – 1978

#2 Goblet 10 oz. 7⅞".................................12.00
#3 Low Goblet 10 oz. 6⅜".........................12.00
#8 Sherbet/Champagne 6 oz. 5⅝".........8.00
#11 Sherbet 6 oz. 4⅜".............................7.00
#21 Cocktail 3½ oz. 5¼"..........................10.00
#29 Cordial 1 oz. 1⅞"..............................18.50
#27 Claret/Wine 3½ oz. 6"........................12.00
#495 Dessert/Finger Bowl.........................8.00
#33 Oyster Cocktail 4 oz. 3¾"..................10.00
#63 Luncheon Goblet/Ice Tea 12 oz. 6"....12.50
#88 Juice, Footed 5 oz. 4⅝"......................10.00
#549 Plate 7"..8.00

~⇒ AURORA Design #651 ⇐~

Crystal with Gold Rim Decoration
See Priscilla Pattern
1954 – 1982
Line reduced to stems in 1974

#2 Goblet 10½ oz. 7¹⁄₁₆" 15.00
#11 Sherbet 7 oz. 5⁷⁄₁₆"............................12.00
#27 Wine/Cocktail 4 oz. 5¼".......................15.00
#63 Luncheon Goblet/Ice Tea 14 oz. 6⅜" ..16.00
#88 Juice, Footed 5½ oz. 4¾" 12.00

#29 Cordial 1½ oz. 3½" 15.00
#495 Dessert/Finger Bowl.........................18.00
#549 Plate 7"..8.00
#550 Plate 8"..8.00
#224 Bowl, Footed 10"..............................30.00
#620 Relish 2 Part...................................12.00
#643 Relish 4 Part...................................15.00
#644 Relish 5 Part...................................18.00
#681 Cream, Footed 14.00
#689 Sugar, Footed 14.00

BAROQUE Pattern #2496

See page 19 for color photo
Crystal, Topaz, Gold Tint, Azure Blue, Ruby
Azure 1936 – 1944
Topaz 1936 – 1938
Gold Tint 1938 – 1944
Ruby 1936 – 1939
Some items also reported in Green, Amber,
  Burgundy, Empire Green
1936 – 1966
Add 50% for Gold Tint and Topaz, 100% for
  Azure Blue, Ruby

Crystal:
Ashtray, oblong 110.00
#137 Bon Bon 3 Toed 7⅜" 15.00
Bowl, Cupped 7".......................................30.00
Bowl, Handled 10".....................................28.00
#221 Bowl, Salad 10½" 25.00
#232 Bowl, Rolled Edge 11"......................28.00
#249 Bowl, Flared 12"...............................33.00
#306 Cake Plate, 2 Handles 10"...............27.00
#315 Candlestick 4" ....pair 30.00
Candlestick 5½" ....pair 34.00
#332 Duo Candlestick 4½" ....pair 36.00
Trindle Candlestick 6" ....pair 50.00
  (Also Burgundy, Ruby, Amber, Green, Blue)
Candelabra 2 Light 8¼" 50.00
Candelabra 3 Light 9½" 65.00
Candle (Lustre) 7¾" 28.00
#344 Candy Box with Cover, 3 part 45.00
Celery 11" 20.00
Cheese, Footed 26.00
Cheese and Cracker 36.00
Cigarette Box with Cover 42.50
Cocktail, Footed 17.50
Cocktail/Old Fashioned 7 oz. 25.00
Comport 5½" 20.00
Comport 6½" 24.00
#681 Cream, Footed 7½ oz. 3¾" 14.50
#688 Cream, Individual 4 oz. 3⅓" 10.00
#697 Cream Soup with Underplate 6½" 30.00
#396 Cup, Footed.....................................10.00
Floating Garden 10" 45.00
Fruit 5" 12.00
Ice Bucket with Metal Handle 57.00
Jelly with Cover..33.00
Jug 3 pint 200.00
Mayonnaise with Plate and Ladle.............40.00
Mayonnaise 2 part 6½" 30.00
Mint Dish, Handled 25.00
Mustard with Cover and Spoon 35.00
Nappy, Regular...13.00
#500 Nappy, Handled, Flared 5" 15.00
Nappy, Flared..13.00
Nappy, Square...13.00

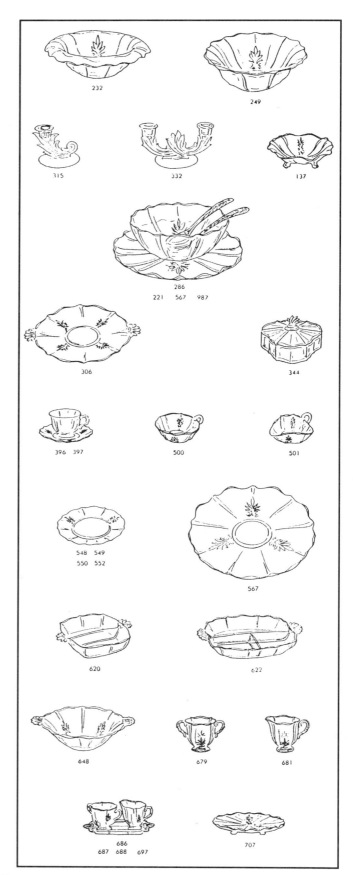

BAROQUE Pattern #2496 Cont.

#501 Nappy, 3 Cornered 4⅝" 14.00
Oil 3½ oz.. .... 33.00
Pickle 8" 13.00
#548 Plate 6" 8.00
#549 Plate 7" 10.00
#550 Plate 8" 13.00
#552 Plate 9" 33.00
Platter oval 12" 33.00
Preserve with Cover 40.00
Punch Bowl, Footed 1½ gallon 375.00
Punch Cup 10.00
#620 Relish 2 Part square 6" 12.00
#622 Relish 3 Part 10" 17.00
Relish 4 part 20.00
Sauce Dish oblong 6½" 12.00
Saucer 5.00
Shaker .... pair 35.00
Sherbet 5 oz. 10.00
#648 Serving Dish with 2 Handles 8½" 18.00
Shaker, individual size .... pair 15.00

#679 Sugar, Footed 11.50
#687 Sugar, Individual 37.50
Sweetmeat 27.50
#707 Tid-Bit 3 Toed, Flat 8¼" 15.00
#567 Torte Plate 14" 32.00
Tumbler, Juice 5 oz. 18.00
Tumbler, Water 9 oz. 20.00
Tumbler, Ice Tea 14 oz. 27.00
Tumbler, Footed 9 oz. 15.00
Tumbler, Footed 12 oz. 17.00
Tray oblong 8" 19.00
Tray, Condiment 20.00
#697 Tray for Individual
   Sugar and Cream 16.00
#686 Tray for Sugar and Cream 6½" 11.00
Tray oval 11" 16.00
Vegetable 9½" 25.00
Vase/Rose Bowl 3½" 20.00
Vase 7" 22.50
Vase 8" 25.00

BEDFORD Pattern #1000

**Crystal Pressed Glass Pattern
1901 – 1904**

Bottle Bitters, no tube 20.00
Bottle Bitters with tube 25.00
Bottle, Water 65.00
Bowl, Royal Berry, 4" 8.00
Bowl, Royal Berry, 4½" 10.00
Bowl, Royal Berry, 7" 14.00
Bowl, Royal Berry, 8" 20.00
Bowl, High Foot, open 6" 20.00
Bowl, High Foot, covered 6" 25.00
Bowl, oval 7" 14.00
Bowl, oval 8" 20.00
Bowl, oval 9" 22.00
Bowl, oval 10" 25.00
Bon Bon 6" 10.00
Butter with Cover 65.00
Celery, Tall 25.00
Celery, Tray 20.00
Claret 18.00
Claret Jug 40.00
Comport, Footed 6" 15.00
Cracker Jar, Covered 65.00
Cracker Jar, Open 40.00
Cream 22.00
Cream, Individual 10.00
Custard 8.50
Finger Bowl 14.00
Goblet 15.00
Horseradish with Stopper
   and Spoon 22.00
Horseradish with Stopper 15.00

Ice Cream Tray 28.00
Jug 75.00
Mug 20.00
Nappy, square 4½" 5.00
Nappy, square 8" 7.00
Nappy, round 4½" 5.00
Nappy, round 7" 6.00
Nappy, round 8" 7.00
Nappy, Handled 5" 10.00
Nappy, Handled 6" 12.00
Oil 52.00
Pickle Dish 16.00
Pickle Jar, no Cover 25.00
Pickle Jar, Covered 38.00
Punch Bowl 12" 45.00
Punch Bowl 12" with Foot 60.00
Punch Bowl 14" 50.00
Punch Bowl 14" with Foot 75.00
Salt Dish, oval 10.00
Shaker, Silver Plate Top 14.00
Shaker, Nickel Top 16.00
Spooner 25.00
Sugar, covered 25.00
Sugar Shaker 18.00
Sugar, Individual, Covered 15.00
Sugar, Individual, Open 9.00
Syrup 35.00
Tankard 98.00
Tumbler 16.50
Toothpick 26.00
Whiskey Jug and Stopper 70.00
Whiskey Tumbler 15.00
Wine 20.00

BELOVED Design #647

Crystal with Platinum Band on Bowl
See Orleans Pattern
1960 – 1982

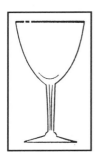

#2 Goblet 11½ oz. 6⅜" 14.00
#11 Dessert/Champagne 7oz. 5⁵⁄₁₆" 12.00
#27 Wine/Cocktail 4½ oz. 5¼" 22.00
#31 Brandy 1½ oz. 4⅛" 12.00
#224 Footed Bowl 10" 25.00
#495 Dessert/Finger Bowl.........................8.00
#549 Plate 7"..8.00
#550 Plate 8"..8.00
#620 Relish, two part 13.00
#643 Relish, four part 17.00

#644 Relish, five part 20.00
#679 Sugar, Footed 12.00
#681 Cream, Footed 12.00

BERKSHIRE Pattern #6105

Crystal Blown Lead Glass Stemware
1966 – 1974
Matching Service Only 1974

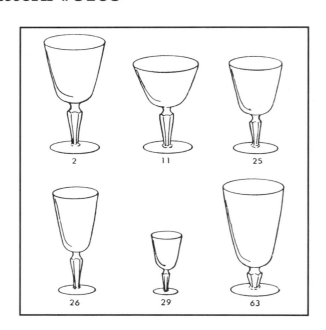

#2 Goblet 11 oz. 7⅛"..................................13.00
#11 Sherbet 9 oz. 5¾" 10.00
#25 Claret 7 oz. 6½" 14.00
#26 Wine 6 oz. 5¾" 12.00
#29 Cordial 1½ oz. 3⅞" 15.00
#63 Luncheon Goblet/Ice Tea 13½ oz. 6⅞" .13.00
#495 Dessert/Finger Bowl.........................8.00
#549 Plate 7"..8.00
#550 Plate 8"..8.00

BETROTHAL Design #673

Crystal with Platinum Band on Bowl
See Inspiration Pattern
1966 – 1971

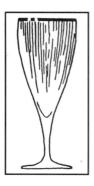

#2 Goblet 11 oz. 8¼"..................................15.00
#11 Sherbet 9 oz. 6⁵⁄₁₆" 13.00
#25 Claret 7½ oz. 5⅞" 14.00
#26 Tulip Wine 6½ oz. 6⅝"........................15.00
#29 Liqueur 2 oz. 4¼" 12.00
#63 Luncheon Goblet/Ice Tea 14 oz. 7¼" ..14.00
#549 Plate 7" (Narrow Rib Optic) 8.00

BISCAYNE Pattern #6122

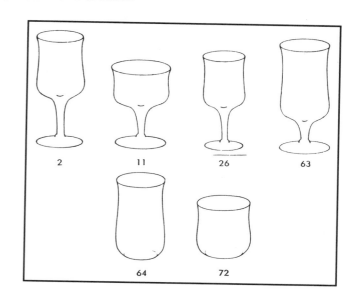

See page 60 for color photo
Blue, Nutmeg, Onyx, Snow, Gold
Line matchings only in Snow and Gold 1973
1970 – 1974

#2 Goblet 11 oz. 6⅜"..................................12.00
#11 Sherbet 9 oz. 4⅝"...............................10.00
#26 Wine 6½ oz. 5½"................................11.00
#63 Luncheon Goblet/Ice Tea 13 oz. 6¼"..12.00
#64 Highball 14 oz. 4¾".............................10.00
#72 On the Rocks 10 oz. 3⅛"....................10.00

BRACELET Design #694

Lead Crystal
Platinum Band on Bowl
See page 62 for color photo
Based on Fairlane Pattern
1982 – Late Line

#29 Cordial 2 oz. 3⅜".................................15.00
#11 Dessert/Champagne 7½ oz. 5¼"...........7.00

#2 Goblet 8½ oz. 6½"..................................8.00
#26 Wine 5½ oz. 5¾".................................8.00

BRAZILIAN Pattern #600

Crystal Pressed Glass Pattern
1898 – 1913

Bottle, Water 70.00
Bowl, Berry 7"...16.00
Bowl, Berry 8" (2 Styles) 20.00
Bowl, oblong 8" 16.50
Bowl, oblong 9" 18.00
Butter, Covered 55.00
Celery, Tall 30.00
Celery Tray..20.00
Comport 8" (2 Styles)..............................27.50
Cracker Jar, covered 60.00
Cream 25.00
Cream, Individual....................................12.00
Custard..9.00
Finger Bowl 14.00
Jug 75.00
Nappy 4½"..8.00
Olive, Handled...15.00

Pickle Dish..17.50
Pickle Jar, Covered..................................42.50
Pickle Jar, Open.......................................25.00
Salt, Regular Top......................................8.00
Salt, Nickel Top.......................................15.00
Salt, Individual..11.50
Spooner..27.50
Sugar, Covered...27.50
Sugar, Individual......................................16.50
Syrup, Regular Top 45.00
Syrup, Nickel Top 45.00
Tankard 100.00
Toothpick..20.00
Tumbler 15.00
Vase 7"..30.00
Vase 9"..40.00
Vase 11"..50.00
Vase/Rose Bowl 32.50
Vinegar (2 styles)....................................50.00

BRILLIANT Pattern #1001

Crystal Pressed Glass Pattern
1901 – 1904

No. 1001. Cracker Jar and Cover.

Berry 7"....................................18.00	Spoon.......................................15.00
Berry 8"....................................20.00	Sugar, Covered........................25.00
Bowl, High Foot 6".....................25.00	Sugar, Individual.....................20.00
Bowl, High Foot 6" Covered 35.00	Syrup Can...............................40.00
Bowl, oval 9"..........................18.00	Toothpick................................20.00
Butter, Cover...........................50.00	Tumbler..................................15.00
Celery, Tall.............................26.00	Vase 7"...................................12.00
Cracker Jar, Covered.................60.00	Vase 9"...................................17.00
Cream......................................22.00	Vase 11".................................20.00
Cream, Individual.....................12.00	
Dipper.....................................45.00	
Jug..75.00	
Nappy 4"....................................6.00	
Nappy 4½"...................................6.00	
Measuring Cup, Boston..............15.00	
Oil 8 oz....................................50.00	
Olive, Handled 6"......................15.00	
Pickle Dish..............................15.00	
Shaker, Nickel or Nickel Plate Top 15.00	

BRILLIANT Pattern #1871

Crystal Pressed Glass Pattern
*Items called Heritage made in 1973. Shakers added to line in 1974.
1914 – 1920

*Bowl 8⅜".................................15.00	Nappy 8".................................10.00
Butter, Covered.........................40.00	*Sugar, Covered......................22.00
*Candy Box and Cover..............45.00	Spooner...................................20.00
*Cream....................................18.00	*Tidbit set (3 pieces)...............45.00
*Double Old Fashioned (Set of 4).............28.00	*Torte Plate............................25.00
*Highball (Set of 4)..................30.00	Tumbler.....................................7.50
*Jug, quart...............................65.00	
Jug 3 pint................................55.00	
*Nappy 4½"................................5.00	

BROCADE Design #674

Crystal with Encrusted Gold Band on Bowl
See Celebrity Pattern
Do not confuse with Brocade Crystal Print #30
on #6124 Line
1966 – 1970

#25 Claret 8 oz. 5¾" 13.00	#63 Luncheon Goblet/Ice Tea 14 oz. 6¾"..10.00
#2 Goblet 12 oz. 7".................11.00	#11 Sherbet 9 oz. 5⁹⁄₁₆"................8.00
#29 Liqueur 2 oz. 3⅝"...............9.00	#26 Tulip Wine 6½ oz. 6½".......12.00
	#495 Dessert/Finger Bowl.........8.00
	#549 Plate 7".............................8.00
	#550 Plate 8".............................8.00

⚒ CAMELOT Pattern #6009 ⚒

Blown lead glass stemware
Crystal, Blue
1980's – 1985

#11 Champagne/Dessert 9 oz. 6⅜" 10.00
#2 Goblet 13 oz. 8³⁄₁₆" 12.00
#63 Luncheon Goblet/Ice Tea 16 oz. 6¾" ..12.00
#35 Magnum 16 oz. 7¾" 20.00
#25 Wine 9 oz. 7⅜" 12.00

⚒ CANDLELIGHT Design #652 ⚒

Crystal with Platinum band on bowl
See Vogue Pattern
1968 – 1973, Matchings only by 1972

#224 Bowl, Footed 10" 16.00
#29 Cordial 1 oz. 3⁹⁄₁₆" 18.00
#27 Cocktail/Wine 4½ oz. 5⁵⁄₁₆" 11.00
#681 Cream, Footed 10.00
#2 Goblet 11 oz. 6⅞" 14.00
#88 Juice, Footed 5½ oz. 4⅞" 11.00
#63 Luncheon Goblet/Ice Tea 14 oz. 6⅝" ..13.00

#620 Relish, 2 part 15.00
#643 Relish, 4 part 17.00
#644 relish, 5 part 19.00
#679 Sugar, Footed 10.00
#11 Sherbet 6½ oz. 5¹⁄₁₆" 7.00
#549 Plate 7" 8.00
#550 Plate 8" 8.00

⚒ CAPRI Pattern #6045 ⚒

Blown lead glass stemware
Solid Crystal and Crystal Bowls on Bitter
**   Green or Cinnamon Base**
1952 – 1965
Add 20% for color

#29 Cordial 1½ oz. 2⅝" 12.00
#27 Claret/Wine 4¾ oz. 4" 10.00
#21 Cocktail 4¾ oz. 3" 10.00
#2 Goblet 15¾ oz. 5⅞" 10.00
#7 Sherbet 9 oz. 3¾" 8.00
#549 Plate 7" 8.00
#550 Plate 8" 8.00
#495 Finger Bowl/Dessert 8.00
#88 Juice, Footed 7¼ oz. 4⅝" 8.00
#51 Ice Tea, Footed 16 oz. 6⅛" 10.00

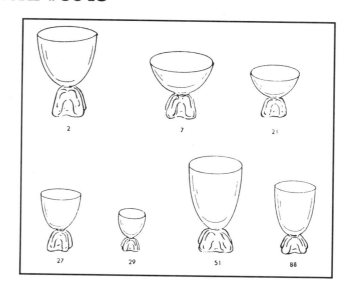

⊸⊷ CARIBBEAN Pattern #2808 ⊷⊸

**Crystal blown lead glass bowls on steel gray
   metal stems
1969 – 1975
All items footed**

#194 Bowl 9" 16.00
#318 Candleholder 5½"...................13.00
#829 Urn, Covered 15" 28.00
#347 Candy, Covered 10" 20.00
#830 Vase 13" 20.00
#3 Goblet 10 oz. 7" 11.00
#12 Sherbet 8 oz. 5⅛"................................9.00
#27 Tulip Wine 5½ oz. 6⁷⁄₁₆".....................10.00
#64 Luncheon Goblet/Ice Tea 14 oz. 7⅛" ..11.00

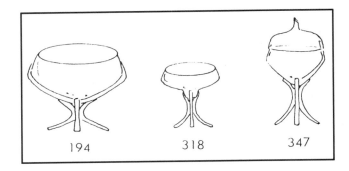

⊸⊷ CASCADE Design #636 ⊷⊸

**Mother of pearl iridescent bowl only
Narrow Rib Optic
See Elegance Pattern
1961 – 1970**

#25 Claret 5¾ oz. 5¾" 18.00
#20 Cocktail 4 oz. 4½" 15.00
#2 Goblet 9¾ oz. 7"..................................18.00
#29 Cordial 1 oz. 3⅜"................................20.00
#63 Luncheon Goblet/Ice Tea 13½ oz. 6⁷⁄₁₆" .18.00

#88 Juice, Footed 5½ oz. 4⅞" 16.00
#33 Seafood Cocktail 7¾ oz. 3⅝"..............12.00
#8 Sherbet/Champagne 8 oz. 5¾".............12.00
#11 Sherbet 7 oz. 4⅝"..............................10.00
#26 Wine 3¼ oz. 5⅛"................................15.00
#549 Plate 7" Narrow Rib Optic 8.00

⊸⊷ CELEBRATION Design #698 ⊷⊸

**Crystal with platinum band on bowl
See page 30 for color photo
Based on Gala Pattern
1980s – 1985**

#11 Champagne/Dessert 9 oz. 5" 10.00
#2 Goblet 12 oz. 7⅜"................................14.00
#63 Luncheon Goblet/Ice Tea 14 oz. 7" 13.00
#25 Wine 9 oz. 6⅝" 14.00

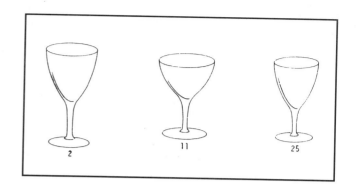 CELEBRITY Pattern #6106

Crystal blown lead glass stemware
1966 – 1971

#25 Claret 8 oz. 5¾" 9.00
#2 Goblet 12 oz. 7" 10.00
#29 Liqueur 2 oz. 3⅝" 9.00
#63 Luncheon Goblet/Ice Tea 14 oz. 6¾" ..10.00
#11 Sherbet 9 oz. 5⁷⁄₁₆" 6.00
#26 Tulip Wine 6½ oz. 6½" 12.00
#495 Dessert/Finger Bowl.........................8.00
#549 Plate 7" 8.00
#550 Plate 8" 8.00

CELESTE Pattern #6072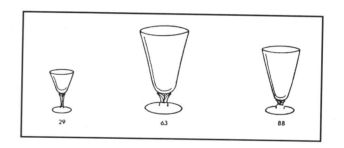

Crystal blown glass stemware
1957 – 1974
Line Matchings only 1974

#29 Cordial 1 oz. 3⅛" 14.00
#495 Dessert/Finger Bowl.........................8.00
#2 Goblet 10 oz. 6⅜" 9.00
#63 Luncheon Goblet/Ice Tea 13 oz. 6⅜" ..11.00
#11 Sherbet 7¼ oz. 5" 6.00
#88 Juice, Footed 5¼ oz. 4⅞" 8.00
#27 Wine/Cocktail 4½ oz. 4⅞" 9.00
#549 Plate 7" 8.00
#550 Plate 8" 8.00

CELLINI Pattern #6024

Crystal blown glass stemware
12 Rib Regular optic
1940 – 1975

#25 Claret 4 oz. 5¾" 15.00
#29 Cordial 1 oz. 3¾" 20.00
#21 Cocktail 3½ oz. 4¾" 12.00
#2 Goblet 10 oz. 7⅛" 16.00
#88 Juice, Footed 5 oz. 4⅝" 12.00
#63 Luncheon Goblet/Ice Tea 12 oz. 5¾" ..12.00
#33 Oyster Cocktail 4½ oz. 3½" 12.00
#11 Low Sherbet 6 oz. 4¼" 10.00
#8 High Sherbet/Champagne 6 oz. 5⅝" 10.00
#72 Water, Footed 9 oz. 5¼" 13.00
#26 Wine 3½ oz. 5⅝" 12.50
#549 Plate 7" Plain 8.00
#549 Plate 7" Optic 8.00
#550 Plate 8" 8.00

CENTURY Pattern #2630

Crystal only
See page 31 for color photo
1949 – 1985
Reduction in line after 1973

#109 Ashtray, Individual 2¾".....................13.00
Basket with Reed Handle 10½" 90.00
#137 Bon Bon 3 Toed 7¼"......................21.00
#449 Bowl, Nappy Handled 4½" 14.00
#421 Bowl, Fruit 5".................................15.00
#393 Bowl, Cereal 6" 20.00
#179 Bowl Flared 8"...............................55.00
#224 Bowl Footed, Flared 10¾"................58.00
#235 Bowl Footed, Rolled Edge 11"..........63.00
#249 Bowl Flared 12" 43.00
#300 Butter with Cover oblong 7½"..........45.00
#306 Cake Plate, Handled 9½" 45.00
#316 Candlestick 4½"...................pair 30.00
#331 Candlestick Duo 7"................pair 60.00
#336 Candlestick Trindle 7¾"..........pair 75.00
#350 Candy Jar, covered 7".....................55.00
#351 Candy Jar 4¾"................................35.00
#369 Cheese and Cracker 11"..................50.00
#370 Cheese, Footed 5⅜"........................15.00
#20 Cocktail 3½ oz. 4⅛"..........................18.00
#388 Comport 4⅜"..................................21.00
#686 Condiment Set.............................130.00
#371 Cracker Plate 11"...........................28.00
#681 Cream, Footed 4¼".........................10.00
#688 Cream, Individual 3½" 8.00
#579 Crescent Salad 7½" 40.00
#396 Cup, Footed 12.50
#2 Goblet 10½ oz. 5¾" 22.00
#63 Luncheon Goblet/Ice Tea 12 oz. 5⅞"..22.00
#424 Ice Bucket with Metal Handle 4⅞"....60.00
#197 Lily Pond 9"...................................53.00
#237 Lily Pond 11¼"...............................60.00
#477 Mayonnaise Plate with Ladle 3¼" 44.00
#480 Mayonnaise, 2 part, 2 Ladles 55.00
#487 Mustard, Covered, with Spoon 4".....50.00
#528 Oil 5 oz. 6"....................................45.00
#33 Oyster Cocktail 4½ oz. 3¾" 16.00
Party Plate and Cup 36.00
Party Plate 8" 25.00
#540 Pickle Dish 8¾"..............................21.00
#453 Pitcher, Cereal, pint 6⅛" 53.00
#456 Pitcher, Ice Lip 3 pint...................150.00
#548 Plate 6"...10.00
#549 Plate 7"...14.00
#550 Plate 8"...18.00
#552 Plate 9"...20.00
#554 Plate, Dinner 10½"..........................32.00

#560 Platter, oval 12" 44.00
#591 Preserve, Covered, Footed 6" 42.00
#592 Preserve, Footed 3⅞".......................25.00
#620 Relish, 2 part 7⅜"...........................22.00
#622 Relish, 3 part 11⅛" 24.00
#190 Salad Bowl 8½"...............................45.00
#221 Salad Bowl 10½"..............................50.00
Salver 12¼ 37.50
#397 Saucer..3.00
#648 Serving Dish, Handled 10½"............43.00
#656 Shakers, Individual 2⅜" ....pair 23.00
#654 Shakers 3¼" ....pair 20.00
#7 Sherbet 5½ oz. 4¼"............................10.00
#666 Snack Bowl 3½"...............................18.00
#687 Sugar, Individual 3⅜" 8.00
#679 Sugar, Footed 4".............................12.00
#707 Tidbit 3 toed 8⅛".............................22.00
#583 Tidbit, Two Tier 10¼" 45.00
#567 Torte Plate 14"...............................30.00
#573 Torte Plate 16"...............................35.00
#659 Tray for Salt & Pepper 4½" 16.00
#697 Tray for Cream & Sugar 7".............22.00
#723 Tray, Lunch, Handled 11¼"..............35.00
#726 Tray, Muffin, Handled 9½" 38.00
#729 Tray, Snack 10½"............................25.00
#732 Tray, Utility, Handled 9⅛"................36.00
#734 Tricorne 3 Toed 7⅛"........................23.00
#88 Tumbler, Footed 5 oz. 4¾"................18.00
#63 Tumbler, Footed 12 oz. 5⅞"..............22.00
#204 Utility Bowl, oval 10" 42.00
#761 Vase, Bud, Footed 6" 18.00
Vase, Handled 7½"..................................58.00
Vase, oval 8½" 100.00
#836 Vegetable Bowl, oval 9½".................36.00
#26 Wine, 3½ oz. 4½".............................30.00

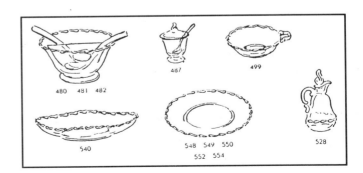

Blown lead glass stemware
Crystal or Crystal with Ebony Stem
1955 – 1965
Add 25% for Ebony

#29 Cordial 1 oz. 2½".................................16.00
#2 Goblet 11 oz. 5⅜".................................13.00
#88 Juice, Footed 5½ oz. 4½"........................9.00
#63 Luncheon Goblet/Ice Tea 14 oz. 5⅞"..12.00
#11 Sherbet 7 oz. 3½".................................8.00
#21 Wine/Cocktail 4½ oz. 3¾" 8.00
#495 Dessert/Finger Bowl.........................8.00
#549 Plate 7"..8.00
#550 Plate 8"..8.00

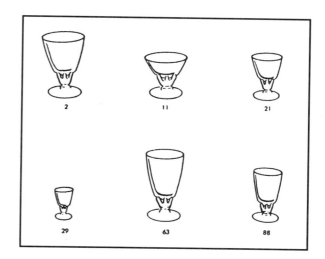

CHATEAU Pattern #6087

Crystal blown lead glass stemware
1959 – 1970

#29 Cordial 1¼ oz. 3½" 15.00
#27 Cocktail/Wine 3¼ oz. 5¼" 7.00
#2 Goblet 8¼ oz. 7".................................8.00
#88 Juice, Footed 5 oz. 5"........................9.00
#63 Luncheon Goblet/Ice Tea 11 oz. 6⅜"....9.00
#11 Sherbet 6½ oz. 5⅞" 5.00
#495 Dessert/Finger Bowl.........................8.00
#549 Plate 7"...8.00
#550 Plate 8"...8.00

CHERISH Design #681

Blown lead glass stemware
Platinum Band on Gray Mist Bowl, Crystal
  Base
See page 30 for color photo
See Glamour Pattern
Late 1982 Design

#31 Brandy 4½ oz.....................................15.00
#25 Claret 7½ oz. 5¾" 13.00
#2 Goblet 12 oz. 7¼"................................13.00
#26 Tulip Wine 7 oz. 6⅜" 13.00
#63 Luncheon Goblet/Ice Tea 14 oz. 6⅝"..13.00
#549 Plate 7" Gray Decorated.....................8.00

CLASSIC GOLD Design #641

Gold band on crystal bowl
See page 56 for color photo
See Fascination Pattern
1958 – 1962

#29 Cordial 1 oz. 3½"................................10.00
#20 Cocktail 4 oz. 4⅜" 8.00

#27 Claret/Wine 4 oz. 5⅛".........................10.00
#2 Goblet 10 oz. 6¾"................................10.00
#11 Sherbet 7 oz. 4¾"...............................8.00
#88 Juice, Footed, 5 oz. 4¼" 8.00
#63 Luncheon Goblet/Ice Tea 13½ oz. 5½".10.00
#549 Plate 7"..8.00
#550 Plate 8"..8.00

☞ CLASSIC Pattern #6011 ☜

Blown lead glass stemware
Solid Crystal
Amethyst with Crystal Base, Green with crystal base
1934 – 1964
Add 25% for color

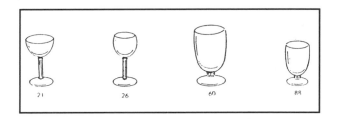

#8 Champagne/High Sherbet 5½ oz. 4¾" 8.00
#21 Cocktail 3½ oz. 4⅝" 8.00
#2 Goblet 10 oz. 6⅜" 10.00
#63 Luncheon Goblet/Ice Tea 13 oz. 5⅜" ..10.00
#88 Juice, Footed 5 oz. 4⅝" 8.00
#11 Sherbet, Low 5½ oz. 3¼" 5.00

#26 Wine 3 oz. 5" 8.00
#495 Dessert/Finger Bowl........................ 8.00
#549 Plate 7"...8.00
#550 Plate 8"...8.00

☞ COIN Pattern #1372 ☜

See pages 32 and 33 for color photos
Crystal, Amber, Olive, Blue, Ruby, Empire Green
1958 – 1982
Add 25% for Amber, Olive
300% for Green, Ruby, Blue
Coin does not conform strictly to the confines of plain patterns, but high interest and the hand molded property of Coin seems to demand a place in this listing.

#114 Ashtray 7½" round..........................22.00
#115 Ashtray 4" oblong 3x4" 12.00
#119 Ashtray 7½" Center Coin.................22.00
#123 Ashtray, One Coin 5" 12.00
#124 Ashtray 10" 25.00
#179 Bowl 8"...45.00
#189 Bowl 9" oval.....................................36.00
#495 Bowl, Nappy 4½".............................30.00
#499 Bowl, Nappy, Handled 5⅜"..............35.00
#316 Candleholder 4½" ....pair 42.00
#326 Candlestick 8" ....pair 25.00
#347 Candy Jar with Cover 6⁵⁄₁₆"..............32.00
#354 Candy Box with Cover 6⅜" 35.00
#381 Cigarette Urn, Footed 3⅜" 16.00
#374 Cigarette Box with Cover 5¾"..........30.00
Cigarette Holder and Ashtray with Cover ..25.00
#199 Compote, Footed 8½" 43.00
#738 Condiment Tray 9⅝" 35.00
#680 Cream 3½"...16.00
#531 Cruet with Stopper 7 oz. 35.00

#400 Decanter with Stopper 90.00
#23 Double Old Fashioned 20.00
#2 Goblet 10½ oz.....................................27.00
#58 Ice Tea 14 oz. 28.00
#448 Jelly, Footed 3¾"..............................16.00
#453 Pitcher, quart 6⁹⁄₁₆".........................65.00
#550 Plate 8"..18.00
#600 Punch Bowl 1½ gallon 14"............250.00
#602 Punch Bowl, Footed 14"..................75.00
#615 Punch Cup 3½".................................13.50
#630 Salver, Cake 10".............................80.00
#652 Shaker, Chrome Top 3¼" 25.00
#7 Sherbet 9 oz. 5⅝" 17.50
#673 Sugar, Covered 5⅜".........................25.00
#64 Tumbler, Ice Tea 12 oz. 5⅛" 37.00
#73 Tumbler, Water 9 oz. 4¼"..................30.00
#81 Tumbler, Juice 9 oz. 3⅝"....................27.00
#829 Urn, Footed with Cover 12¾"...........68.00
#799 Vase, Bud 8"....................................15.00
#162 Wedding Bowl with Cover 8¼".........50.00
#26 Wine 5 oz. 5³⁄₁₆"................................35.00
#310 Lamp, Oil 9¾" 90.00
   Handled Courting Lamp also Electric #311
#459 Lamp, Patio 16⅝"...........................165.00
   Also Electric #466
#324 Lamp, Coach 13½".........................165.00
   Also Electric #321

⊷⊶ COLFAX Pattern #6023 ⊷⊶

Crystal blown lead glass stemware
1940 – 1976

#29 Cordial 1 oz. 3⅜"................................16.00
#8 Champagne 6 oz. 4⅞" 14.00
#27 Claret/Wine 4 oz. 4¾".......................12.50
#21 Cocktail 3¾ oz. 4⅜"..........................10.00
#2 Goblet 9 oz. 6⅜"................................12.50
#63 Luncheon Goblet/Ice Tea 12 oz. 5¾"..12.50
#88 Juice, Footed 5 oz. 4½" 9.00
#11 Low Sherbet 6 oz. 4⅛"........................6.00
#33 Oyster Cocktail 4 oz. 3⅝" 8.00
#72 Water, Footed 9 oz. 5⅛" 11.00
#495 Dessert/Finger Bowl 8.00
#549 Plate 7"..8.00
#550 Plate 8"..8.00

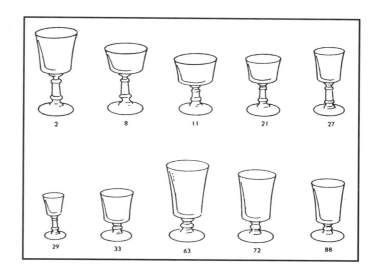

⊷⊶ COLONIAL Pattern #2222 ⊷⊶

Crystal pressed glass
1920 – 1929

Items made in 1928 – 1933 in Amber and Green, named Tea Room then. See Tea Room for pricing and identification.

No. 2222—Pint Jug
Actual Capacity, 19 oz.
Height, 5 inches.

⊷⊶ COLONIAL DAME Pattern #5412 ⊷⊶

Companion Stemware to Colony Pattern #2412
Blown lead glass stemware
Solid Crystal and Empire Green with Crystal Base
1948 – 1982

#27 Claret/Wine 3¾ oz. 4⅝"......................10.00
#29 Cordial 1 oz. 3¼"................................15.00
#21 Cocktail 3½ oz. 4" 8.00
#2 Goblet 11 oz. 6⅜"................................10.00
#88 Juice, Footed 5 oz. 4⅝" 8.00
#63 Luncheon Goblet/Ice Tea 12 oz. 6" 10.00
#33 Oyster Cocktail 4½ oz. 3⅞"...................8.00
#11 Sherbet 6½ oz. 4⅝" 6.00
#495 Dessert/Finger Bowl...........................8.00
#549 Plate 7"...8.00
#550 Plate 8"...8.00

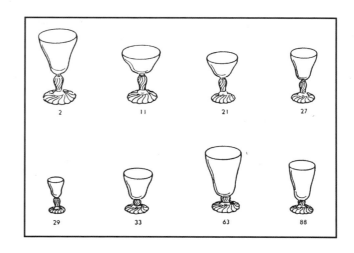

⚓ COLONIAL PRISM Pattern #2183 ⚓

Crystal pressed glass
See page 20 for color photo
1918 – 1928

Boat 8½"	10.00
Boat 11"	14.00
Bowl, Combination	40.00
Bowl, Footed, Flared	25.00
Bowl, Footed, Crimped	25.00
Butter, Covered	40.00
Butter, Covered, 2 Handles	45.00
Cabarette 12"	16.00
Celery, Tall	15.00
Celery Tray 10"	12.00
Celery Tray 12"	15.00
Comport, 5½"	14.00
Comport, Covered 5½"	18.00
Condiment Set (2 Oils, 2 Shakers, 1 Tray)	75.00
Condiment Tray	15.00
Cream (2 Styles)	15.00
Cream, Hotel	14.00
Crushed Ice, Hotel 9¾x7"	20.00
Custard	6.00
Custard, Flared	6.00
Dish, oval 6"	8.00
Dish, oval 7½"	10.00
Dish, oval 9"	12.00
Dish, oval 10½"	14.00
Finger Bowl	9.00
Finger Bowl Plate	5.00
Fruit Bowl 12¼"	18.00
Fruit Bowl 14¾"	20.00
Fruit Salad	30.00
Grapefruit, Footed	8.00
Grapefruit Plate	5.00
Grapefruit Liner	8.00
Ice Tea (2 Styles)	14.00
Ice Tea Plate 4½"	5.00
Ice Tub 4"	20.00
Ice Tub 6½"	24.00
Ice Tub Plate 8"	6.00
Jar, Footed, Covered	28.00
Jelly, Footed 5"	12.00
Jelly, Footed, Covered 4½"	18.00
Lemon Dish	6.00
Lemon Dish, Covered	15.00
Nappy 3¼"	6.00
Nappy 4½"	7.00
Nappy 5"	7.00
Nappy 6"	7.50
Nappy 7"	8.00
Nappy 8"	10.00
Nappy, Flared to 4¾"	7.00
Nappy, Flared to 6"	7.50
Nappy, Flared to 7"	8.00
Nappy, Flared to 8"	10.00

Nappy, Flared to 9"	12.00
Nappy, Shallow 7"	8.00
Nappy, Shallow 8"	10.00
Nappy, Deep 8"	12.00
Nappy, Deep, Flared to 10"	12.00
Nappy, Handled 4½"	7.00
Nappy, Handled, 3 Cornered 5"	7.00
Nappy, Handled, square 4¼"	7.00
Nappy, Handled, Flared 5"	7.00
Nut Bowl	8.00
Oil, Drop Stopper 5½ oz.	25.00
Oil, Drop Stopper 6½ oz.	28.00
Oil, Ground Stopper 5½ oz.	30.00
Oil, Ground Stopper 6½ oz.	35.00
Olive Dish 5¾"	10.00
Orange Bowl, square 8½"	40.00
Pickle Dish 8"	10.00
Pickle Jar, Covered	28.00
Pickle Tray 10"	14.00
Pitcher, Milk 10½ oz.	20.00
Pitcher, Ice Lip, 3 quart	40.00
Pitcher, Ice Lip, ½ gallon	35.00
Pitcher, ½ gallon	35.00
Pitcher, quart	22.00
Plate 9¼"	9.00
Preserve, 2 Handled 5½"	25.00
Punch Bowl	60.00
Punch Bowl with Foot	75.00
Shaker, Nickel or Silver or Glass or Pearl Tops	12.00
Sherbet, Footed	5.00
Sherbet, Footed, Flared	5.00
Sugar, Covered (2 Styles)	22.00
Sugar, Hotel (2 Styles)	15.00
Sugar, Covered, 2 Handles	22.00
Tankard, Footed	55.00
Toothpick	17.50
Tumbler, Table (2 Styles)	9.00
Tumbler, Handled 12 oz.	10.00
Vase 8"	10.00
Vase 10"	12.00
Vase 12"	14.00
Vase, Swung 13"	15.00

COLONY Pattern #2412

Crystal

Rooted in the much older twisted Cascade #112 pattern, Queen Anne (1926 – 1929) became the immediate forerunner of the very popular Colony pattern listed here. Colonial Dame, the stemware companion to Colony, is listed separately. Maypole became the 1982 version of this complicated line.
1938 – 1979

Almond Footed 2¾" 16.00
Ashtray, Individual 3" 11.00
Ashtray, round 3" 11.00
Ashtray, 3½" 12.00
Ashtray, 4½" 15.00
Ashtray, round 4½" 13.00
Ashtray, round 6" 18.00
#137 Bon-Bon 3 toed 7" 14.00
#135 Bon-Bon 5" 13.00
#495 Bowl, round Nappy 4½" 10.00
#506 Bowl, round Nappy 5" 10.00
Bowl, Cupped 8" 43.00
Bowl, Flared 8¼" 48.00
#648 Bowl, Serving, Handled 8½" 38.00
Bowl, Rolled Edge 9" 42.00
#836 Bowl, Vegetable, oval, 10½" 48.00
Bowl, Vegetable, 2 part oval, 10½" 55.00
Bowl, Low Footed, 10½" 68.00
Bowl, Footed, oval 11" 75.00
Bowl, Flared 11" 43.00
#300 Butter with Cover 7½" 55.00
#306 Cake Plate Handled 10" 40.00
#630 Cake Salver 12" 45.00
Candlestick Lustre 6" ....pair 70.00
Candlestick Lustre 7½" ....pair 110.00
Candlestick Lustre 14" ....pair 200.00
#323 Candlestick 7" ....pair 45.00
#332 Candlestick, Duo 6¼" ....pair 60.00
#314 Candlestick 3" ....pair 33.00
Candy, Covered 6½" 48.00
#360 Celery 9⅝" 20.00
Celery 10½" 25.00
#363 Centerpiece Bowl 13" 50.00
Cheese and Cracker Set 40.00
Cheese, Footed 5¼" 17.00
Cigarette Box with cover 75.00
#20 Cocktail 3½ oz. 4" 17.00
Comport and Cover 6⅜" 35.00
#389 Comport 4" 18.50
Cracker Plate 12½" 20.00
#681 Cream, Footed 7 oz. 3⅞" 9.00
#688 Cream, Individual 4 oz. 3¼" 10.00
#669 Cream Soup 5" 43.00
#396 Cup Footed 6 oz. 9.00

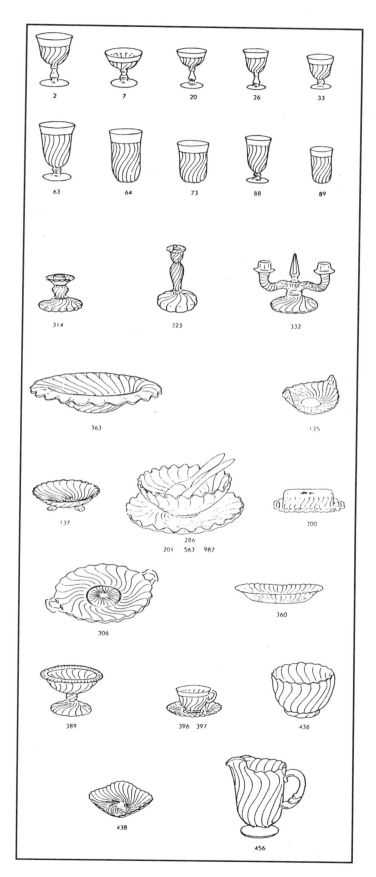

⊷⊷ COLONY Pattern #2412 Cont. ⊷⊷

Finger Bowl 12.00
Fruit Bowl 10½" 45.00
Fruit Bowl, Footed 10½" 55.00
Fruit Bowl, Low 14" 60.00
Fruit Bowl, High Footed.............................65.00
#2 Goblet 9 oz. 5⅛"....................................18.00
#436 Ice Bowl 4½" 85.00
Ice Bowl 6¼" 100.00
#438 Ice Cream Bowl, square 5½".............30.00
Jelly, Covered 6"...38.00
Lemon Dish 6½"...35.00
Lily Pond Bowls 9"......................................32.00
    10"..40.00
    13"..45.00
#477 Mayonnaise, Underplate, Ladle........45.00
Nut Bowl 17.00
Oil with Stopper 4 oz. 5⅞"..........................50.00
Olive, Rectangular 6¼"...............................15.00
#33 Oyster Cocktail 4 oz. 3⅜" 20.00
Pickle 8" 14.00
    9½"..18.00
    Rectangular 8"..14.00
#456 Pitcher, Ice lip 3 pint 8½"................165.00
Pitcher, Ice 2 quart 7¾" 85.00
Pitcher, Cereal pint 5⅞" 70.00
#548 Plate 6"...6.00
#549 Plate 7"...7.00
#550 Plate 8"...8.00
#552 Plate 9"...20.00
#563 Plate, Torte 13"..................................33.00
Plate, Torte 15"..42.00
Plate, Torte 18"..105.00
Platter 12½"..48.00
#600 Punch Bowl 2 gal. 13¼" 400.00

#615 Punch Cup 18.00
#620 Relish, 2 part rectangular 7¼"..........16.00
#622 Relish, 3 part rectangular 10" 18.00
Rose Bowl 6" 48.00
#201 Salad Bowl 9¾"..................................30.00
#397 Saucer...3.00
#656 Shakers, individual 1⅞" ....pair 16.00
#654 Shakers 3⅝".......................................15.00
#659 Shaker Tray, individual 4½" 13.00
#7 Sherbet 5 oz. 3⅝"....................................9.00
#687 Sugar, individual 2¾".........................10.00
#679 Sugar, Footed 3⅜"..............................10.00
Sweetmeat, Handled 5".............................13.00
Sweetmeat, Divided, Rectangular..............26.00
Tid Bit, 3 Toed...18.00
Tid Bit, Footed 7" 30.00
#723 Lunch Tray, Handled 11½"..............32.00
Tray, Snack 10½" 19.00
#726 Tray, Muffin Handled 8⅜" 30.00
#88 Tumbler, Footed 5 oz. 4½"................17.50
#89 Tumbler, Flat 5 oz. 3⅝"......................15.00
#73 Tumbler, Flat 9 oz. 3⅞".......................20.00
#64 Tumbler, Flat 12 oz. 4⅞".....................25.00
#63 Luncheon Goblet/Ice Tea
    Footed 12 oz. 4⅞" 20.00
Urn, Covered 45.00
Urn, Covered, Footed..................................50.00
#763 Vase, Bud, Flared and Footed 6"......20.00
Vase, Cupped and Footed 7"....................55.00
Vase, Footed and Flared 7½"....................65.00
Vase, Cornucopia 9¼"..............................125.00
#840 Whipped Cream Bowl,
    Handled 4¾"..16.00
#26 Wine 3¼ oz. 4⅛"..................................22.00

⊷⊷ CONTINENTAL Pattern #6052½ ⊷⊷

Crystal stemware
See also Moon Ring
1956 – 1973

#29 Cordial 1¼ oz. 3⅛" 15.00
#27 Claret/Wine 4¼ oz. 4⅜".......................11.00
#20 Cocktail 4¾ oz. 3⅞"...............................9.00
#2 Goblet 9¾ oz. 5⅛".................................11.00
#60 Ice Tea 13 oz. 9⅛".................................9.00
#88 Juice, Footed 5½ oz. 4⅞".......................8.00
#7 Sherbet 6½ oz. 4⅜" 6.00
#495 Dessert/Finger Bowl.............................8.00
#549 Plate 7"...8.00
#550 Plate 8"...8.00

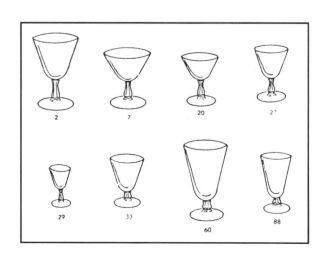

⌘ CONTOUR Pattern #2638, #6060, #2666 ⌘

Crystal, Crystal with Pink
1955 – 1977
In 1972 line matchings only were available.

CONTOUR #2638

#116 Ashtray 1 Lip 3"..................................	6.00
#117 Ashtray 2 Lips 7"..................................	8.00
#118 Ashtray 3 Lips 6"	10.00
#152 Bowl 5½"	8.00
#153 Bowl, square 5½"	8.00
#169 Bowl, Deep 7"	15.00
#174 Bowl, 3 cornered 7½"	14.00
#189 Bowl, oval 8½"	15.00
#191 Bowl, square 8½"	16.50
#220 Bowl, oblong 10½"	18.50
#223 Bowl, High Flared 10¾"......................	20.00
#316 Candlestick 4½" ....pair	25.00
#720 Tray 7"	10.00

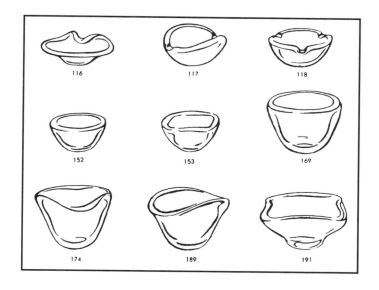

CONTOUR #2666

#136 Bon Bon 6⅞"......................................	12.00
#189 Bowl, oval 8¼"	15.00
#195 Bowl, Salad 9"	18.00
#238 Bowl, Salad 11"	20.00
#300 Butter with Cover, oblong 7"	30.00
#309 Canape Plate 7⅜"...............................	10.00
#680 Cream 8½ oz.......................................	8.00
#688 Cream, Individual 5½"	8.00
#396 Cup 8 oz...	8.00
#360 Celery 9"...	14.00
#579 Crescent Salad Plate 7¼"	14.00
#311 Flora-Candle 6" ....pair	25.00
#477 Mayonnaise with Plate and Ladle	30.00
Mayonnaise Ladle..	12.00
#453 Pitcher, pint 5¼"	26.00
#454 Pitcher, quart 6⅞"...............................	35.00
#455 Pitcher, 3 pint 8¾"	43.00
#549 Plate 7"...	7.00
#500 Preserve, Handled 6½"	18.00
#620 Relish 2 part 7⅜"	13.00
#622 Relish, 3 part 10¾"	16.00
#630 Salver 11¼"...	25.00
#557 Sandwich Plate 11½"...........................	25.00
#639 Sauce Pitcher with Plate 8½"...........	30.00
#397 Saucer...	4.00
#654 Shaker 3¼" ....pair	15.00
#655 Shaker 2⅝"	13.00
#729 Snack Plate 10"	15.00
#677 Sugar 2⅝"...	8.00
#687 Sugar, Individual 2½"	8.00
#567 Torte Plate 14"	28.00
#573 Torte Plate 16"	32.00
#697 Tray for Sugar and Cream	8.00
#723 Tray, Lunch, Handled 11¼"..............	25.00

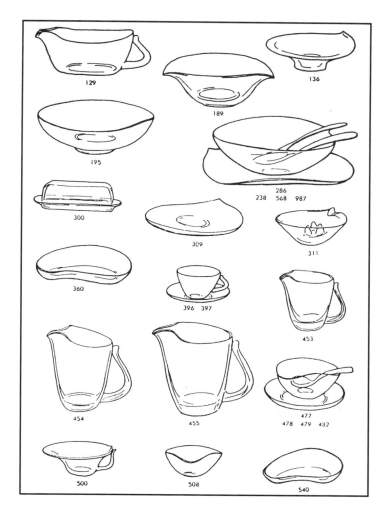

CONTOUR Pattern #2638, #6060, #2666 Cont.

CONTOUR #6060

#2 Goblet 10½ oz. 5⅞" 20.00
#11 Sherbet 6½ oz. 4½" 15.00
#21 Wine/Cocktail 5 oz. 4½".....................15.00
#29 Cordial 1 oz. 2⅞"...............................22.00
#63 Luncheon Goblet/Ice Tea,
    Footed 14 oz. 20.00
#88 Juice, Footed 6 oz. 4¾" .... Crystal 15.00
.... Pink 20.00
#549 Plate, coupe shape 7".......................8.00
#550 Plate 7"..8.00

CONTRAST Pattern #6120

White bowl with Onyx base
See Eloquence Pattern
1970 – Matching Service only after 1978

#25 Claret 9 oz. 5¹⁵⁄₁₆................................15.00
#2 Goblet 14 oz. 7"...................................14.00
#29 Liqueur 2 oz. 3⅝"...............................12.00

#63 Luncheon Goblet/Ice Tea 15 oz. 6⅞"..14.00
#11 Sherbet 10 oz. 5⅝".............................10.00
#549 Plate, Onyx 7"..................................10.00

CORONET Pattern #2560

Crystal dinnerware
Do not confuse with Coronet Design #656
1938 – 1960

Bon Bon, 3 Toed 7¼" 8.00
Bon Bon 5¾" 8.00
Bowl, Cereal 6"..7.00
Bowl, Cupped 8½" 15.00
Bowl, Handled 8½".....................................15.00
Bowl, Handled 11".....................................22.00
Bowl, Crimped 11½" 20.00
Bowl, Flared 12" 22.00
Bowl, Serving, Handled 20.00
Cake Plate, Handled 10½"..........................16.00
Candlestick 4".................................pair 20.00
Candlestick 4½".............................pair 30.00
Candlestick Duo 5⅛" ....pair 32.00
Cheese, Footed 17.00
Cheese and Cracker 25.00
Celery Tray, 11".......................................17.00
Compote 6" 16.00
Cracker Plate...14.00

Cream, Footed 4⅛" 7.00
Cream, Individual......................................7.00
Cup, Footed 5½ oz. 8.00
Fruit, Individual 5".....................................6.00
Fruit Bowl 13"..19.00
Ice Bucket, Chrome Handle 25.00
Lemon Plate 6¼".......................................8.00
Lunch Tray, Handled 11½" 28.00
Mayonnaise with Underplate and Ladle 38.00
Mayonnaise, 2 part with Underplate and
    2 Ladles 50.00
Muffin Tray, Handled 8½" 17.00
Nut Bowl 3 Toed, Crimped........................9.00
Oil, Footed with Stopper 28.00
Olive 6¾"..11.00
Pickle 8¾"..14.00
Plate 6" 3.00
Plate 7" 5.00
Plate 8" 7.00

⇥ CORONET Pattern #2560 Cont. ⇤

Plate 9" 17.00
Relish, 2 part 6½" 13.00
Relish, 3 part 10" 17.00
Relish, 4 part 21.00
Relish, 5 part 25.00
Salad Bowl 10" 21.00
Salad Bowl, 2 part 23.00
Saucer 3.00
Shakers, Footed ....pair 13.00
Sugar, Footed 3½" 7.00

Sugar, Individual...7.00
Sweetmeat Bowl 5½"..................................10.00
Tid-Bit, Flat 3 Toed 13.00
Torte Plate 13"...22.00
Torte Plate 14"...25.00
Tray for Sugar and Cream 7½".....................10.00
Tray for Individual Sugar and Cream........10.00
Vase, 3¾" Pansy 8.00
Vase, Handled 6" 12.00
Whipped Cream 5" 10.00

⇥ CORSAGE PLUM Pattern #6126 ⇤

Blown lead glass stemware
Crystal Bowl with Plum Stem and Base
See page 59 for color photo
See also Gazebo and Wimbledon
1973 – 1978

#11 Champagne/Dessert 9 oz. 5⅝".............9.00
#63 Luncheon Goblet/Ice Tea 13 oz. 6" 12.00
#2 Goblet 12 oz. 7"...................................13.00
#26 Wine 7 oz. 5¾"...................................12.00
#549 Plate 7"...8.00

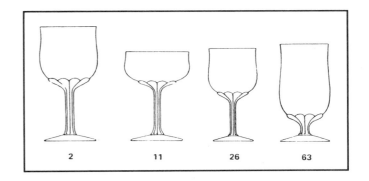

⇥ COURTSHIP Pattern #6051½ ⇤

Crystal blown lead glass stemware
1956 – Matching service only after 1978

#27 Claret/Wine 4 oz. 4½"........................11.00
#20 Cocktail 3¼ oz. 3⅞"...........................12.00
#29 Cordial 1¼ oz. 3⅛" 15.00
#2 Goblet 10½ oz. 6³⁄₁₆" 11.00
#88 Juice, Footed 5 oz. 4" 9.00
#63 Luncheon Goblet/Ice Tea 12¼ oz. 6⅛".11.00
#33 Oyster Cocktail 4½ oz. 3¾"...................8.00
#7 Sherbet 6½ oz. 4⅜" 6.00
#495 Dessert/Finger Bowl........................ 8.00
#549 Plate 7"...8.00
#550 Plate 8"...8.00

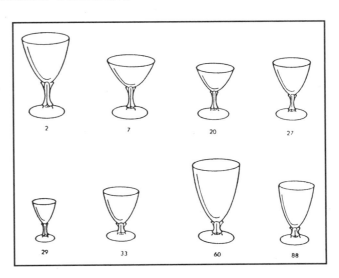

CRYSTAL TWIST Pattern #6101

Crystal blown lead glass stemware
1962 – 1971

#29 Cordial 1½ oz. 3⅛" 12.00
#2 Goblet 10 oz. 6⅛".......................................8.00
#63 Luncheon Goblet/Ice Tea 14 oz. 6⅛"..10.00
#88 Juice, Footed 6 oz. 5" 6.00
#11 Sherbet 7 oz. 4⅜"....................................5.00
#27 Wine/Cocktail 5 oz. 4⅞"....................6.00
#495 Dessert/Finger Bowl.........................8.00
#549 Plate 7"...8.00
#550 Plate 8"...8.00

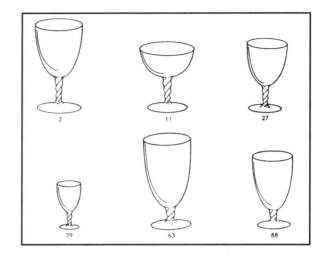

DEBUTANTE Pattern #6100

Crystal blown lead glass stemware
See page 34 for color photo
Crystal or Grey Mist Bowl with Crystal Base
1962 – 1985

#31 Brandy 1½ oz. 2¹³⁄₁₆" 8.00
#25 Claret 7½ oz. 5⁵⁄₁₆" 10.00
#2 Goblet 11 oz. 6⅝".................................10.00
#63 Luncheon Goblet/Ice Tea 14½ oz. 6⅝"10.00
#11 Sherbet 7½ oz. 4⅛" 8.00
#26 Tulip Wine 5½ oz. 5⁹⁄₁₆".....................10.00
#495 Dessert/Finger Bowl.........................8.00
#549 Plate 7" Grey 8.00
#550 Plate 8" Grey 8.00

DECORATOR Pattern #2691

Crystal
1956 – 1960

Ashtray, Individual 2⅝" 3.00
Bowl, Sauce with Underplate and
   Ladle 2¾"..8.00
Cigarette Holder 2½"..................................8.00
Cream 3¼"..10.00
Cup 7½ oz. 7.00
Cup, Demitasse 2¼ oz. 8.00
Dessert 4⅞"...7.00
Plate 7" 8.00

Preserve, Handled 4" 10.00
Saucer, regular 4.00
Saucer, Demitasse.......................................5.00
Server, 2 part 1½ x 6⅜"..........................15.00
Server, 3 part 9⅜ x 7½"...........................18.00
Shaker, chrome top 3".....................each 7.00
Sugar, covered 3¼" 12.00
Soup 4¾"..7.00
Tray for Sugar and Cream 10.00

DIADEM Pattern #2430

Crystal, Azure, Rose, Green, Amber, Topaz
Selected items in Ebony
Early: 1929 – 1944

Bowl 11".....................................15.00	Mint 5½"......................................13.00
Candy jar with Cover ½ lb. 24.00	Vase 8"..18.00
Jelly 7"......................................14.00	Tall Candlesticks reported in color 65.00

DIADEM Pattern #6056

Crystal blown lead glass
1954 – 1965

Claret/Wine 4¼".....................................6.00
Cocktail 3⅜" 5.00
Cordial 3"...15.00
Goblet 5⅝"..10.00
Ice Tea, Footed 6⅜"................................8.00
Juice, Footed 4⅞".................................8.00
Oyster Cocktail 4¹⁄₁₆" 6.00
Sherbet 4" 6.00

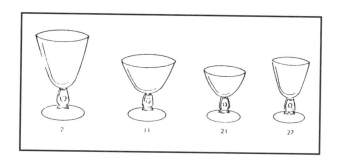

DIANA Pattern #601

Crystal pressed glass
Plain, Scalloped Edge Pattern
1898 – 1913

Butter, Covered 20.00
Berry Bowl 4½"......................................7.00
Berry Bowl 7" 10.00
Berry Bowl 8" 19.00
Bowl, Open, High Foot 7"........................22.50
Bowl, Open, High Foot 8"........................25.00
Bowl, Covered, High Foot 7" 37.50
Bowl, Covered, High Foot 8" 44.00
Bowl, Low Foot 7"...................................38.50
Bowl, Low Foot 8"...................................52.00
Celery..18.50
Comport 4"..10.00
Cream 16.00
Jelly 5"...12.50
Jug ½ gallon...32.50
Salver 9"..32.50
Salver 10"...35.00
Shaker, Nickel Top 7.50
Spooner 17.50
Syrup...27.50
Sugar, Covered....................................20.00

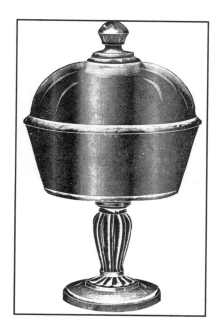

Tankard ½ gallon....................................50.00
Tumbler 5.00

DISTINCTION Pattern #6125

See pages 35, 59 and 60 for color photos
**Crystal, Blue Bowl with Crystal Base, Plum
Bowl with Crystal Base, Cobalt Bowl with
Crystal Base.
1972 – 1985**

#11 Champagne/Dessert 9 oz. 4½" 14.00
#2 Goblet 11 oz. 7⅜" 18.00
#63 Luncheon Goblet/Ice Tea 13 oz. 6¾" ..18.00
#26 Wine 6½ oz. 6¼" 16.00
#549 Plate 7" 8.00

2   11   26   63

DRAPE Pattern #1300

**Crystal pressed glass
See page 20 for color photo
1904 – 1906
Some items reproduced in 1969 Centennial
II Collection.**

Bon Bon, Handled 10.00
Bowl, Footed 7" 16.00
Bowl, Footed 8" 20.00
Bowl, Footed 10½" 22.00
Bowl, Footed 11½" 25.00
Butter, Covered 56.00
Celery, Tall...30.00
Comport 4"..6.00
Comport 4½" 6.00
Comport 7"...8.00
Comport 8"..20.00
Comport 9"..22.00
Comport 10"..24.00
Comport 11"..26.00
Comport, Cupped 11".............................15.00
Cracker Jar...56.00
Cracker Jar and Cover 60.00
Cream...22.00
Cream, Individual....................................10.00
Custard...9.00
Finger Bowl..14.00

Fruit Bowl 13"...35.00
Ice Cream 5"..10.00
Jelly, Footed 5"..15.00
Molasses Can, Nickel or Tin Top 45.00
Nappy, Handled 5" 10.00
Nicknack..14.00
Pitcher, ½ gallon.....................................70.00
Plate 5" 4.00
Plate 6"...6.00
Plate 9"...8.00
Punch Bowl 16"..35.00
Punch Bowl 16" with Stand 50.00
Rose Bowl 26.00
Salver 9"...30.00
Shaker...15.00
Sherbet, Footed 8.00
Sugar, Covered...27.00
Sugar, Individual......................................16.00
Toothpick..23.50
Tumbler 16.00
Vinegar or Oil, Cut or Stopper 50.00
Water Bottle..65.00

⇥ EDGEWOOD WARE #675 ⇤

Crystal pressed glass
1898 – 1908
Re-issued in lead crystal 1974 – 75

Bottle, Water 65.00
Butter, Covered 44.00
Berry Bowl 4½" 12.50
Berry Bowl 8" 16.50
Bowl, oval 9" 24.00
Celery Stand 24.00
Celery Tray...12.50
Cream 18.00
Custard...8.00
Finger Bowl...7.50

Oil and Vinegar (2 styles)..................pair 38.00
Pickle Jar, Open.......................................22.00
Pickle Jar, Covered..................................33.00
Shaker (2 styles)...........................pair 17.00
Spooner..20.00
Sugar Shaker 25.00
Sugar, Covered...25.00
Syrup, Nickel Top or Regular Top 42.00
Tankard 95.00
Tumbler 15.00

⇥ ELEGANCE Pattern #6064½ ⇤

Crystal blown lead glass stemware
Narrow Rib Optic
1956 – 1971

#29 Cordial 1 oz. 3⅝".................................15.00
#25 Claret 5¾ oz. 5¾" 10.00
#20 Cocktail 4 oz. 4½" 10.00
#8 Champagne 8 oz. 5¾" 8.00
#2 Goblet 9¾ oz. 7".....................................11.00
#63 Luncheon Goblet/Ice Tea 13½ oz. 6⁷⁄₁₆".11.00
#11 Sherbet, Low 7 oz. 4⅝"..........................8.00
#33 Seafood Cocktail 7¾ oz. 3⅝" 8.00
#88 Juice, Footed 5½ oz. 4⅞".......................8.00
#26 Wine 3¼ oz. 5⅛"...................................10.00
#549 Plate, Narrow Rib Optic 7" 8.00

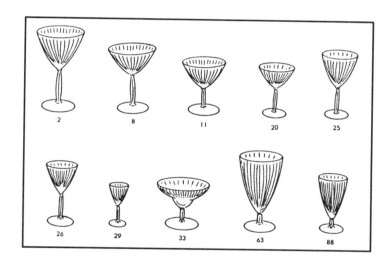

⇥ ELOQUENCE Pattern #6120 ⇤

Crystal blown glass stemware
See page 59 for color photo
See also Contrast Pattern
Eloquence Onyx Crystal Bowl with Onyx
Base, Eloquence Gold #686 Gold Band at
Rim, Eloquence Platinum #687 Platinum
Band at Rim, Eloquence Gold in Matchings
Only in 1973
1971 – 1978

#25 Claret 9 oz. 6"......................................15.00
#2 Goblet 14 oz. 7" 16.00
#63 Luncheon Goblet/Ice Tea 15 oz. 6⅞" ..16.00
#29 Liqueur 2 oz. 3⅜"..................................14.00
#11 Sherbet 10 oz. 5⅝"...............................12.00

#495 Dessert/Finger Bowl.........................8.00
#549 Plate 7"...5.00
#550 Plate 8"...6.00

⇒ EMBASSY Pattern #6083 ⇐

Crystal blown lead glass stemware
1959 – 1974
Line Matchings Only in 1973, 1974

#29 Cordial 1¼ oz. 3⁵⁄₁₆" 12.00
#27 Cocktail/Wine 4 oz. 4⁹⁄₁₆" 6.50
#2 Goblet 11½ oz. 6¼" 7.50
#63 Luncheon Goblet/Ice Tea 14 oz. 6¼" 8.00
#11 Sherbet 7¾ oz. 4¾" 5.00
#88 Juice, Footed 5½ oz. 4¾" 6.00
#549 Plate 7"...8.00
#550 Plate 8"...8.00

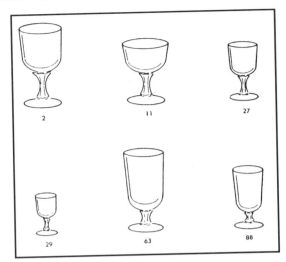

⇒ ENCHANTMENT Pattern #6074 ⇐

Crystal blown lead glass stemware
1958 – 1965

#29 Cordial 1 oz. 3¼"................................15.00
#20 Cocktail/Wine 4 oz. 5" 11.00
#2 Goblet 9½ oz. 6¼" 9.00
#11 Sherbet 6 oz. 4¾"..............................7.00
#88 Juice, Footed 5 oz. 4¾" 11.00
#63 Luncheon Goblet/Ice Tea 13 oz. 6⅜" ..14.00
#549 Plate 7"...8.00
#550 Plate 8"...8.00

⇒ ENGAGEMENT Design #648 ⇐

Crystal with Platinum Band on bowl
See page 35 for color photo
Based on Priscilla Pattern
1960 – 1985

#29 Cordial 1½ oz. 3½" 15.00
#27 Cocktail/Wine 4½ oz. 5¼" 8.00
#2 Goblet 10½ oz. 7"...............................10.00

#63 Luncheon Goblet/Ice Tea 14 oz. 6⅜" ..15.00
#88 Juice, Footed 5½ oz. 4¾" 19.00
#11 Sherbet 7 oz. 5⁷⁄₁₆" 10.00
#495 Dessert/Finger Bowl........................8.00
#550 Plate 8"...8.00

⇒ ENVOY Pattern #6027 ⇐

Crystal blown lead glass stemware
1940 – 1957

Cordial 1 oz. 2¾" 15.00
Cocktail 3½ oz. 3⅞"..................................8.00
Goblet 10 oz. 5¼".....................................10.00
Oyster Cocktail 4 oz. 3"............................8.00

Saucer champagne 5½ oz. 4¼" 8.00
Sherbet 5½ oz. 3¼" 7.00
Juice, Footed 5 oz. 4" 8.00
Ice Tea, Footed 12 oz. 5½".........................10.00

ESSEX Pattern #1372

Crystal pressed glass
See page 20 for color photo
1905 – 1925

Bon Bon	4.00
Butter, Covered	45.00
Cabaret 10"	10.00
Cabaret 11"	12.00
Celery	20.00
Claret	10.00
Cocktail	10.00
Champagne, Saucer	8.00
Champagne, Tall	10.00
Comport 4½"	6.00
Comport 8"	12.00
Comport 9"	15.00
Cordial	12.00
Cream	15.00
Cream, Hotel	15.00
Custard	8.00
Dish, oval 7"	14.00
Dish, oval 8"	15.00
Dish, oval 9"	16.00
Finger Bowl	16.00
Finger Bowl Plate	18.00
Goblet	14.00
Ice Cream 5½"	10.00
Jug, ½ gallon	35.00
Nappy 5"	6.00
Nappy 6"	7.00
Nappy 7"	8.00
Nappy 8"	10.00
Olive	10.00
Oyster Cocktail & Liner	18.00
Pickle Dish	15.00
Punch Bowl 10"	28.00
Punch Bowl Footed 10"	35.00
Shaker, Silver or Nickel Plated Top	15.00
Spoon	15.00
Sugar, Covered	20.00
Sugar, Hotel	14.00
Sugar Shaker	15.00
Sundae	4.00
Syrup, Britannia or Nickel Top	25.00
Syrup Ewer	25.00
Toothpick	15.00
Tumbler	12.00
Tumbler, Ice Tea	14.00
Tumbler, Footed	16.00
Violet Bouquet Holder	12.00

EXETER Pattern #6109

Henry Ford Museum Line
Blown lead glass stemware
See page 64 for color photo
Solid Crystal, Solid Amethyst
1967 – 1971
Add 25% for color

#2 Goblet 10 oz. 7½"	12.00
#63 Luncheon Goblet/Ice Tea 12 oz. 6¾"	14.00
#11 Sherbet 7 oz. 5⅞"	19.00
#27 Sherry/Liqueur 3½ oz. 5⅜"	10.00
#26 Wine 6 oz. 5⅝"	14.00
#549 Plate 7"	8.00
#550 Plate 8"	8.00

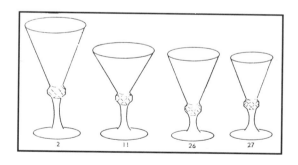

FAIRFAX Pattern #2375

Dinnerware Line
Crystal; Amber, Green 1927 – 1941; Orchid 1927 – 1928; Rose, Azure 1928 – 1941; Topaz 1929 – 1936; Selected items in Ebony 1930 – 1942; Selected items in Ruby 1935 – 1939

1927 –1960
300% for Azure and Orchid, 200% for Rose and Green, 150% for Topaz, Gold Tint, Amber

Ashtray	15.00
Baker, oval 9"	22.00

FAIRFAX Pattern #2375 Cont.

Baker, oval 10½"	25.00
Bon Bon	10.00
Bouillon	10.00
Bottle, Salad Dressing	60.00
Bowl, round 8"	14.00
Bowl 12"	18.00
Bowl, Whipped Cream, Handled 5½"	35.00
Butter and Cover	100.00
Cake Plate, 2 Handles 10"	15.00
Canape Plate	5.00
Candlestick 3"	pair 20.00
Candlestick 6"	pair 30.00
Celery 11½"	12.00
Centerpiece, oval	22.00
Centerpiece 12"	18.00
Centerpiece 15"	21.00
Cereal Bowl	12.50
Cheese, Footed	12.00
Cheese & Cracker	20.00
Chop Plate 13"	30.00
Cigarette Box, Covered	30.00
Comport 7"	22.00
Cracker Plate	8.00
Cream	15.00
Cream, Footed, Tea	8.00
Cream Soup, Footed	10.00
Cream Soup Plate	5.00
Cup	6.00
Cup, Footed	8.00
Cup, After Dinner	10.00
Dessert Tray, 2 Handles	18.00
Flower Holder, oval	30.00
Fruit 5"	7.00
Grill Plate 10"	15.00
Ice Bucket	35.00
Lemon Dish	10.00
Lunch Tray, Handled	75.00
Mayonnaise	15.00
Mayonnaise Plate	5.00
Mayonnaise Ladle	20.00
Nappy, round 7"	15.00
Oil Cruet, Footed	88.00
Pickle Dish 8½"	10.00
Plate 6"	5.00
Plate, Salad 7"	6.00
Plate, Salad 8"	7.00
Plate, Dinner 9"	10.00
Plate Dinner 10"	18.00
Platter 10½" oval	25.00
Platter 12" oval	30.00
Platter 15" oval	40.00
Sauce Boat	25.00
Sauce Boat Plate	14.00
Saucer	3.00
Saucer, After Dinner	6.00
Shaker, Footed	pair 50.00
Sugar	10.00
Sugar, Footed	10.00
Sugar, Footed, Covered	24.00
Sugar, Tea	6.00
Sweetmeat	8.00

FAIRLANE Pattern #2916

Lead Crystal
See page 36 for color photo
Late pattern still made in 1982

#29 Cordial 2 oz. 3⅜"	12.00
#11 Dessert/Champagne 9 oz. 5 11/16"	8.00
#23 Double Old Fashioned 11 oz. 3½"	6.00
#2 Goblet 11 oz. 7 5/16"	9.00
#64 Highball 14 oz. 5½"	5.00
#63 Luncheon Goblet/Ice Tea 14 oz. 6⅝"	9.00
#26 Wine 6½ oz. 6 3/16"	10.00

FAIRMONT Pattern #2718

Crystal, Blue, Green, Amber
1958 - 1965

#360 Celery 9¼"	8.00
#681 Cream, Footed 4¼"	6.00
#421 Dessert Bowl 5"	5.00
#2 Goblet 10½ oz. 5⅞"	7.00
#63 Luncheon Goblet/Ice Tea 13 oz.	7.00
#88 Juice, Footed 5 oz. 5⅛"	5.00
#447 Jelly, Covered 6"	8.00

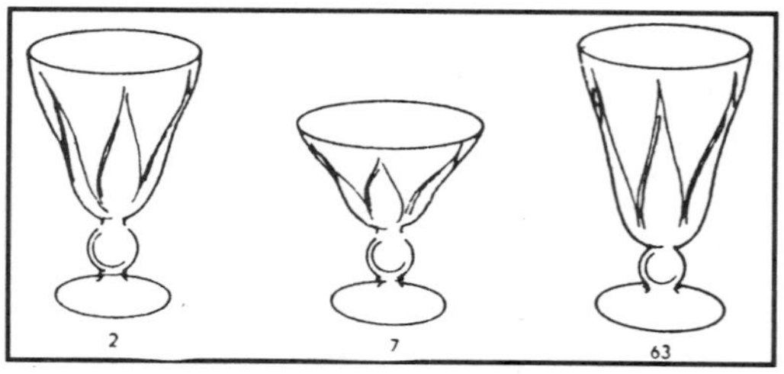

FAIRMONT Pattern #271 Cont.

#540 Pickle Dish 7¾"..................................7.00
#550 Plate 8"..8.00
#620 Relish, 2 part 9⅛"...........................10.00

#635 Sauce Dish with Cover 4"................10.00
#7 Sherbet 6 oz. 4⅜"................................6.00
#679 Sugar, Footed 3½"............................8.00

FASCINATION Pattern #6080

Blown lead glass stemware
See page 36 and 56 for color photos
Crystal; Lilac Bowl with Crystal Base; Ruby
   Bowl with Crystal Base
1958 – 1985

#29 Cordial 1 oz. 3½"...............................15.00
#27 Claret/Wine 4 oz. 5⅛"........................12.00
#25 Claret, Large 6 oz. 5¾"........................16.00
#20 Cocktail 4 oz. 4⅜"..............................10.00
#2 Goblet 10 oz. 6¾"................................12.00
#63 Luncheon Goblet/Ice Tea 13½ oz. 5½".12.00
#11 Dessert/Champagne 7 oz. 4¾"..............8.00
#88 Juice, Footed 5 oz. 4¼".......................10.00

FESTIVE Pattern #6127

See page 36 for color photo
Crystal or Blue Bowl on Crystal Base
Custom order in Yellow
Late 1970's – 1982

#25 Claret 7 oz. 6¼"..................................7.00
#11 Dessert/Champagne 9 oz. 5¾".............5.00

#2 Goblet 12 oz. 7⅜"................................8.00
#63 Luncheon Goblet/Ice Tea 15 oz. 7"......7.00

FIRELIGHT Design #657

Mother of Pearl Iridescent Bowl Only
Loop Optic
See page 59 for color photo
See Fascination Pattern
1963 – 1985
Matching Service only in 1981

#27 Claret/Wine 4 oz. 16.00
#20 Cocktail 4 oz.....................................14.00
#29 Cordial 1 oz. 18.00
#88 Juice, Footed 5 oz..............................13.00

#2 Goblet 10 oz. 16.00
#63 Luncheon Goblet/Ice Tea 13½ oz. 16.00
#11 Sherbet 7 oz. 10.00
#549 Plate, Loop Optic 7" 8.00

FLEMISH Pattern #1913

Crystal pressed glass
1913 – 1928
Some items produced in 1969

Basket 11"...50.00	
Butter and Cover...45.00	
Caster, 3 Bottle 60.00	
Celery Dip, Large 10.00	
Celery Dip, Small 8.00	
Celery Tall...15.00	
Celery Tray..8.00	
Cream...15.00	
Cream, Individual..10.00	
Cracker Jar and Cover 60.00	
Custard 8.00	
Finger Bowl..10.00	
Finger Bowl Plate 5.00	
Fruit Bowl 11"...20.00	
Goblet 9 oz. 10.00	
Jelly Bowl, Covered.....................................30.00	
Jug, quart "Hall Boy"..................................20.00	
Jug, ½ gallon 30.00	
Nappy 4" 6.00	
Nappy 4½"..6.00	
Nappy 7" 9.00	
Nappy 8" 10.00	
Nappy 9" 10.00	
Match Box/Toothpick Box..........................15.00	
Molasses Can...30.00	
Oil with Stopper 5 oz. 25.00	
Oil, Tall with Stopper 7 oz. 30.00	
Orange Bowl 9" 40.00	
Pickle Tray 14.00	
Pickle Jar, Covered.....................................28.00	
Punch Bowl..60.00	
Punch Bowl with Stand 75.00	

Sherbet, Low 6.00
Sherbet, Medium..7.00
Sherbet, Tall..8.00
Sherry 2 oz..8.00
Sugar, Covered..20.00
Sugar, Individual..15.00
Sugar Sifter..25.00
Shaker ....pair 10.00
Shaker, Restaurant ....pair 10.00
Syrup, Metal Handle....................................30.00
Toothpick 15.00
Tumbler, Ice Tea...12.00
Tumbler, Table..10.00
Tumbler, Milk 11 oz. 9.00
Tumbler, Split 8 oz. 8.00
Vase, Bud 6" 9.00
Vase 6"..9.00
Vase 8"..12.00
Vase 10"...15.00
Wine 4½ oz. 8.00
Whiskey 2 oz. 7.00

FRISCO Pattern #1229

Crystal pressed glass
See page 21 for color photo
1903 – 1905
Aqua and Peach Milk Glass 1937 – 1958
***Items made in Milk Glass in 1954 – 1964**
Late production of Candy Jar in Lead Crystal

Bowl 7"...16.50
Bowl, Covered 7" 45.00
Butter 35.00
Butter, Covered 50.00
Cabaret 15.00
*Candy Jar & Cover.....................................30.00

↬ FRISCO Pattern #1229 Cont. ↫

Comport 4½" 6.00
Comport 6" 8.00
Comport 7" 10.00
Comport 8" 12.00
Cream 20.00
Fruit Bowl 9" 35.00
Oil 35.00
Pitcher, ½ gallon (2 Styles) 65.00
Shaker, Nickel Top 16.00

Spoon...22.00
*Spooner 28.00
*Toothpick..................................20.00
Tumbler 16.00
Vase 3½" 8.00
Vase 6" 12.00
*Vase Bud 6" 15.00
*Vase, Swung 10" 30.00
Vase 13" 18.00

↬ GALA Pattern #6147 ↫

Crystal blown lead glass stemware
See page 30 for color photo
1981 –1985

#11 Dessert/Champagne 9 oz. 5" 7.00
#2 Goblet 12 oz. 7⅜"..7.00

#63 Luncheon Goblet/Ice Tea 14 oz. 7" 8.00
#25 Wine 9 oz. 6⅝".......................................8.00

↬ GAZEBO Pattern #6126 or GA01/GA02 ↫

Blowl lead glass stemware
See page 37 for color photo
See Corsage Plum and Wimbledon
Crystal Bowl with Ebony Stem
Crystal Bowl with Rust Stem
1980 – 1985

#11 Dessert/Champagne 9 oz. 5⅝" 10.00
#2 Goblet 12 oz. 7" 8.00
#63 Luncheon Goblet/Ice Tea 13 oz. 6" 10.00
#26 Wine 7 oz. 5¾" 10.00

↬ GLACIER Design #2510 ↫

Crystal
Sun Ray #2510 with ribs in Silver Mist
Acid etched
1935 –1944
See Sun-Ray
Do not confuse with Glacier gift line

Ashtray, Square 6.00
Ashtray, Individual......................6.00
Bon Bon, Handled 10.00
Bowl, 13"....................................20.00
Bowl, Handled............................18.00
Candlestick 3".................pair 25.00
Candlestick 5½".............pair 30.00

Candlestick 2 Light ....pair 45.00
Candelabra/Candlestick Duo 40.00
Candy Jar with Cover 30.00
Celery, Handled......................................13.00
Cheese or Butter Tray 25.00
Cigarette Box with Cover 30.00
Cigarette Box with Cover, oblong............25.00

GLACIER Design #2510 Cont.

Claret 4½ oz. 8.00	Relish, 4 part 15.00
Cocktail, Footed 4 oz 8.00	Rose Bowl 3½" 16.00
Comport 15.00	Rose Bowl 5" 25.00
Cream, Footed 8.00	Shaker ....pair 16.00
Cream, Individual.........................8.00	Shaker, Individual...............pair 17.00
Cream Soup with Underplate.............20.00	Salad Bowl 13".........................25.00
Cup...6.00	Salt Dip...................................5.00
Decanter with Stopper 18 oz.............35.00	Sandwich Plate 12"....................30.00
Fruit 5" 6.00	Saucer 2.00
Fruit Cocktail 8.00	Sherbet 5 oz. 6.00
Frozen Dessert 11.00	Sugar, Footed...........................8.00
Goblet 9 oz. 12.00	Sugar, Individual.......................7.00
Ice Bucket, Chrome Handle 30.00	Sweetmeat, Divided, Handled 15.00
Jelly, Covered...........................25.00	Torte Plate 11"..........................25.00
Jug, Ice Lip 55.00	Torte Plate 15"..........................35.00
Jug 2 quart 55.00	Tray for Shakers........................12.50
Mustard, Covered with Spoon...........22.00	Tray for Sugar and Cream 15.00
Mayonnaise with Plate and Ladle.......25.00	Tray, Handled, oval 30.00
Nappy, Tri-Cornered 10.00	Tray, Square 10" 22.00
Nappy, Square...........................10.00	Tray, Oblong 10½".....................20.00
Nappy, Flared 15.00	Tumbler, Footed 5 oz...................8.00
Nappy, Regular..........................10.00	Tumbler, Footed 9 oz...................9.00
Oil with Stopper 3 oz. 30.00	Tumbler, Footed 13 oz.................10.00
Onion Soup with Cover..................25.00	Tumbler, 5 oz...........................15.00
Pickle Dish, Handled 8.00	Tumbler, 9 oz...........................18.00
Plate 6" 6.00	Tumbler, 13 oz..........................22.00
Plate 7" 6.00	Tumbler, Old Fashioned 8.00
Plate 8" 8.00	Vase, 6" 25.00
Plate 9" 8.00	Vase, 7" 30.00
Plate, Flat 16".............................35.00	Vase, Square Footed 30.00
Relish, 2 part 14.00	Vase, Sweet Pea........................30.00
Relish, 3 part 15.00	Whiskey, 2 oz. 7.00

GLAMOUR Pattern #6103

Crystal blown lead glass stemware
See pages 30 and 37 for color photos
Green Mist Bowl with Crystal Base added in
   1968; Gray Mist Bowl with Crystal Base
   1969; Crystal Bowl with Onyx Base 1969;
   Blue Bowl with Crystal Base 1969
1964 – 1982

#31 Brandy 4½ oz. 3⅞" 8.00
#25 Claret 7½ oz. 5¾" 10.00
#2 Goblet 12 oz. 7¼".......................10.00
#63 Luncheon Goblet/Ice Tea 14 oz. 6⅝" ..10.00
#11 Sherbet 8 oz. 5⅛"......................6.00
#26 Tulip Wine 7 oz. 6⅜" 10.00
#495 Dessert/Finger Bowl...................8.00
#549 Plate 7" 8.00
#550 Plate 8" 8.00

⤙⤙ GOLDEN BELLE Design #677 ⤙⤙

Crystal with Gold Band on Bowl
See Promise
1968 – Late 1970s

#224 Bowl, Footed 10".................................8.00
#681 Cream, Footed 7.00
#2 Goblet 11 oz. 12.00
#11 Sherbet 7 oz. 6.00
#29 Liqueur 2 oz. 8.00

#63 Luncheon Goblet/Ice Tea 14 oz. 12.00
#26 Wine 7 oz. 12.00
#549 Plate 7"..8.00
#550 Plate 8"..8.00
#620 Relish, 2 part.....................................8.00
#643 Relish, 4 part...................................10.00
#644 Relish, 5 part...................................15.00
#679 Sugar, Footed 7.00

⤙⤙ GOLDEN FLAIR Design #643 ⤙⤙

Gold Band on Crystal Bowl
See Chateau Pattern
1959 – 1970
Matching Service Only 1969

#29 Cordial 1¼ oz. 3½" 12.00
#27 Cocktail/Wine 3¼ oz. 5¼" 8.00

#2 Goblet 8¼ oz. 7"...................................10.00
#88 Juice, Footed 5 oz. 5" 7.00
#63 Luncheon Goblet/Ice Tea 11 oz. 6⅜"..10.00
#11 Sherbet 6½ oz. 5⁷⁄₁₆" 8.00
#549 Plate 7"..8.00
#550 Plate 8"..8.00

⤙⤙ GOLDEN GRAIL Design #644 ⤙⤙

Crystal with Encrusted Gold Band on Bowl
See Embassy Pattern
1959 – 1974
Matchings Only after 1971

#29 Cordial 1¼ oz. 3⁵⁄₁₆" 14.00
#27 Cocktail/Wine 3¾ oz. 4⁹⁄₁₆" 10.00
#2 Goblet 11½ oz. 6¼" 12.00
#63 Luncheon Goblet/Ice Tea
   14 oz. 6⅜"...12.00
#88 Juice, Footed 5½ oz. 4¾" 11.00
#11 Sherbet 7¾ oz. 4¾" 8.00

#549 Plate 7"..8.00
#550 Plate 8"..8.00

⤙⤙ GOLDEN TRIUMPH Pattern #6112 ⤙⤙

Crystal blown lead glass with metal stem
See page 64 for color photo
See also Caribbean
1969 – 1973

#3 Goblet 10 oz. 7" 11.00
#64 Luncheon Goblet/Ice Tea 14 oz. 7⅛" ..11.00
#12 Sherbet 8 oz. 5⅛".................................7.00
#27 Tulip Wine 5½ oz. 6⁷⁄₁₆".......................11.00
#495 Dessert/Finger Bowl 8.00
#549 Plate 7"..8.00
#550 Plate 8"..8.00

3   12   27   64

⇌ GOURMET Pattern #2785 ⇌

Crystal handmolded dinnerware
Platinum Decoration #668 and Gold Decoration #669 added in 1966
1965 – 1970

#224 Bowl, Footed 10" 4½" 10.00
#681 Cream, Footed 4" 12.00
#620 Relish, 2 part 7" 10.00
#643 Relish, 4 part 11⅝" 10.00
#644 Relish, 8 part 11⅛" 10.00
#653 Shaker, Chrome Top 3⅜" ....pair 12.00
#679 Sugar, Footed 3½" 10.00
#567 Torte Plate, 14" 20.00

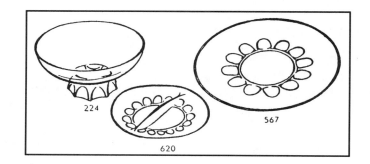

⇌ GREENBRIER Pattern #6026 ⇌

Crystal
16 Rib Regular Optic
1940 – 1976

#29 Cordial 1 oz. 3⅞" 18.00
#27 Claret/Wine 4 oz. 5⅜" 11.00
#21 Cocktail 4 oz. 5" 10.00
#2 Goblet 9 oz. 7⅝" 12.50
#3 Low Goblet 9 oz. 6⅛" 10.00
#11 Low Sherbet 6 oz. 4⅜" 7.00
#8 High Sherbet/Champagne 6 oz. 5½" 9.00
#88 Juice, Footed 5 oz. 4¾" 8.00
#60 Luncheon Goblet/Ice Tea 13 oz. 6" 11.00
#33 Oyster Cocktail 4 oz. 3⅝" 9.00
#549 Plate (Niagara Optic) 7" 8.00
#550 Plate 8" 8.00

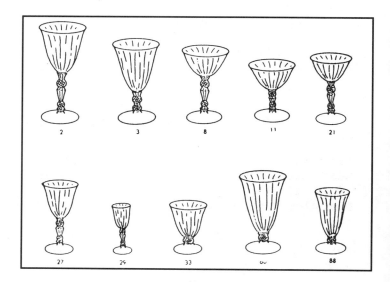

⇌ HALO Design #689 ⇌

Onyx with Platinum Band
See Biscayne Pattern
1970 – 1974

#2 Goblet 11 oz. 14.00
#63 Luncheon Goblet/Ice Tea 13 oz. 15.00

#11 Sherbet 9 oz. 14.00
#26 Wine 6½ oz. 15.00

⇌ HARTFORD Pattern #501 ⇌

Crystal pressed glass
1898 – 1901

Basket for Spoons 45.00
Berry Bowl 5½" 12.50

Berry Bowl 6" 15.00
Berry Bowl 7" 16.00
Berry Bowl 8" 22.00

HARTFORD Pattern #501 Cont.

Bowl, oblong 7"	19.00
Bowl, oblong 8"	19.00
Bowl, oblong 9"	23.00
Butter	68.00
Celery, Tall	45.00
Comport 4½"	15.00
Comport 5½"	16.00
Comport 6"	21.00
Comport 7"	22.00
Comport 8"	35.00
Cream	25.00
Dessert Bowl, Handled 5½"	22.50
Finger Bowl	16.00
Olive	26.50
Salt, Individual	13.50
Salt Shaker	21.00
Spooner	29.00
Sugar, Covered (2 Styles)	32.50
Syrup, Nickel Top	45.00
Syrup, Regular Heavy Top	35.00
Tumbler	18.00

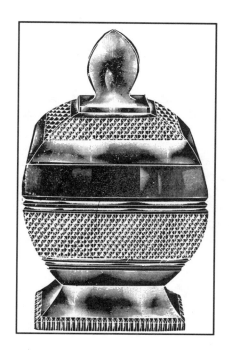

HARVEST Pattern #6097, HA01

Blown lead glass stemware
See page 38 for color photo
See also Sheraton
Rust Bowl on Crystal Base
Late Pattern: 1980s

#25 Claret 7 oz. 6"	13.00
#11 Dessert/Champagne 7 oz. 5¼"	13.00
#2 Goblet 10 oz. 6⅝"	15.00
#63 Luncheon Goblet/Ice Tea 12 oz. 6½"	14.00
#35 Magnum 16 oz. 6¾"	20.00

HERITAGE Pattern #HE03

Lead Crystal Stemware, Giftware, Barware
Barware Coordinates with Radiance Stemware
See page 63 for color photo
Late 1970s – 1985

#894 Bowl 5"	12.00
#194 Bowl Large	15.00
#639 Cake Stand/Chip & Dip	16.00
#732 Cake Knife	20.00
#334 Candy with Cover	19.00
#380 Coasters, Utility	each 4.00
#382 Coasters, Executive	each 5.00
#163 Compote, footed	16.00
#2 Goblet 10½ oz. 7¼"	9.00
#11 Dessert/Champagne 8 oz. 4⅞"	7.00
#23 Double Old Fashioned 10 oz. 4"	8.00
#64 Highball 12 oz. 5¼"	6.00
#63 Luncheon Goblet/Ice Tea 12 oz. 7⅛"	9.00
#493 Napkin Rings	set of four 10.00
#733 Pastry Server	16.00
#550 Plate 8"	8.00
#509 Server & Spoon Set	20.00
#649 Shakers	pair 10.00
#583 Tidbit, Handled	13.00
#578 Server, Two Tiered	16.00
#757 Vase, Two Styles	9.00
#26 Wine 6½ oz. 6"	10.00

☞ HERMITAGE Pattern #2449 ☜

Crystal, Green, Amber 1931 – 1942, Topaz
1932 – 1938; Gold Tint 1938 – 1944; Wiste-
ria 1932 – 1938; Selected items in Ebony
1932 – 1938
1932 – 1945
Add 25% for Amber, Gold Tint, Green; 50% for
Topaz; 100% for Ebony and Wisteria

Ashtray set, 4 stacking	20.00
Ashtray	10.00
Bar Bottle with Stopper	28.00
Beer Mug, Footed 9 oz.	30.00
Beer Mug, Footed 12 oz.	33.00
Bowl Deep 8"	25.00
Bowl Shallow 10"	28.00
Bowl Flared 10"	25.00
Candlestick 6"	pair 32.00
Celery 11"	15.00
Cereal 6"	12.00
Claret 4 oz.	12.50
Coaster	5.00
Cocktail 4 oz.	10.00
Comport 6"	18.00
Condiment Tray	25.00
Coupe Salad 6½"	16.00
Coupe Salad 7½"	18.00
Cream, Footed	10.00
Crescent Salad Plate	20.00
Cup, Footed	10.00
Decanter with Stopper	60.00
Finger Bowl	10.00
Fruit 5"	9.00
Fruit Cocktail 5 oz.	6.50
Goblet 9 oz.	15.00
Grapefruit	26.00
Grapefruit Liner	8.00
Ice Dish	30.00
Ice Dish Plate 7"	12.50
Ice Tea, Footed 12 oz.	15.00
Ice Tub	38.00

Jug, 3 pint, Footed	45.00
Jug, "Hall Boy"	65.00
Jug, Ice Lip, quart	55.00
Mayonnaise	20.00
Mayonnaise Plate	5.00
Mustard with Cover	28.00
Mustard with Spoon	12.00
Nappy 7"	10.00
Oil 3 oz.	50.00
Pickle Dish 8"	12.00
Pitcher, pint, Cereal	35.00
Plate 6"	8.00
Plate 7"	8.00
Plate 8"	10.00
Plate, Luncheon 8"	15.00
Plate 9"	14.00
Plate, Sandwich 12"	15.00
Relish, 2 part	12.00
Relish, 3 part	15.00
Salver 11"	35.00
Salt, Individual	7.00
Saucer	5.00
Shaker	pair 25.00
Sherbet, High 5½ oz.	10.00
Sherbet, Low 7 oz.	8.00
Soup 7"	10.00
Sugar, Footed	10.00
Tumbler, Old Fashioned 6 oz.	10.00
Tumbler, Footed 2 oz.	10.00
Tumbler, Footed 5 oz.	12.00
Tumbler, Footed 9 oz.	14.00
Tumbler, Footed 12 oz.	15.00
Tumbler 2 oz.	10.00
Tumbler 5 oz.	10.00
Tumbler 9 oz.	12.00
Tumbler 13 oz.	16.00
Vase 6"	30.00

☞ HOLIDAY Pattern #2643 ☜

Crystal hand molded
1949 – 1960

Coaster 4"	4.00
Cocktail 4 oz. 2½"	8.50
Cocktail Mixer 20 oz. (Ice Lip Pitcher)	20.00
Cocktail Mixer 30 oz.	25.00
Decanter with Stopper 24 oz. 10¼"	22.00

Ice Bowl 6⅝ x 5"	12.00
Tumbler, Scotch & Soda 9 oz. 4½"	6.00
Tumbler, Double Old Fashioned 12 oz. 3¾"	8.00
Tumbler, Highball 12 oz. 5¼"	8.00
Tumbler, Old Fashioned 6 oz. 3"	5.00
Whiskey 1½ oz. 2⅛"	4.00

⇌ HORIZON ⇌

Combination Line #2650 Tableware, #5650
Tumblers, #5650 Stemware
Crystal, Spruce Green, Cinammon
1951 – 1955

Bowl, Cereal 5.00
Bowl, Dessert 6.00
Bowl, Fruit....................................4.00
Bowl, Salad 8½" 12.00
Bowl, Salad 10½"..........................14.00
Bowl, Serving, 4 part 11½"..............20.00
Bowl, Serving, Handled 15.00
Coaster 5.00
Cream 3½"...................................5.00
Cup 8½ oz. 5.00

Ice Tea/Highball 6".....................................5.00
Juice/Cocktail 3⅜" 4.00
Mayonnaise with Plate and Ladle..............25.00
Plate, Salad 7"..4.00
Plate, Dinner 10".....................................14.00
Plate, Sandwich 11".................................12.00
Platter, Oval 12" 15.00
Relish, 3 part 12½" 18.00
Sherbet/Old Fashioned 3⅜".......................5.00
Sugar 3½"...5.00
Torte Plate 14".......................................15.00
Water/Scotch & Soda 5"..............................5.00

⇌ ICICLE Pattern ⇌

Blown lead glass stemware
Crystal, Blue, Yellow
See Gala Pattern
Late 1980's line

#2 Goblet 12 oz. 7⅜"..................................10.00
#11 Dessert/Champagne 9 oz. 5" 8.00
#25 Wine 9 oz. 6⅝".....................................10.00
#63 Luncheon Goblet/Ice Tea 14 oz. 7" 10.00

⇌ ILLUSION Pattern #6111 ⇌

Crystal blown lead glass stemware
See page 39 for color photo
1969 Line Matchings Only from 1974 –1985

#25 Claret 7½ oz. 6" 8.00
#29 Cordial 2 oz. 3⅞"................................10.00
#2 Goblet 12 oz. 7⅛"..................................10.00
#63 Luncheon Goblet/Ice Tea 15 oz. 6⅝"..10.00
#11 Sherbet 9 oz. 5⅛".................................6.00
#26 Wine 7 oz. 6⅛"....................................10.00
#495 Dessert/Finger Bowl............................8.00
#549 Plate 7"...8.00
#550 Plate 8"...8.00

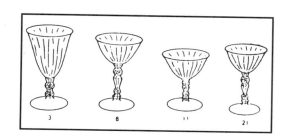

⇌ INSPIRATION Pattern #6107 ⇌

Crystal blown lead glass stemware
1966 Line matchings only in 1971

#25 Claret 7½ oz. 5⅞" 12.00
#2 Goblet 11 oz. 8¼"..................................15.00
#29 Liqueur 2 oz. 4¼".................................8.00
#63 Luncheon Goblet/Ice Tea 14 oz. 7¼"...15.00
#11 Sherbet 9 oz. 6⁵⁄₁₆"..............................10.00

❧ INSPIRATION Pattern #6107 Cont. ❧

#26 Tulip Wine 6½ oz. 6⅝"........................15.00
#495 Dessert/Finger Bowl.......................8.00

#549 Plate 7"...8.00
#550 Plate 8"...8.00

❧ INVITATION Design #660 ❧

Crystal with Platinum Band on Bowl
See page 39 for color photo
See Silhouette Pattern
1964 – 1980s

#224 Bowl, Footed 10".............................10.00
#31 Brandy 4 oz. 12.00
#25 Claret 7½"...12.00
#681 Cream, Footed 7.00
#2 Goblet 10 oz. 12.00
#63 Luncheon Goblet/Ice Tea 14 oz. 8.00
#11 Sherbet/Dessert/Champagne 8 oz.......8.00
#26 Tulip Wine 5½ oz. 5⅞" 10.00

#24 Wine 11 oz. 8" 12.00
#495 Dessert/Finger Bowl.........................8.00
#549 Plate 7"..8.00
#550 Plate 8"..8.00
#620 Relish, 2 part....................................8.00
#634 Relish, 4 part....................................9.00
#644 Relish, 5 part....................................12.00
#679 Sugar, Footed 7.00

❧ JAMESTOWN Pattern #2719 ❧

See pages 40 and 41 for color photos
Azure, Azure Tint, Pink, Crystal, Green,
  Amber, Ruby, Smoke
1958 – 1985
Crystal Stems and Plate Matching Service
  only in 1971
By 1973 only stems and 8" plate active
Add 50% for Ruby, Azure, Pink

#211 Bowl, Salad 10" Crystal 10.00
#421 Bowl, Dessert 4½".............................25.00
#648 Bowl, Serving...................................30.00
#300 Butter with Cover 8".........................38.00
#306 Cake Plate, Handled 9½"...................18.00
#316 Celery 9"..16.00
#681 Cream, Footed 4" 12.00
#2 Goblet 9½ oz. 5¾" 12.00
#7 Sherbet 6½ oz. 4¼" 8.00
#63 Luncheon Goblet/Ice Tea
    11 oz. 6"...15.00
#447 Jelly/Cover 6⅛"................................35.00
#88 Juice, Footed 5 oz. 4¾" 12.00

#726 Muffin Tray, Handled 9⅜" 30.00
#540 Pickle Dish 7⅝"..............................16.00
#456 Pitcher, Ice Lip 3 pint 7⁵⁄₁₆" 85.00
#550 Plate 8"...8.00
#620 Relish 2 part 9⅛" 20.00
#567 Torte Plate 14" Crystal 28.00
#630 Salver round 10" 35.00
#635 Sauce Dish with Cover 4½" 42.00
#653 Shakers...................................pair 18.00
#679 Sugar 10.00
#73 Tumbler, Water 9 oz. 4¼"...................12.00
#64 Tumbler 12 oz. 5⅛"............................15.00
#26 Wine 4 oz. 4⁵⁄₁₆" 12.00

⇌ JEFFERSON Pattern #6104 ⇌

Crystal blown lead glass stemware
1964 – 1973

#25 Claret 7 oz. 5".....................................12.00
#29 Cordial 1½ oz. 5⅝"...........................15.00
#2 Goblet 11 oz. 6⅞"...............................14.00
#63 Luncheon Goblet/Ice Tea 13½ oz.
   6½"...14.00
#11 Sherbet 9 oz. 5"..................................8.00
#26 Wine 6 oz. 5⅝".................................16.00
#495 Dessert/Finger Bowl.........................8.00
#549 Plate 7"..8.00
#550 Plate 8"..8.00

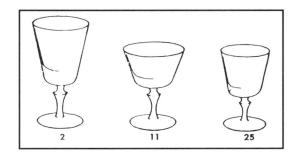

⇌ JUBILEE Design #699 ⇌

Crystal with Gold Band on bowl
See page 30 for color photo
See Gala Pattern
1980s line

#11 Dessert/Champagne 9 oz. 5" 8.00
#2 Goblet 12 oz. 7⅜"................................10.00

#63 Luncheon Goblet/Ice Tea 14 oz. 7" 10.00
#25 Wine 9 oz. 6⅝" 10.00

⇌ KENT Pattern #2424 ⇌

Hand molded crystal
1939 – 1944

Almond 5.00
Ashtray 6.00
Bowl 8"..15.00
Bowl, Flared 9½"......................................18.00
Candlestick 3½".............................pair 18.00
Candlestick Duo..16.00
Candy Jar with Cover 20.00
Cigarette Box with Cover 20.00
Comport with Cover 5½" 20.00

Fruit Bowl 11½".......................................25.00
Mayonnaise with Plate and Ladle.............30.00
Plate 12"...18.00
Salt, Individual 5.00
Sweetmeat...10.00
Urn 5½"..13.00
Urn, Footed, Flared 5" 17.00
Urn, Footed, Flared 6½"...........................18.00
Urn, Footed 7½".......................................23.00

↭ KENT Pattern #6069 ↜

**Crystal blown double lead glass stemware
1958 – 1971**

#27 Claret/Wine 4⅞" 8.00
#20 Cocktail 3⅞" 8.00
#29 Cordial 3⅜" 16.50
#2 Goblet 6½" 10.00
#63 Luncheon Goblet/Ice Tea 6¼" 10.00
#88 Juice, Footed 4¾" 8.00
#11 Sherbet 5" 8.00

↭ KIMBERLY Pattern #2990 ↜

**Made in lead crystal
See page 42 for color photo
Do not confuse with Kimberly Cutting #855
Late 1970s – 1985
Add 50% for Kimberly Gold and Platinum
  Banded Decorations**
> **KIMBERLY GOLD with gold band
> at rim: Goblet, Dessert/Cham-
> pagne, Wine, Luncheon Goblet/Ice
> Tea.
> KIMBERLY PLATINUM with Plat-
> inum band at rim: Goblet,
> Dessert/Champagne, Wine, Lun-
> cheon Goblet/Ice Tea.**

#8 Dessert/Champagne 8 oz. 6" 7.00
#84 Flute Champagne/Parfait 8 oz. 7½"....11.00
#2 Goblet 10 oz. 7½" 9.00
#63 Luncheon Goblet/Ice Tea 14 oz. 6⁹⁄₁₆" .10.00
#35 Magnum 16 oz. 7½" 12.00
#26 Wine 7 oz. 6½" 10.00

↭ LAFAYETTE Pattern #2440 ↜

**Crystal 1931 – 1960; Wisteria 1931 – 1938;
  Rose, Green, Amber 1933 – 1938; Topaz
  1932 – 1938; Gold Tint 1938 – 1944; Regal
  Blue, Burgundy, Empire Green 1935 – 1942;
  Ruby 1935 – 1939.
1931 – 1960
Add 100% for Wisteria**

Almond, Individual 8.00
Baker, oval 10" 12.00
Bon Bon, Handled 5" 12.00
Bowl 7" 12.00
Bowl 10" 14.00
Cake Plate, oval 10½" 17.00
Celery 11½" 15.00
Cereal Bowl 6" 8.00
Cream, Footed 13.00
Cream Soup 13.00
Cup..6.00
Cup and Saucer, After Dinner ....set 10.00
Fruit Bowl 5" 7.00
Lemon Dish, Handled 5½" 12.00

Mayonnaise, 2 part 6½" 15.00
Nappy round 8" 10.00
Olive Dish 6½"...11.00
Pickle Dish 8½"...13.00
Plate 6" 5.00
Plate 7" 6.00
Plate 8" 8.00
Plate 9" 11.00
Plate 10" 14.00
Platter 12" 22.00
Relish, Handled, 2 part 15.00
Relish, Handled, 3 part.............................18.00
Salad Bowl 12" 18.00
Sauce Dish, oval 6½" 14.00
Saucer 5.00
Sugar, Footed 13.00
Sweetmeat, Handled 4½" 14.00
Torte Plate 13"...22.00
Tray, oval 8½"...18.00
Vase, 7"...14.00

⇜ LEGACY Design #635 ⇝

Platinum band on crystal bowl
See Symphony Pattern
1956 – 1971
Matching Service only after 1969

#315 Candlestick 4" ....pair 18.00
#29 Cordial 1 oz. 15.00
#21 Cocktail/Wine 4 oz. 12.00
#680 Cream 3½"...7.00
#396 Cup 5.00
#495 Dessert/Finger Bowl.........................8.00
#2 Goblet 11 oz. 12.00
#63 Luncheon Goblet/Ice Tea 12 oz. 12.00
#688 Individual Cream...............................7.00

#687 Individual Sugar................................7.00
Tray for Individual Sugar and Cream........10.00
#88 Juice, Footed 6 oz................................8.00
#477 Mayonnaise 5½" with Plate 6¾"
   and Ladle 30.00
#549 Plate 7"...8.00
#550 Plate 8"...8.00
#397 Saucer...3.00
#195 Salad Bowl 9" 12.00
#7 Sherbet 7½ oz..8.00
#677 Sugar 2⅝"..7.00

⇜ LINCOLN Pattern #1861 ⇝

Crystal pressed glass
1912 – 1928

Bowl, High Footed 8" 32.50
Bowl, High Footed, Covered 8".................35.00
Catsup with Ground Stopper....................38.00
Celery Dip (2 styles)....................................7.50
Celery, Tall...15.00
Celery Tray...13.00
Chow Chow with Ground Stopper............22.00
Butter, Covered 38.00
Comport 4"..7.50
Comport 4½"..7.50
Comport, Covered 4½" 10.00
Comport 6"..9.50
Comport, Covered 6" 12.50
Comport 7"...11.00
Comport 8"...12.50
Comport, Covered 8" 30.00
Comport, Covered, Deep 8".......................40.00
Cracker Jar...44.00
Cracker Jar Covered..................................50.00
Cream 12.50
Cream, Individual...9.00
Custard..7.50
Dish, oval 7"...10.00
Dish, oval 8"...12.00
Dish, oval 9"...12.50
Dish, oval 10"...13.50
Finger Bowl...8.00
Finger Bowl Plate 6"....................................7.00
Fruit Bowl...15.00
Fruit Salad (2 pieces)................................40.00
Goblet 9.00
Jelly 15.00

Jelly with Cover...22.00
Marmalade..19.00
Marmalade, Covered.................................27.50
Molasses Can, Nickel or Silver Top 38.50
Mustard with Cover, large 24.00
Mustard with Cover, small.......................22.50
Nut Bowl...8.00
Nut Dish, Footed, Individual.....................8.00
Oil Tall, Ground Stopper 6 oz. 29.00
Oil Squat, Ground Stopper 6 oz. 30.00
Olive Tray...10.00
Pickle Tray 11.00
Pitcher, ½ gallon.......................................44.00
Punch Bowl...70.00
Punch Bowl, Footed..................................45.00
Salver 10"..40.00
Shaker (3 Styles) 15.00
Sherbet, High Footed 6.00
Sherbet, High Footed, Flared 6.00
Sherbet, Low Footed...................................5.00

⇜ LINCOLN Pattern #1861 Cont. ⇝

Sherbet, Low Footed, Flared 5.00
Spoon..22.00
Spoon, 2 Handled......................................24.00
Sugar, Covered...22.00
Sugar, 2 Handled..20.00
Sugar, 2 Handled, Covered 25.00
Sugar, Individual..14.00

Sugar Sifter...23.00
Syrup Can, Nickel or Silver Top 32.00
Toothpick 15.00
Tumbler, Ice Tea 17 oz. 10.00
Tumbler, Ice Tea 14 oz. 9.00
Tumbler, Ice Tea Plate 5"............................4.00
Wine 9.00

⇜ LOTUS Pattern #6144 ⇝

See pages 42 and 43 for color photos
Crystal Bowl with Crystal Mist Base
Crystal Bowl with Ebony Base
Crystal Bowl with Peach Mist Base
1980 – 1985

#318 Candlestick 5½" ....pair 24.00
#323 Candlestick 7½" ....pair 30.00
#84 Flute Champagne 6 oz. 8⅞".............16.00
#27 Claret 10 oz. 7¼" 15.00

#11 Dessert/Champagne 8 oz. 6½" 11.00
#2 Goblet 11 oz. 8¼".................................16.00
#63 Luncheon Goblet/Ice Tea 14 oz. 7½"..15.00
#789 Vase, Bud 8"......................................18.00

⇜ LOUISE Pattern #1121 ⇝

Pressed glass
Crystal or Crystal with Gold Decoration
1902 – 1907
Limited number of items produced in 1969,
Footed Compote 1974 – 1976 in Lead Crystal

Bowl, High Footed 5" 14.00
Bowl, High Footed 6" 16.00
Bowl, Low Footed 7" 14.00
Bowl, Low Footed 8" 16.00
Bowl, High Footed 5" Flared to 6" 14.00
Bowl, High Footed 6" Flared to 7" 16.00
Bowl, Low Footed 7" Flared to 8½" 14.00
Bowl, Low Footed 8" Flared to 9½" 16.00
Bowl, High Footed/Covered 5" 25.00
Bowl, High Footed/Covered 6" 30.00
Butter, Covered 65.00
Butter, Covered, Small 40.00
Cabaret 8½"...11.00
Cabaret 9½"...12.00
Cabaret 11" 15.00
Candy Tray 5x7"...15.00
Candy Tray 6x8"...20.00
Celery...30.00
Comport 4½" 12.50
Comport 5" 16.00
Confection...10.00
Cream 25.00

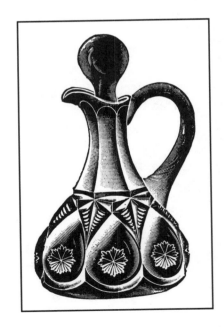

Custard...6.00
Finger Bowl 14.00
Jelly Flared 4½" 15.00
Jelly Covered 4½" 20.00

⤌⇒ LOUISE Pattern #1121 Cont. ⇐⤍

Jelly Stand 15.00
Molasses Can, Blown, Nickel Top 16 oz. ...45.00
Molasses Can, Blown, Tin Top 16 oz. 45.00
Nappy, Not Polished 4" 5.00
Nappy, Not Polished 4½" 5.00
Nappy, Not Polished 6" 6.00
Nappy, Not Polished 7" 8.00
Nappy, Not Polished 8" 10.00
Nappy, Handled 5" 6.00
Nappy 4" 5.00
Nappy 4½" 5.00
Nappy 6" 6.00
Nappy 7" 8.00
Nappy 8" 10.00
Nappy Flared 6" to 7" 7.00
Nappy Flared 7" to 8½" 10.00

Nappy Flared 8" to 9½" 12.00
Oval Dish 9" 10.00
Oval Dish Not Polished 7" 6.00
Oval Dish Not Polished 8" 8.00
Pickle Dish 8.00
Pickle Dish Not Polished 8" 8.00
Pitcher ½ gallon 65.00
Plate 8" 8.00
Salver 10" 32.00
Salver 11" 38.00
Shaker, Nickel Top 15.00
Sugar, Covered 26.50
Spoon...25.00
Toothpick 18.00
Tumbler 15.00
Vinegar 22.00

⤌⇒ LOVELIGHT Design #671 ⇐⤍

Crystal with platinum band on bowl
See Inspiration Pattern
1966 – 1971
Matching Service Only after 1971

#25 Claret 7½ oz....................................14.00
#2 Goblet 11 oz. 14.00
#11 Sherbet 9 oz. 10.00
#26 Tulip Wine 6½ oz. 14.00

#29 Liqueur 2 oz. 10.00
#63 Luncheon Goblet/Ice Tea 14 oz. 14.00
#495 Dessert/Finger Bowl........................8.00
#549 Plate 7"...8.00
#550 Plate 8"...8.00

⤌⇒ LUCERE Pattern #1515 ⇐⤍

Crystal pressed glass
1907 – 1915
***Gold decorated, named Lucere Gold**

*Bowl 4½" 10.00
*Bowl, Berry 8".......................................20.00
Berry Saucer 4½".....................................3.00
Bowl, Low Footed, Flared 7"....................14.00
Bowl, Low Footed, Star Shape 7" 14.00
Bowl, High Footed, Flared 7" 15.00
Bowl, High Footed, Star Shape 7" 15.00
Bowl, High Footed, Flared 8" 20.00
Bowl, High Footed, Star Shape 8" 20.00
Bowl, High Footed, Covered 7"..................28.00
Bowl, High Footed, Covered 8"..................28.00
Brandy..10.00
Butter, Covered 47.50
Celery Tray 15.00

Champagne, Tall 15.00
Champagne, Saucer 15.00
*Cider Goblet...15.00
Claret..12.00
Cocktail 3 oz. 10.00
Cologne with Drop Stopper 4 oz. 25.00

LUCERE Pattern #1515 Cont.

Cologne, Cut with Ground Stopper 4 oz. ...35.00
Comport 4½" 6.00
Comport 7" 8.00
Comport, Star Shape 7" 8.00
Comport, Square 7" 8.00
Comport 8" 20.00
Comport, Star Shape 8" 20.00
Comport, Square 8" 20.00
Cordial 10.00
Cracker Jar 45.00
Cracker Jar and Cover 55.00
Cream 20.00
*Cream, Individual 15.00
Creme de Menthe 2½ oz. 8.00
*Custard 8.00
Dish, oval 7" 6.00
Dish, oval 8" 8.00
Dish, oval 9" 10.00
Dish, oval 10" 12.00
Finger Bowl 8.00
Fruit Bowl 14.00
Goblet 12.00
Ice Bowl Plate 7½" 8.00
*Jelly, Low Footed 4" 10.00
*Jelly, High Footed 4½" 12.00
Jelly, High Footed, Flared 4½" 12.00
*Jug ½ gallon..65.00
Molasses Can, Britannia or Nickel or
   Silver Plate Tops 45.00
*Nappy, Handled 5" 12.00
*Nappy, Star Shape 4½"...............................12.00
Nut Bowl 8.00
Oil 2 oz...45.00
Oil 4 oz...50.00
Oil 6 oz...55.00
Oil, Cut with Ground Stopper 2 oz...........48.00
Oil, Cut with Ground Stopper 4 oz...........52.00

Oil, Cut with Ground Stopper 6 oz............55.00
*Olive Dish 5" 12.00
*Pickle Dish...12.00
Pickle Jar and Cover....................................35.00
Pitcher ½ gallon...45.00
Plate 8½" 8.00
Salt, Individual, Footed 10.00
*Sherbet, Footed..6.00
Sherry..8.00
Spoon...22.00
*Spoon Tray 12.00
Sugar, Covered...22.00
*Sugar, Individual 18.00
Sundae 6.00
Shaker, Nickel or Cut or
   Non Corrosive Tops...............................15.00
Syrup, Silver Plate Top and Handle
   2 Styles 45.00
*Tumbler, Table..14.00
*Tumbler, Ice Tea 14.00
Tumbler Plate..6.00
Vase 9"...25.00
Vase 10"...30.00
Vase 12"...35.00
*Wine 10.00

LYRIC Pattern #6061

Crystal and Pink bowl with Crystal base
1955 – 1965
Add 30% for Pink

#21 Cocktail/Wine/Seafood 4 oz. 3⅞" 5.00
#29 Cordial 1 oz. 2½"................................10.00
#2 Goblet 11 oz. 5⅛" 8.00
#11 Sherbet 7½ oz. 4"...................................6.00
#88 Juice, Footed 6 oz. 4¾" 6.00
#63 Luncheon Goblet/Ice Tea 12 oz. 6" 8.00
#549 Plate 7" 8.00
#550 Plate 8"..8.00

MADEMOISELLE Pattern #6033

Crystal blown lead glass
1949 – 1975
Line Matchings Only in 1972

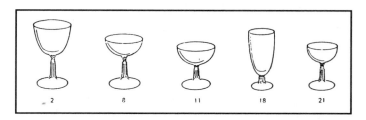

#27 Claret/Wine 4 oz. 4¾" 11.00
#21 Cocktail 4 oz. 4¼" 8.00
#29 Cordial 1 oz. 3⅝" 15.00
#2 Goblet 10 oz. 6¼" 12.50
#33 Oyster Cocktail 4 oz. 3¾" 9.00
#60 Ice Tea, Footed 13 oz. 5⅞"................12.00
#18 Parfait 6 oz. 5⅝"................................10.00
#8 Saucer Champagne 6 oz. 4¾"...............10.00
#11 Sherbet 6 oz. 4" 7.00

#495 Dessert/Finger Bowl..........................8.00
#549 Plate 7"...8.00
#550 Plate 8"..8.00

MANTILLA Design #675

Crystal with encrusted platinum at bowl rim
See Inspiration Pattern
1966 – 1971

#25 Claret 8 oz. 14.00
#2 Goblet 12 oz. 14.00
#63 Luncheon Goblet/Ice Tea 14 oz. 14.00
#29 Liqueur 2 oz. 12.00

#11 Sherbet 9 oz. 10.00
#26 Tulip Wine 6½ oz. 14.00
#495 Dessert/Finger Bowl..........................8.00
#549 Plate 7"...8.00
#550 Plate 8"..8.00

MARILYN Pattern #6055

Crystal blown lead glass stemware made in
Loop Optic
See also Rhapsody Pattern
1954 – 1977
Reduction to stems in 1973

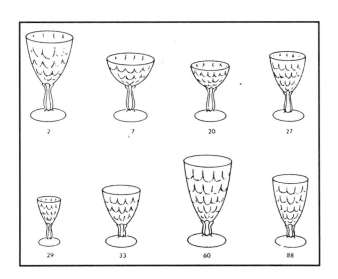

#27 Claret/Wine 4½ oz. 4⅝".....................12.00
#20 Cocktail 3½ oz. 3⅞"............................10.00
#29 Cordial 1¼ oz. 3⁵⁄₁₆" 18.00
#2 Goblet 10 oz. 6⅛".................................13.00
#60 Ice Tea, Footed 12¼ oz. 6⅛" 14.00
#33 Oyster Cocktail 4¾ oz. 4" 10.00
#7 Sherbet 6 oz. 4½".................................9.00
#88 Juice, Footed 5½ oz. 4⅞".....................9.00
#549 Plate (Loop Optic) 7" 8.00
#550 Plate (Loop Optic) 8" 8.00

MAYFAIR Pattern #2419

Crystal
Azure, Green 1930 – 31; Topaz, 1930 – 1938; Gold Tint 1938 – 1944; Amber, Rose 1930 – 1942; Selected items in Ebony, Wisteria, Ruby 1930 – 1942; Ashtray, Cream/Sugar may be found in Burgundy and ashtray in Silver Mist
1930 – 1944
Add 50% for Topaz, Ebony, Rose
Add 100% for Empire Green, Wisteria, Azure, Ruby

Ashtray	9.00
Baker 10"	14.00
Bon Bon, 2 Handles	12.50
Cake Plate, 2 Handles	22.00
Celery 11"	11.50
Cereal 6"	10.00
Comport 6"	15.00
Cream	12.00
Cream, Footed	13.00
Cream, Tea	8.00
Cream, Soup	13.00
Cup, Footed	6.00
Cup, After Dinner	7.00
Fruit 5"	8.00
Jelly, 2 Handles	14.00
Lemon Dish, 2 Handles	17.00
Mayonnaise, 2 Handles	27.00
Oil with Glass Stopper 6 oz.	65.00
Pickle 8½"	14.00
Plate, Bread & Butter 6"	7.00
Plate, Salad 7"	9.00
Plate, Luncheon 8"	10.00
Plate, Dinner 10"	22.00
Platter 12"	25.00
Platter 15"	35.00
Relish 8½"	13.00
Relish, 4 part	14.00
Relish, 5 part	16.00
Sauce Boat and Stand	22.00
Saucer	3.00
Saucer, After Dinner	3.00
Shaker	pair 35.00
Soup 7"	13.00
Sugar	12.50
Sugar, Footed	13.00
Sugar, Tea	8.00
Syrup, Covered	25.00
Syrup Underplate	10.00
Tray, Condiment	28.00
Tray, Handled Lunch	25.00

MAYPOLE Pattern #6149, MA08, MA09, MA10

Reissue of Colony in 1982
Blown lead glass stemware and giftware
See page 44 for color photo
Light Blue, Yellow, Peach; selected items in Milk Glass and Ruby
1982 – 1983

#195 Bowl 9"	30.00
#314 Candlestick 3"	pair 18.00
#319 Candlestick 9"	pair 40.00
#11 Dessert/Champagne 9 oz. 5⅜"	9.00
#2 Goblet 12 oz. 7½"	12.00
#63 Luncheon Goblet/Ice Tea 15 oz. 7¹⁄₁₆"	12.00
#567 Torte Plate 12"	25.00
#25 Wine 8½ oz. 6¾"	12.00
#764 Vase, Bud 6 oz. 6¾"	15.00

MESA Pattern #4186

See pages 45 and 46 for color photos
Crystal, Olive Green, Brown, Amber, Blue,
  Ruby with Crystal Foot
Line Matchings only in 1974
1968 – 1976

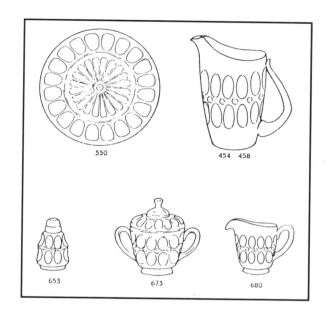

#380 Coaster 3⅝" 3.00
#680 Cream 4½" 7.00
#495 Dessert 4¾" 4.00
#23 Double Old Fashioned 12 oz. 3¾".........5.00
#2 Goblet 13 oz. 5⅛" 8.00
#58 Ice Tea 15 oz. 5⅝" 8.00
#84 Juice 7 oz. 4¼" 6.00
#72 On The Rocks/Wine 9 oz. 4¼"............7.00
#454 Pitcher 1 qt. 7⅝" 17.50
#458 Pitcher 2 qt. 8⅞" 25.00
#550 Plate 8" 5.00
#653 Shaker 3½" ....pair 9.00
#7 Sherbet 8 oz. 4.00
#673 Sugar, Handled 5" 7.00

MISTY Pattern #6129

See page 47 and 62 for color photos
Blue, Yellow, Brown
Late 1970's – 1982
Misty Platinum with band on rim could be
  custom ordered

#27 Claret 7 oz. 5¾" 8.00
#11 Dessert/Champagne 7 oz. 4⁹⁄₁₆" 7.00

#2 Goblet 10 oz. 6¾"...............................10.00
#63 Luncheon Goblet/Ice Tea 13 oz. 6⅝"..10.00
#35 Magnum 16 oz. 5⅞" 12.00

MODULE Pattern #2824

Crystal, Dusk, Sunrise
1971 – 1974
Line Matchings Only in 1972

#2 Goblet 9 oz. 7.00
#64 Ice Tea 13 oz. 8.00
#89 Juice/Wine 5 oz. 5.00
#506 Nappy 5" 4.00
#549 Dessert Plate 6¾"...............................8.00

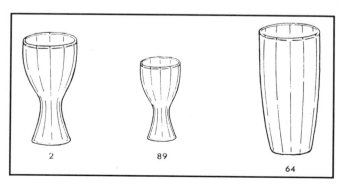

⇌ MONARCH BARWARE M011 ⇌

See page 63 for color photo
1970's – 1985

#23 Double Old Fashioned 10 oz. 3½".........6.00
#64 Highball 12 oz. 5¾"...............................7.00
Goblet 8.00

Dessert/Salad 8.00
Wine 5.00
Luncheon Goblet/Ice Tea 10.00

⇌ MONET STEMWARE ⇌

Dark Blue, Light Blue, Lilac, Peach
1980 – 1985

#891 Goblet 10.00

#893 Ice Tea...10.00
#892 Wine...10.00

⇌ MOON MIST Design #684 ⇌

Silver Mist decorated stem
See Versailles Design #683
1969 – 1972
Matching Service Only in 1972

#31 Brandy 2½ oz......................................12.00
#25 Claret 9 oz..10.00
#2 Goblet 14 oz. 12.00

#63 Luncheon Goblet/Ice Tea 15 oz. 11.00
#549 Plate 7" Not Decorated 8.00
#11 Sherbet 10 oz. 7.00
#26 Wine 8 oz. 9.00

⇌ MOON RING Pattern ⇌

Stems #6052, Tumblers #4132
Crystal
1953 – 1965

#2 Goblet 9¾ oz. 5⅞" 10.00
#7 Sherbet 6½ oz. 4⅜" 6.00
#20 Cocktail 4¾ oz. 3⅞"..............................6.00
#27 Claret/Wine 4¼ oz. 4⅜".......................6.00
#29 Cordial 1¼ oz. 3⅛" 12.00
#33 Oyster Cocktail 4½ oz. 3⅞"..................7.00
#60 Ice Tea, Footed 13 oz. 9⅛"..................11.00
#88 Juice, Footed 5½ oz. 4⅞"......................8.00
#22 Old Fashioned 7½ oz. 3⅛"....................7.00
#23 Double Old Fashioned 13 oz. 3⅝".........8.00
#64 Highball 14 oz. 4⅞"...............................9.00
#73 Scotch & Soda 9 oz. 4⅝" 7.00
#89 Whiskey Sour 5 oz. 3⅝" 6.00
#100 Whiskey 1½ oz. 2⅛" 7.00
#549 Plate 7"...8.00
#550 Plate 8"...8.00

◅═ MOONSTONE Pattern #2882 ═▻

See page 47 for color photo
Blue, Apple Green, Pink, Yellow, Dark Blue,
    Taupe
Late 1970's – 1982
Crystal Moonstone Stems were custom order
    items in 1982

#23 Old Fashioned 6.00
#64 Tumbler 6.00
#2 Goblet 10 oz. 6½" 6.00
#63 Luncheon Goblet/Ice Tea 13 oz. 6½" 7.00
#7 Sherbet 7 oz. 5⅛" 4.00
#26 Wine 5 oz. 5⅛" 6.00

◅═ NEO CLASSIC Pattern #6011 ═▻

Crystal
Crystal base with colored bowl; Regal Blue,
    Burgundy, Ruby; Amber base with Crystal
    bowl
1934 – late 1950's
Add 25% for color

Brandy 1 oz. 12.00
Cocktail 3 oz. 11.00
Claret 4½ oz. 13.00
Cordial 1 oz. 15.00
Creme de Menthe 2 oz. 11.00
Decanter, Footed with Stopper..................65.00
Goblet 10 oz. 10.00
Jug, Footed 44.00

Oyster Cocktail 4 oz. 8.00
Rhine Wine 4½ oz. 7.00
Saucer Champagne 4½ oz. 10.00
Sherbet 5½ oz. 8.00
Sherry 2 oz. 10.00
Tumbler, Footed 5 oz. 9.00
Tumbler, Footed 10 oz. 10.00
Tumbler, Footed 13 oz. 12.00
Whiskey, Footed 2 oz. 7.00
Wine 3 oz. 9.00

◅═ NIAGARA Pattern #793 ═▻

Pressed glass
Crystal or Gold Decorated Crystal
1900 – 1901

Berry Bowl 7" 20.00
Berry Bowl 8" 19.00
Berry Bowl 9" 22.50
Butter 40.00
Celery, Tall...27.50
Cream 22.50
Jug/Tankard..100.00
Nappy 4" 12.00

Nappy 4½" 14.00
Shaker, Nickel Top 14.00
Spooner...25.00
Sugar, Covered 30.00
Syrup, Nickel Top 42.50
Syrup, Regular Top 42.50
Vinegar or Oil, Plain Stopper ....each 32.00
Vinegar or Oil, Cut Stopper ....each 32.00

⊸⇒ NIAGARA Pattern #6026/2 ⇐⊷

**Crystal
Niagara Optic
See also Greenbrier Pattern
1940 – 1965**

#27 Claret/Wine 4½ oz. 5⅜"......................11.00
#21 Cocktail 4 oz. 5" 10.00
#29 Cordial 1 oz. 3⅞".............................14.00
#2 Goblet 9 oz. 7⅝"...............................13.00
#3 Low Goblet 9 oz. 6⅛".........................13.00
#60 Luncheon Goblet/Ice Tea 13 oz. 6" 12.00
#33 Oyster Cocktail 4 oz. 3¾" 9.00
#8 Sherbet/Champagne 6 oz. 5½"..............9.00
#11 Low Sherbet 6 oz. 4⅜"........................7.50
#88 Juice, Footed 5 oz. 4¾" 9.00
#549 Plate Niagara Optic 7"......................5.00

⊸⇒ NORDIC Pattern #6077 ⇐⊷

**Crystal blown lead glass stemware
1958 – 1965**

#20 Cocktail/Wine 4 oz. 4¼"......................8.00
#29 Cordial 1 oz. 3"................................12.00
#2 Goblet 10 oz. 5⅝"................................8.00
#11 Sherbet 7 oz. 4¼"..............................5.00
#88 Juice, Footed 5½ oz. 4⅜".....................5.00
#63 Ice Tea, Footed 13 oz. 5⅝"...................7.00
#549 Plate 7"...4.00
#550 Plate 8"...5.00

⊸⇒ OLD ENGLISH Pattern #1460 ⇐⊷

**Crystal pressed glass
See also Crystal Wedding in Giftware
1906 – 1908**

Bouquet Holder 9"...................................30.00
Bowl, Footed 10" 22.00
Butter with Cover 55.00
Celery Tray 11".......................................16.50
Comport 4½" 6.00
Comport 7"...8.00
Comport 8"..15.00
Comport 10"..16.50
Comport, Belled 10" to 12" 16.50
Cream...28.00

Custard Cup 8.00
Molasses Can 35.00

OLD ENGLISH Pattern #1460 Cont.

Nappy 4½"	10.00	Shaker	16.00
Nappy, Handled 5"	10.00	Spoon	28.00
Nappy 8"	30.00	Sundae	6.00
Olive Dish	11.00	Sugar, Covered	32.00
Pickle Dish	15.00	Tumbler	16.00
Pitcher ½ gallon	50.00	Vinegar 6 oz.	50.00

ORLEANS Pattern #6089

Crystal blown lead glass stemware
Do not confuse with Orleans Cutting #194
1960 – 1977

#31 Brandy 1½ oz. 4¹⁄₁₆" 12.50
#27 Cocktail/Wine 4½ oz. 5¼" 7.00
#2 Goblet 11½ oz. 6³⁄₁₆" 10.00
#11 Sherbet 7 oz. 5⁵⁄₁₆" 6.00
#88 Juice, Footed 5 oz. 4¾" 8.00
#63 Luncheon Goblet/Ice Tea 13 oz. 6³⁄₁₆" .10.00
#495 Dessert/Finger Bowl 5.00
#549 Plate 7" 5.00
#550 Plate 8" 7.00

PATRICIAN Pattern #6064

Crystal blown lead glass stemware
See also Elegance Pattern
1956 – 1971

#29 Cordial 1 oz. 3⅝" 15.00
#25 Claret 5¾ oz. 5¾" 10.00
#20 Cocktail 4 oz. 4½" 10.00
#2 Goblet 9¾ oz. 7" 11.00
#63 Luncheon Goblet/Ice Tea
     13½ oz. 6⁷⁄₁₆" 11.00
#88 Juice, Footed 5½ oz. 4⅞" 8.00
#33 Seafood Cocktail 7¾ oz. 3⅝" 8.00
#11 Sherbet Low 7 oz. 4⅝" 6.00
#8 Sherbet, High/Champagne 8 oz. 5¾" 8.00
#26 Wine 3¼ oz. 5⅛" 10.00
#495 Dessert/Finger Bowl 6.00
#549 Plate 7" 5.00
#550 Plate 8" 6.00

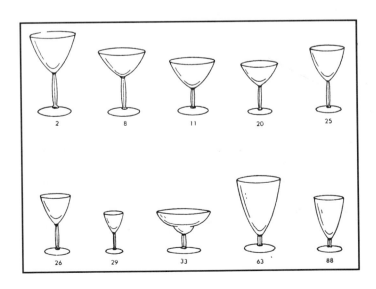

PAVILION Pattern #6143

Optic blown lead glass stemware
See page 48 for color photos
Crystal, Grey
Late Pattern still made in 1985

#11 Dessert/Cocktail 7 oz. 6⅛".................5.00
#2 Goblet 10 oz. 7⅞"................................8.00

#63 Luncheon Goblet/Ice Tea 14 oz. 6⁵⁄₁₆"...8.00
#25 Wine 7½ oz. 7⁷⁄₁₆"...............................7.50

PEBBLE BEACH Pattern #2806

See page 49 for color photos
Crystal Ice, Black Pearl, Lemon Twist, Pink
  Lady, Flaming Orange
1969 – 1972

#558 Cake Plate 11"..................................6.50
#2 Goblet 10 oz. 6"....................................4.50
#58 Ice Tea 14 oz. 5¾"..............................4.50
#72 On the Rocks/Wine 8 oz. 4⅛"............4.50
#7 Sherbet 7 oz. 2¾".................................3.50
#84 Juice 7 oz. 4".....................................3.50
#680 Cream 3¼"..4.00
#421 Dessert Bowl 4¾"..............................6.00
#454 Pitcher, quart 7⅛".............................20.00
#550 Plate 8"..6.00
#600 Punch Bowl 9 qt. 11½"......................40.00
#615 Punch Cup 6½ oz..............................3.50
#622 Relish, 3 part 10"..............................9.00
#211 Salad Bowl 10"..................................9.00
#652 Shaker with Chrome Top 2⅞"......pair 5.50
#676 Sugar with Cover 4"...........................6.50
#567 Torte Plate 14".................................10.00

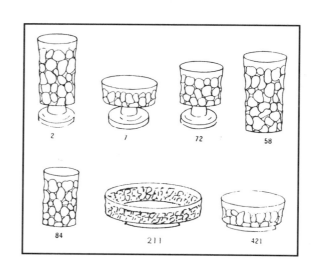

PETITE Pattern #6085

Crystal blown lead glass stemware
1959 – 1978

#29 Cordial 1¼ oz. 3½" 15.00
#27 Cocktail/Wine 4 oz. 5"........................8.00
#63 Ice Tea, Footed 11¾ oz. 6³⁄₁₆" 9.00
#88 Juice, Footed 5½ oz. 4⁹⁄₁₆"....................8.00
#2 Goblet 8¾ oz. 6½" 10.00
#11 Sherbet 6 oz. 5³⁄₁₆"..............................8.00
#549 Plate 7"...5.00
#550 Plate 8"...7.00

╾╼ PIONEER Pattern #2350 ╾╼

Crystal; Amber, Green 1926 – 1941; Blue
1926 – 1927; Selected item in Rose, Azure
1929 – 1936; Selected items in Ebony 1929
– 1941; Selected items in Ruby, Regal Blue,
Burgundy and Empire Green 1934 – 1941
Late production or Cream/Sugar in Ruby and
Ebony and Ashtrays in Ebony
1926 – 1960

Large Ashtray	10.00
Small Ashtray	5.00
Baker oval 9"	16.00
Baker oval 10½"	18.00
Bouillon	17.00
Bouillon, footed	18.00
Bowl, Cereal 6"	9.00
Bowl, Soup 7"	10.00
Butter with Cover	38.00
Celery 11"	12.50
Comport 8"	12.00
Cream	12.00
Cream, Footed	9.00
Cup	5.00
Cup, Footed	6.00
Cup, After Dinner	6.00
Egg Cup	25.00
Fruit Bowl 5"	9.00
Grape Fruit	14.00

Grape Fruit Liner	10.00
Nappy 8"	13.00
Nappy 9"	14.00
Pickle 8"	15.00
Plate, Bread & Butter 6"	9.00
Plate, Salad 7"	10.00
Plate, Salad 8"	14.00
Plate, Dinner 9"	17.00
Plate, Dinner 10"	18.00
Plate, Chop 12"	19.00
Plate, Chop 13"	25.00
Plate, Torte 15"	27.00
Platter, oval 10½"	22.00
Platter, oval 12"	23.00
Platter, oval 15"	25.00
Relish, 3 part	15.00
Salad Bowl 10"	15.00
Sauce Boat	15.00
Sauce Boat Plate	9.00
Saucer, After Dinner	5.00
Soup, Cream	11.00
Soup, Cream Plate	7.00
Sugar with Cover	14.00
Sugar, Footed with Cover	15.00

╾╼ PRECEDENCE Pattern #6108 ╾╼

Blown lead glass stemware
See pages 59 – 61 and 64 for color photos
Crystal, Gray Mist Bowl with Crystal Base,
Onyx Bowl with Crystal Base
1967 – 1975

#25 Claret 8 oz. 6⅛"	12.50
#2 Goblet 12 oz. 7⁷⁄₁₆"	12.50
#63 Luncheon Goblet/Ice Tea 14 oz. 6½"	13.00
#29 Liqueur 2 oz. 3⅞"	10.00
#11 Sherbet 9 oz. 5¾"	13.00
#26 Tulip Wine 7 oz. 5¾"	13.00
#495 Dessert/Finger Bowl	6.00
#549 Plate 7"	5.00
#550 Plate 8"	6.00

⊶ PRELUDE Pattern #6071 ⊷

Crystal blown lead glass stemware
1957 – 1970

#29 Cordial 1¼ oz. 3¼" 12.00
#27 Cocktail/Seafood 4½ oz. 5" 8.00
#2 Goblet 11½ oz. 6⅜" 10.00
#11 Sherbet 7 oz. 4¾" 6.00
#88 Juice, Footed 5¼ oz. 4½" 7.00
#63 Ice Tea, Footed 13 oz. 6" 8.00
#549 Plate 7" 5.00
#550 Plate 8" 6.00

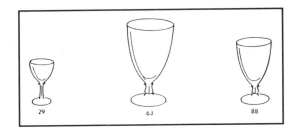

⊶ PRESSED GLASS Pattern #956 ⊷

Crystal
1901 – 1903

Berry Bowl 8" 22.50
Bowl, High, Footed, Open 6" 25.00
Bowl, High, Footed, Open 7" 28.00
Bowl, High, Footed, Open 8" 32.00
Bowl, High, Footed, Covered 6" 30.00
Bowl, High, Footed, Covered 7" 40.00
Bowl, High, Footed, Covered 8" 52.00
Butter, Covered 28.00
Cream 20.00
Nappy 4½" 10.00
Oil Bottle..30.00
Pickle Dish 12.00
Salver 10"..42.50
Shaker, Nickel Top 10.00
Spooner..21.00
Sugar, Covered...25.00

Syrup...32.50
Tankard 105.00
Tumbler 10.00

⊶ PRESSED GLASS Pattern #1223 ⊷

Crystal
1903 – 1908

Bowl, oval 7" 8.00
Bowl, oval 8" 10.00
Candy Tray 5x7"..8.00
Candy Tray 6x8"...10.00
Finger Bowl...12.00
Nappy 4" 5.00
Nappy 4½" 5.00

Nappy 6" 6.00
Nappy 7" 6.00
Nappy 8" 8.00
Plate 8" 10.00
Pickle Dish 8"..8.00
Tray, oval 7"..6.00
Tray, oval 8"..8.00

PRESSED GLASS Pattern #1231

**Crystal
1903 – 1908**

Berry Bowl, oval 10" 24.00
Custard..8.50
Cream..20.00
Finger Bowl...14.00
Nappy 4½" 5.00
Pickle Jar with Cover...............................35.00

Punch Bowl with Stand 60.00
Rose Bowl 22.00
Sugar 20.00
Sherbet, Footed 3½ oz. 15.00
Tankard, 2qt. 88.00
Tumbler 16.00

PRESSED GLASS Pattern #1299

**Crystal
1904 – 1913**

Bouquet Holder 14" 12.00
Bouquet Holder 17" 15.00
Butter, Covered 50.00
Celery, Tall 25.00
Celery Tray 17.50
Comport 4" 5.00
Comport 4½" 6.00
Comport 7" 8.00
Comport 8" 10.00
Comport 9" 12.00
Cracker Jar 30.00
Cracker Jar with Cover............................45.00
Cream 13.50
Cream, Individual....................................10.00
Custard..8.00
Dish, oblong 7" 8.00
Dish, oblong 8" 9.00
Dish, oblong 9" 10.00
Dish, oblong 10" 12.00

Ice Cream 5"...14.00
Oil or Vinegar, Cut or Drop Stopper.........25.00
Pickle Dish 17.50
Pickle Jar, Covered..................................25.00
Pitcher ½ gallon 75.00
Punch Bowl 18".......................................50.00
Punch Bowl, Footed 18"...........................85.00
Salt, Individual..8.00
Shaker, Silver or Nickel Top.....................15.00
Spoon..18.00
Sugar, Covered 25.00
Sugar, Individual.....................................12.00
Syrup, Swelled Silver or Straight
    Silver Top..35.00
Tankard, ½ gallon 45.00
Toothpick...18.00
Tumbler, Belled 15.00
Tumbler, Restaurant 20.00
Tumbler, Ice Tea......................................25.00

PRESSED GLASS Pattern #1303

**Crystal
1904 – 1925**

Butter, Covered 35.00
Butter, Individual....................................35.00

Cream 20.00
Spoon..20.00
Sugar & Cover 27.50

PRESSED GLASS Pattern #1641

1909 – 1913
Some items made in 1969 under Sovereign Pattern as part of Centennial II Collection

Almond, Salted 8.00
Bon Bon, Handled, 3 Cornered 11.00
Butter, Covered 45.00
Celery, Tall...20.00
Celery Tray...13.00
Comport 4"..8.00
Comport 4½"..9.00
Comport, Flared 6" to 7" 8.00
Comport, Flared 7" to 8" 9.00
Comport, Flared 8" to 9" 10.00
Confection..11.00
Cracker Jar, Covered...............................60.00
Cream 16.50
Cream, Individual....................................12.50
Finger Bowl 9.00
Ice Cream 5"..12.00
Jelly, Low Foot 14.00
*Lemonade/Custard....................................8.50
Olive, 3 Cornered 13.00
Olive, Square..13.00
Oil, Drop Stopper 26.50
Molasses Can, Pressed Silver or
    Britannia Top 42.50
Molasses Can, Blown, Silver or
    Nickel Top 45.00

*Nappy, Handled 5" 13.00
*Nut Bowl...12.50
*Pickle Dish..17.00
Pickle Jar, Covered 30.00
Pitcher, quart 34.00
Pitcher ½ gallon 75.00
Punch Bowl, Footed................................110.00
Salver, Footed 10" 50.00
Shaker, Tall, Nickel Top...........................15.00
Shaker, Large, Glass or Silver or
    Nickel Top 15.00
Shaker, Small, Nickel or Silver Plate Top ..15.00
*Sugar, Individual 12.50
Sugar Sifter..25.00
Sugar, Covered...20.00
Tumbler, Table 12.00
Tumbler, Whiskey 10.00
Wafer Dish 12.00
Wine 12.00

PRESIDENT'S HOUSE Pattern #7780 Morgantown

Blown lead glass stemware
Crystal
1961 – Line Matchings only in 1974

Brandy 2½ oz. 10.00
Brandy Inhaler 9 oz....................................10.00
Cocktail 5 oz. 9.00
Cordial 1½ oz...16.00
#2 Goblet 11 oz. 6⅞"..................................16.00
#63 Ice Tea, Footed 12 oz. 5⅞".................18.00
#89 Juice 5 oz. 3⅞" 10.00
#22 Old Fashioned 8 oz. 3½" 13.00
#8 Saucer Champagne 6 oz. 4½"..............12.00
#11 Sherbet 6 oz. 3" 10.00
#24 Tulip Champagne 11 oz. 8" 14.00
#30 Burgundy Wine 9½ oz. 5¾" 14.00

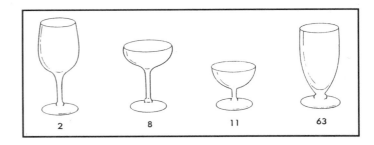

#28 Wine 8 oz. 5¾" 12.00
#26 Wine 5 oz. 5" 12.00
#84 Whiskey Sour/Parfait 6 oz. 6¾".........12.00
#64 Highball 11 oz. 5⅛"............................8.00
Finger Bowl/Nappy 6.00
Plate 7" 5.00

⤝⤞ PRINCESS Pattern #6123 ⤝⤞

Blown lead glass stemware
See page 50 for color photo
Crystal; Blue Bowl with Crystal Base; Green
Mist Bowl with Crystal Base; Grey Mist Bowl
with Ebony Base; Princess Platinum Design
#690 with platinum band.
1972 – 1982

#2 Goblet 8½ oz. 6½" 15.00
#63 Luncheon Goblet/Ice Tea 11½ oz. 6" ..14.00
#11 Sherbet 7½ oz. 5¼" 10.00
#26 Wine 5½ oz. 5¾".................................14.00
#549 Plate 7"...5.00
#550 Plate 8"..6.00

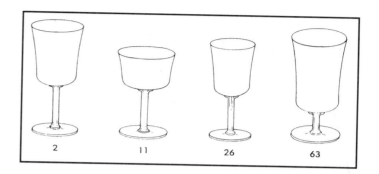

⤝⤞ PRISCILLA Pattern #6092 ⤝⤞

Crystal blown lead glass stemware
See pages 35 and 50 for color photos
1960 – 1985

#29 Cordial 1½ oz. 3½" 15.00
#27 Cocktail/Wine 4 oz. 5¼".......................8.00
#2 Goblet 10½ oz. 7¹⁄₁₆"...........................10.00
#63 Ice Tea, Footed 14 oz. 6³⁄₈".................10.00
#88 Juice, Footed 5½ oz. 4¾"......................7.00
#11 Sherbet 7 oz. 5⁷⁄₁₆"..............................6.00
#549 Plate 7"...5.00
#550 Plate 8"...5.00

⤝⤞ PRISCILLA Pattern #2321 ⤝⤞

Crystal, Amber, Blue, Green 1925 – 1930
*Items in Rose and Azure 1929 – 1930
Do not confuse with Priscilla Pattern #6092
 or early Priscilla Pattern #676
1925 – 1930

Bouillon 10.00
*Cream..9.00
Cup...6.00
Custard, Footed, Handled.............................9.00
Goblet 9 oz. 12.00
Luncheon Goblet 7 oz...............................12.00

Mayonnaise...26.00
Ice Tea, Footed 12.00
Jug, 3 pint 60.00
Plate, Luncheon 8" 6.00
Saucer 4.00
*Sugar...10.00
Sherbet 8.00
Tumbler, Footed, Handled 13.00

PRISCILLA Pattern #676

Pressed glass
Crystal, also items with Gold Decoration
1898 – 1901

Butter 55.00
Berry Bowl 8½" 27.50
Bowl, High Footed 6" 35.00
Bowl, High, Footed, Covered 6" 47.50
Cream 22.50
Custard..12.50
Celery...27.50
Egg Dish 20.00
Jug 60.00
Nappy 4½" 22.00
Pickle Dish (2 Styles) 15.00
Shaker, Large, Nickel Top.........................13.00
Shaker, Small, Silver Plated Top 18.00
Shaker, Large, Silver Plated Top 20.00
Spooner..21.00
Sugar 22.00

Syrup, Nickel Top 38.00
Toothpick 18.00
Tumbler 15.00
Vinegar or Oil 40.00
Water Bottle 65.00

PROMISE Pattern #6110

Crystal blown lead glass stemware
1967 – 1978

#2 Goblet 11 oz. 7¾"..................................12.50
#63 Luncheon Goblet/Ice Tea 14 oz. 6⅜" ..12.50
#11 Sherbet 7 oz. 6⅛".................................8.00
#29 Liqueur 2 oz. 4⅛".................................9.00
#26 Wine 7 oz. 6⅜".....................................11.00
#495 Dessert/Finger Bowl.........................6.00
#549 Plate 7"..5.00
#550 Plate 8"...6.00

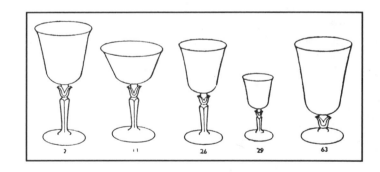

PURITAN Pattern #6068

Crystal blown lead glass stemware
1957 – 1971

#29 Cordial 1¼ oz. 3".................................15.00
#27 Cocktail/Wine/Seafood 4¼ oz. 4½" 7.00
#2 Goblet 10 oz. 5¾"..................................10.00
#11 Sherbet 6½ oz. 4⅝" 6.00
#63 Ice Tea, Footed 13 oz. 5⅞"....................8.00
#88 Juice, Footed 5 oz. 4½" 7.00
#549 Plate 7"..5.00
#550 Plate 8"...6.00

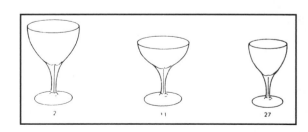

PURITAN Pattern #1432

**Crystal pressed glass table accessory line
1906 – 1925**

Cream, Hotel	14.00
Finger Bowl	6.00
Molasses Can, Silver or Nickel Top	25.00
Oil, Drop or Cut Stopper 6 oz.	20.00
Salt	3.00
Salt, Individual	3.00
Shaker, Plated Top or Non-corrosive Top	6.50
Sugar, Hotel	16.00
Sugar Sifter	15.00
Tumbler	7.00
Tumbler, Ice Tea	8.00

QUEEN ANNE Design #2412

**See page 21 for color photo
Crystal, Amber, Blue, Green
1926 – 1929
Queen Anne Design became part of Colony
Pattern in 1938
Do not confuse with Queen Anne etched pattern or Queen Anne Cutting
Add 50% for color**

Candlestick 9"	pair 75.00
Candlestick 5"	pair 50.00
Candlestick 2"	pair 30.00
Candleholder with Bobache and Prisms, 14½"	pair 175.00
Candelabra, 2 Light with Bobaches and Prisms	pair 250.00
Centerpiece 9"	50.00

Centerpiece 12"	53.00
Centerpiece 15"	70.00
Bowl, Low Footed 9"	75.00
Bowl, High Footed 9"	82.00
Bowl, High Crystal Bowl, Colored Foot 9"	150.00
Bowl, oval, Footed 10"	85.00
Bowl, oblong 13"	85.00
Flower Block 3¾"	20.00
Flower Block oval 4½"	25.00
Mint dish	20.00
Vase 12"	70.00
Vase 14"	90.00

RADIANCE Pattern #3013

**Lead Crystal coordinating with Heritage Barware
See page 50 for color photo
1980 – 1982**

#2 Goblet 10 oz. 7⁵⁄₁₆"	7.00
#63 Luncheon Goblet/Ice Tea 14 oz. 6⁹⁄₁₆"	7.00
#11 Dessert/Champagne 8 oz. 5¹³⁄₁₆"	5.00
#26 Wine 6½ oz. 6⁵⁄₁₆"	8.00

RADIANCE Pattern #2700

Crystal
Designed by Raymond Loewy
See page 20 for color photo
1956 – 1958

Bowl, Salad 12" 14.00	Plate, Dinner 10" 11.00
Beverage, Footed 10 oz. 5¾".....................5.00	Platter 15" 16.00
Cereal/Dessert 5½" 4.00	Sauce Bowl with Plate and Ladle 22.00
Cream 3¼"...5.00	Serving Dish 11"...................................12.50
Cup and Saucer 4.00	Server, 3 part 12⅝"...............................12.50
Juice 5½ oz. 4½" 5.00	Shaker with Gold Top 2½" ....pair 10.00
Plate, Buffet 14" 9.00	Sherbet 6 oz. 3" 5.00
Plate, Salad/Dessert 7" 5.00	Sugar 2¾"..6.00

RAINBOW Design #638

Mother of Pearl Iridescent Bowl only
Narrow Rib Optic
See Victoria Pattern 6068½
1957 – 1968

#27 Cocktail/Wine 4¼ oz...........................10.00	#63 Ice Tea, Footed 13 oz. 12.00
#29 Cordial 1¼ oz....................................15.00	#88 Juice, Footed 5¼" 10.00
#2 Goblet 10 oz. 14.00	#11 Sherbet 6½ oz....................................8.00
	#549 Plate Narrow Rib Optic 7" 6.00

RALEIGH Pattern #2574

Crystal
1939 – 1966

Bon bon 13.00	
Bowl, Handled 9½" 15.00	
#249 Bowl, Flared 12" 19.00	
#306 Cake Plate 10" 14.00	
Candlestick 4".................................pair 15.00	
#332 Candlesticks Duo 5¼".............pair 20.00	
Celery 10½" 11.00	
Comport 5"..9.00	
#681 Cream, Footed 7 oz.........................6.50	
#688 Cream, Individual.............................8.00	
#396 Cup, Footed 6.00	
Fruit Bowl 13" 19.00	
Ice Tub..22.00	
Lemon Dish...12.00	
Mayonnaise with Plate and Ladle.............33.00	
Muffin Tray, Handled 8" 15.00	

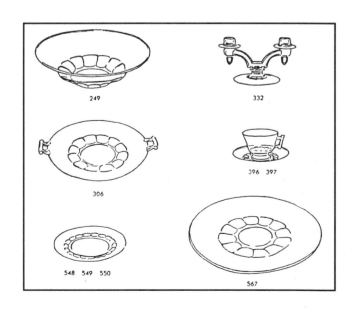

249   332
306
396 397
548 549 550   567

RALEIGH Pattern #2574 Cont.

#528 Oil, Ground Stopper 4½".................25.00
#397 Saucer.....................................2.50
#654 Shaker, Silver Top 3¼"............pair 18.00
#679 Sugar, Footed............................6.00
#687 Sugar, Individual 7.50
Sweetmeat......................................7.00
Olive Dish 6".....................................7.50
Pickle Dish 8"..................................10.00

#548 Plate 6"....................................5.00
#549 Plate 7"....................................5.00
#550 Plate 8"....................................6.00
Serving Dish, Handled 8½"...................15.00
#622 Relish, 3 part..........................16.50
#567 Torte Plate 14"..........................18.00
#697 Tray For Sugar & Cream 6¾"............9.00
Whipped Cream................................28.00

RAMBLER Pattern #1827

Crystal pressed glass
1911 – 1915
Some items reproduced 1969

Berry 4½" 9.00
Berry 4¾"...9.00
Custard..9.00
Nappy 8"..18.00
Nappy 10".......................................20.00
Nappy, Flared 8" to 10"......................24.00
Nappy, Flared 10" to 12......................26.00
Pitcher, ½ gallon...............................60.00
Punch Bowl & Foot 10".....................160.00
Punch Bowl & Foot, Flared 10" to 12".....210.00
Tumbler 12.00
Vase 7"..18.50
Vase 9"..22.00
Vase 13"...30.00

No. **1827.** 10 in. Deep Punch Bowl and Foot.
Made also in 12 inch Flared.

RECEPTION Design #676

Crystal with platinum band on bowl
See page 64 for color photo
See Promise Pattern
1968 – 1978

#224 Bowl, Footed 10"........................10.00
#581 Cream, Footed 7.00
#2 Goblet 11 oz. 15.00
#63 Luncheon Goblet/Ice Tea 14 oz. 14.00
#29 Liqueur 2 oz. 10.00
#620 Relish, 2 part..............................8.00
#643 Relish, 4 part............................10.00

#644 Relish, 5 part............................12.00
#11 Sherbet 7 oz. 10.00
#679 Sugar, Footed............................7.00
#26 Wine 7 oz. 15.00
#495 Dessert/Finger Bowl......................6.00
#549 Plate 7"....................................5.00
#550 Plate 8"....................................6.00

REFLECTION Design #625

Crystal blown lead glass
Platinum Band on Bowl
See Mademoiselle Pattern
Matchings only in 1973
1949 – 1973

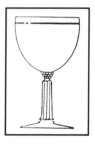

#315 Candlestick 4" ....pair 18.00
#27 Claret/Wine 4 oz. 3.00
#21 Cocktail 4 oz..9.00
#29 Cordial 1 oz. 18.00
#680 Cream 7.00
#699 Individual Cream 7.00
#396 Cup 5.00
#2 Goblet 10 oz. 14.00
#60 Ice Tea, Footed 13 oz. 13.00
#88 Juice, Footed 5 oz.............................10.00
#477 Mayonnaise with Plate and Ladle 33.00
#33 Oyster Cocktail 4 oz...........................7.50
#18 Parfait 6 oz. 10.00
#195 Salad Bowl 9" 15.00
#397 Saucer...3.00
#11 Sherbet 6 oz. 8.00

#8 Sherbet/Champagne 6 oz. 10.00
#677 Sugar 7.00
#687 Sugar, Individual.............................7.00
#495 Dessert/Finger Bowl.........................6.00
#549 Plate 7"..5.00
#550 Plate 8"..6.00

REGAL Pattern #2000

Crystal pressed glass pattern
1914 – 1928

Almond, Footed 6.00
Berry Bowl 4½"...5.00
Berry Bowl 4¾"...5.00
Butter, Covered (2 Styles) 35.00
Celery Tray..13.00
Condiment Set (5 pieces) 60.00
Condiment Tray 5x7"................................15.00
Cream 12.00
Cream, Hotel 10.00
Custard..7.00
Finger Bowl (2 styles) 7.00
Finger Bowl Plate 5.00
Fruit Salad Bowl 8" with
  Stand Flared to 12"................................45.00
Goblet 9 oz..8.00
Goblet 11 oz. 10.00
Goblet 13 oz. 12.00
Jelly, Low Footed......................................14.00
Jelly, High Footed......................................16.00
Jug, 2½ gallon 35.00

Jug, 3 pint 30.00
Jug, Ice Lip ½ gallon 35.00
Lemon Dish...6.00
Liner, Footed..8.00
Loaf Sugar..8.00

☞ REGAL Pattern #2000 Cont. ☜

Mayonnaise & Plate ....set 16.00	Salt, Individual or Celery 8.00
Mayonnaise Plate 5.00	Salt, Footed Individual 10.00
Mint Dish, Footed 10.00	Shakers, (3 styles) Nickel or Silver Plate or
Molasses Can, Nickel or Silver Top 36.00	Glass Top 15.00
Mustard, Covered......................................22.00	Sherbet, Footed 5 oz. 5.00
Nappy 5" 8.00	Sherbet, Footed 6 oz. 6.00
Nappy 6" 10.00	Sherbet, Footed 6½ oz. 6.00
Nappy 8" 12.00	Sherbet, High Footed 7 oz.......................7.00
Nappy 10" 15.00	Sugar, Covered...15.00
Nappy, Flared 5" to 6½" 10.00	Sugar, Hotel 12.00
Nappy, Flared 6" to 8" 12.00	Sugar Shaker 20.00
Nappy, Flared 7" to 9" 14.00	Sweetmeat...8.00
Nappy, Flared 8" to 10" 18.00	Syrup Can, Metal Handle, Nickel or
Nappy, Flared 10" to 12"...........................22.00	Silver Top 35.00
Oil, Ground Stopper 4 oz. 27.00	Tumbler, Table (4 Styles) 7.00
Oil, Ground Stopper 6 oz. 29.00	Tumbler, Table, Optic 7.00
Oil, Ground Stopper 8 oz. 32.00	Tumbler, Ice Tea (4 Styles).......................10.00
Oil, Drop Stopper 4 oz. 20.00	Tumbler, Ice Tea, Optic 10.00
Oil, Drop Stopper 6 oz. 22.00	Tumbler, Split (2 Styles) 8.00
Oil, Drop Stopper 8 oz. 25.00	Tumbler, Whiskey 3½ oz. (3 styles) 6.00
Olive Dish/Pickle Dish 10.00	Tumbler, Whiskey, Optic 6.00
Oyster Cocktail & Liner 8.00	Tumbler, Wine..8.00
Oyster Cocktail, Footed, & Liner..............10.00	Tumbler, Wine, Optic 8.00
Punch Bowl & Stand 10" 55.00	Tumbler, Footed 10.00
Punch Bowl & Stand Flared to 12"...........75.00	Water Bottle 25.00

☞ REGAL Design #693 ☜

Stainless Steel on Crystal
See Priscilla Pattern 6092
1973 – late 1970's
Do not confuse with Regal Cutting #842

#2 Goblet 10½ oz.....................................10.00	#11 Dessert/Champagne 7 oz. 8.00
#63 Luncheon Goblet/Ice Tea 14 oz. 10.00	#27 Wine/Cocktail 4 oz. 11.00

☞ REGENCY Pattern #RE10 ☜

Crystal blown lead glass stemware
See page 51 for color photo
Late 1970's

	#2 Goblet 10 oz. 16.50
#25 Claret 7 oz. 14.50	#63 Luncheon Goblet/Ice Tea...................15.00
#11 Dessert/Champagne 7 oz. 14.50	

⚡ REGIS Design #697 ⚡

Crystal blown lead glass stemware
Gold Band on Bowl
See page 51 for color photo
See Wilma Pattern
1980 – 1983

#27 Claret 6½ oz. 6½" 12.00
#63 Luncheon Goblet/Ice Tea 13 oz. 5⅞"..11.00
#2 Goblet 10 oz. 7⅛".............................12.00
#8 Dessert/Champagne 6 oz. 5⅝"..............9.00

⚡ REHEARSAL Design #667 ⚡

Crystal blown lead glass
Gold Band on Bowl Rim
See Glamour Pattern
1964 – 1978

#224 Bowl, Footed 10"............................10.00
#31 Brandy 4½ oz....................................12.00
#25 Claret 7½ oz.....................................15.00
#681 Cream, Footed 7.00
#2 Goblet 12 oz. 15.00
#63 Luncheon Goblet/Ice Tea 14 oz. 14.00
#11 Sherbet 8 oz. 10.00

#679 Sugar, Footed 7.00
#26 Tulip Wine 7 oz.................................15.00
#620 Relish, 2 part..................................8.00
#634 Relish, 4 part..................................10.00
#644 Relish, 5 part..................................12.00
#495 Dessert/Finger Bowl........................6.00
#549 Plate 7"..5.00
#550 Plate 8"..6.00

⚡ REMEMBRANCE Design #670 ⚡

Crystal blown lead glass
Gold Band at Bowl Rim
See Inspiration Pattern
1966 – 1971
Available for Matching Service after 1970

#25 Claret 7½ oz.....................................15.00
#2 Goblet 11 oz. 15.00
#63 Luncheon Goblet/Ice Tea 14 oz. 14.00
#29 Liqueur 2 oz. 10.00

#11 Sherbet 9 oz. 10.00
#26 Tulip Wine 6½ oz. 15.00
#495 Dessert/Finger Bowl........................6.00
#549 Plate 7"..5.00
#550 Plate 8"..6.00

⚡ RHAPSODY Pattern #6055½ ⚡

Blown lead glass stemware
Crystal, Turquoise Bowl with Crystal Base
Line Matchings only after 1973
1955 – 1975
Add 25% for color

#27 Claret/Wine 4¼ oz. 4⅝"........................8.00
#20 Cocktail 3½ oz. 3⅞"............................7.00
#29 Cordial 1¼ oz. 4".................................15.00

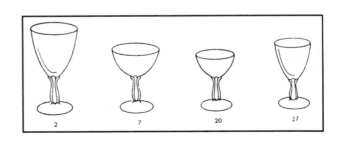

⇒ RHAPSODY Pattern #6055½ Cont. ⇐

#88 Juice, Footed 5½ oz. 4⅞"......................8.00
#2 Goblet 10 oz. 6⅛"..................................10.00
#60 Luncheon Goblet/Ice Tea 12¼ oz. 6⅛" 10.00
#33 Oyster Cocktail 4¾ oz. 3⁵⁄₁₆"................6.00

#7 Sherbet 6 oz. 4½"..................................7.00
#495 Dessert/Finger Bowl........................6.00
#549 Plate 7"..5.00
#550 Plate 8"..6.00

⇒ RICHMOND Design #654 ⇐

Crystal blown lead glass stemware
Gold Band on Bowl Rim
See page 52 for color photo
See Sheraton Pattern
1961 – 1985

#47 Bell 5½"...45.00
#224 Bowl, Footed 10"..............................30.00
#25 Claret 7 oz..15.00
#27 Cocktail/Wine 3½ oz..........................12.00

#29 Cordial 1 oz..18.00
#681 Cream, Footed 8.00
#11 Dessert/Champagne..........................12.00
#2 Goblet 10 oz...18.00

⇒ RINGLET Pattern #6051 ⇐

Blown lead glass stemware
Crystal
1953 – 1965

#27 Claret/Wine 4 oz. 4½".......................10.00
#20 Cocktail 3¼ oz. 3⅞".............................7.50
#29 Cordial 1¼ oz. 3⅛".............................13.00
#2 Goblet 10½ oz. 6³⁄₁₆".............................10.00
#33 Oyster Cocktail 4¼ oz. 3¾"..................6.00
#7 Sherbet 6½ oz. 4⅜"...............................6.00
#60 Ice Tea, Footed 12¼ oz. 6⅛" 9.00
#88 Juice, Footed 5 oz. 4" 7.00
#549 Plate 7"..5.00
#550 Plate 8"..6.00

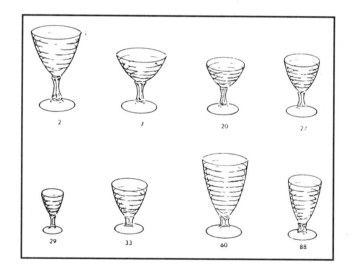

⇒ ROBIN HOOD WARE #603 ⇐

Crystal pressed glass
1898 – 1903

Butter, Covered 72.50
Bowl, High, Open 6" 25.00
Bowl, High, Open 7" 28.00

Bowl, High, Open 8" 35.00
Bowl, High, Covered 6" 42.50
Bowl, High, Covered 7" 50.00

⇝ ROBIN HOOD WARE #603 Cont. ⇜

Bowl, High, Covered 8"	58.00	Nappy, Unpolished 7"	9.00
Berry Bowl 6"	21.00	Nappy, Unpolished 8"	10.00
Berry Bowl 7"	22.50	Oil	30.00
Berry Bowl 8"	24.00	Pickle Dish	15.00
Celery, Tall	35.00	Salver 9"	50.00
Cream	20.00	Salver 10"	52.00
Jug	65.00	Shaker, Nickel Top	10.00
Mug	47.50	Spooner	25.00
Nappy 4½"	10.00	Sugar, Covered	32.50
Nappy, Unpolished 4"	6.00	Syrup, Nickel Top	37.50
Nappy, Unpolished 6"	8.00	Tumbler	12.50

⇝ ROSBY Pattern #1704 ⇜

Crystal or Gold Decorated pressed glass
See page 21 for color photo
1910 – 1928
Some milk glass, short production in 1950s.
Punch Bowl and Cups produced as gift items
for extended period. Some items reproduced
in 1965 as part of Centennial II Collection.

Berry Bowl 4½"	8.50
Berry Bowl 7"	10.00
Berry Bowl 8"	10.00
Berry Bowl 10" Regular	12.00
Berry Bowl 10" Belled	12.00
Berry Bowl 10" Cupped	12.00
Bowl 7½"	10.00
Butter, Covered	58.00
Celery Tray	15.00
Comport 8" Regular	16.00
Comport 8" Belled	16.00
Comport 8" Star	16.00
Cracker Jar	58.00
Cracker Jar, Covered	66.00
Cream	17.50
Custard	10.00
Dish, oval 7"	8.00
Dish, oval 8"	10.00
Dish, oval 9"	12.00
Flower Bowl	16.00
Jelly, High, Footed 4½"	14.00
Jelly, High, Footed, Square 4½"	14.00
Jelly, Low, Footed, Star 5"	12.00
Jelly, Low, Footed, square 5"	12.00
Molasses Can, Britannia or Silver Plate or Nickel Top	40.00
Nappy, Regular 4¾"	10.00

Nappy, Handled 4½"	10.00
Nappy, Handled, square 4½"	10.00
Nappy, Handled, 3 cornered 4½"	10.00
Nappy, square 7"	12.00
Nappy, square partitioned 7"	12.00
Olive tray 6"	11.00
Pickle Dish 8"	10.00

✐ ROSBY Pattern #1704 Cont. ✐

Pickle Jar, Covered 45.00
Pitcher, ½ gallon 60.00
Plate 5" 5.00
Preserve, Footed 12.50
Punch Bowl No Foot 10" 145.00
Punch Bowl, Footed 10" 195.00
Punch Bowl No Foot 15" 240.00
Punch Bowl, Footed 15" 290.00
Punch Bowl, No Foot 16" 290.00
Punch Bowl, Footed 16" 395.00
Punch Cup 8.00
Relish Tray 10¼" 15.00

Salad, oval 12" 14.00
Serving Plate 10" 26.00
Shaker, Tall, Glass or Nickel or
    Silver Tops 15.00
Shaker, Small, Glass or Nickel or
    Silver Tops 20.00
Sugar, Covered 22.50
Spooner 18.00
Syrup, Silver Plate Top and Handle...........35.00
Toothpick 15.00
Tumbler 11.50
Vinegar, Cut or Drop Stopper 6 oz. 26.00

✐ RUTLEDGE Pattern #6036 ✐

Blown lead glass stemware
Crystal
1951 – 1977

#27 Claret/Wine 3¼ oz. 4¾"......................10.00
#21 Cocktail 3½ oz. 4⅛".............................7.50
#29 Cordial 1 oz. 3¼"................................13.00
#2 Goblet 9½ oz. 6⅞" 12.00
#63 Ice Tea, Footed 12 oz. 6⅛".................12.00
#88 Juice, Footed 5 oz. 4⅞" 9.00
#33 Oyster Cocktail 4 oz. 3¾".....................5.00
#18 Parfait 5½ oz. 5⅞" 10.00
#8 Sherbet/Champagne 6 oz. 4¾".............10.00
#11 Sherbet 6 oz. 4⅛"................................7.00
#495 Dessert/Finger Bowl.........................6.00
#549 Plate 7"..5.00
#550 Plate 8"...6.00

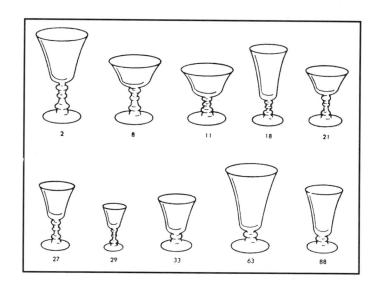

✐ SCEPTRE Pattern #6017 ✐

Blown lead glass stemware
Topaz or Azure Bowl
Gold Band at Rim
1938 – 1976

#25 Claret 4 oz. 5⅞" 12.00
#21 Cocktail 3½ oz. 4⅞"...........................10.00
#29 Cordial ¾ oz. 3⅞" 15.00

#2 Goblet 9 oz. 7⅜"..................................13.00
#63 Luncheon Goblet/Ice Tea 12 oz. 6" 12.00
#33 Oyster Cocktail 4 oz. 3⅝" 8.00

SCEPTRE Pattern #6017 Cont.

#11 Sherbet 6 oz. 4½"...................................7.00
#8 Sherbet/Champagne 6 oz. 5½"..............9.00
#88 Juice, Footed 5 oz. 4¾"......................9.00
#72 Water, Footed 9 oz. 5½"...................11.50
#26 Wine 3 oz. 5½"....................................11.50
#495 Dessert/Finger Bowl.........................6.00
#549 Plate 7"...5.00
#550 Plate 8"...6.00

SHEFFIELD Design #653

Crystal blown lead glass
Platinum band on bowl
See page 52 for color photo
See Sheraton Pattern
1961 – 1985

#224 Bowl 10"...17.00
#315 Candlestick 4"........................pair 25.00
#15 Claret 7 oz. 18.00
#29 Cordial 1 oz. 25.00
#680 Cream 7.00
#688 Cream, Individual.............................7.00
#396 Cup 6.00
#2 Goblet 10 oz. 16.00
#63 Ice Tea, Footed 12 oz. 6½"................17.00

#88 Juice, Footed 5 oz.............................14.00
#477 Mayonnaise with Plate and Ladle.....28.00
#549 Plate 7"...5.00
#550 Plate 8"...6.00
#195 Salad Bowl 9"..................................17.00
#397 Saucer...3.00
#11 Sherbet 7 oz. 10.00
#677 Sugar 9.00
#687 Sugar, Individual.............................7.00
#27 Wine 3½ oz. 17.00

SHELL PEARL Design #633

Mother of Pearl Iridescent on Bowl Only
Loop Optic
See Marilyn Pattern
1954 – 1977

#189 Bowl, oval..8.00
#309 Canape Plate 20.00
#27 Claret/Wine 4½ oz. 16.00
#20 Cocktail 3½ oz. 16.00
#29 Cordial 1 oz. 22.00
#680 Cream 8.00
#688 Cream, Individual.............................6.00
#311 Flora-Candle.....................................10.00
#2 Goblet 10 oz. 20.00
#88 Juice, Footed 5½ oz..........................15.00
#63 Ice Tea, Footed 12¼ oz.....................18.00

#477 Mayonnaise with Plate and Ladle.....25.00
#33 Oyster Cocktail 4¾ oz. 10.00
#549 Plate Loop Optic 7" 5.00
#620 Relish, 2 part...................................10.00
#622 Relish, 3 part...................................12.00
#568 Serving Plate 14" 18.00
#654 Shaker, Chrome Top.................pair 8.00
#7 Sherbet 6 oz. 12.00
#729 Snack Plate 10" 14.00
#677 Sugar 8.00
#687 Sugar, Individual.............................6.00

⇌ SHERATON Pattern #6097 ⇌

Crystal blown lead glass stemware
See page 52 for color photo
1961 – 1978

#25 Claret 7 oz. 5³⁄₁₆" 15.00
#27 Cocktail/Wine 3½ oz. 5"....................16.00
#29 Cordial 1 oz. 3⁹⁄₁₆"............................25.00
#2 Goblet 10 oz. 6⅝".............................18.00
#88 Juice, Footed 5 oz. 4¹¹⁄₁₆.....................11.00
#63 Ice Tea, Footed 12 oz. 6⁷⁄₁₆"................15.00
#11 Sherbet 7 oz. 5³⁄₁₆".........................10.00
#495 Dessert/Finger Bowl.........................6.00
#549 Plate 7"...5.00
#550 Plate 8"...6.00

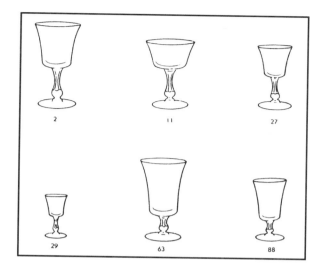

⇌ SILHOUETTE Pattern #6102 ⇌

Blown lead glass stemware
See pages 39 and 53 for color photos
Crystal, Solid Pink, Mother of Pearl
Late additions in Ebony or Blue were Silhou-
ette Classics
1964 – 1985

#31 Brandy 3 oz. 3⅜" 15.00
#25 Claret 7½ oz. 5¾" 16.00
#27 Large Claret 10 oz. 6¾" 16.00
#21 Cocktail/Sherry 4 oz. 5½" 14.00
#84 Flute Champagne 7 oz. 7⁹⁄₁₆"..............16.00
#2 Goblet 10 oz. 7" 18.00
#24 Goblet, Large 11 oz. 8"......................18.00
#63 Luncheon Goblet/Ice Tea 14 oz. 6⅝" ..21.00
#11 Sherbet 8 oz. 5⅛".............................9.00
#26 Tulip Wine 5½ oz. 5⅞".......................17.00
#495 Dessert/Finger Bowl.........................6.00
#549 Plate 7"...5.00
#550 Plate 8"...6.00

⊶ SILVER FLUTES Pattern #6037 ⊷

Crystal blown lead glass stemware
Matching Service only in 1972
1949 – 1972

#27 Claret/Wine 4 oz. 6" 12.00
#21 Cocktail 4 oz. 5" 10.00
#29 Cordial 1 oz. 4" 15.00
#2 Goblet 9 oz. 7⅛" 12.00
#3 Goblet 9 oz. 6⅜" 12.00
#63 Luncheon Goblet/Ice Tea 9 oz. 6⅜"....10.00
#33 Oyster Cocktail 4½ oz. 4" 9.00
#18 Parfait 6 oz. 6⅛" 13.00
#8 Saucer Champagne 7 oz. 6" 12.00
#11 Sherbet 7 oz. 4¾" 8.00
#88 Juice, Footed 5 oz. 4⅞" 10.00

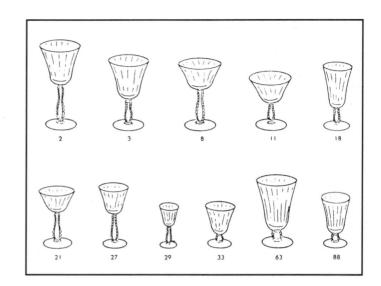

⊶ SILVER TRIUMPH Pattern #6112 ⊷

Crystal blown lead glass with metal stem
See Golden Triumph Pattern
1969 – 1972

#2 Goblet 10 oz. 7" 16.00
#63 Luncheon Goblet/Ice Tea 14 oz. 7⅛"..14.00
#11 Sherbet 8 oz. 5⅛" 10.00

#26 Tulip Wine 5½ oz. 6⁷⁄₁₆" 15.00
#495 Dessert/Finger Bowl 6.00
#549 Plate 7"..5.00
#550 Plate 8"...6.00

⊶ SIMPLICITY Design #618 ⊷

Crystal blown lead glass
Gold band on bowl and foot
See Sceptre Pattern
1938 – Matching Service Only in 1969

#259 Bowl 13"...16.00
#315 Candlestick 4" ....pair 18.00
#332 Candlestick Duo ....pair 22.50
#29 Cordial ¾ oz....................................15.00
#25 Claret 4 oz......................................14.00
#21 Cocktail 3½ oz.................................10.00
#679 Cream, Footed 5.00
#396 Cup, Footed....................................5.00
#2 Goblet 9 oz. 14.00
#63 Ice Tea, Footed 12 oz. 14.00
#88 Juice, Footed 5 oz. 10.00
#251 Lily Pond 12" 16.00

#477 Mayonnaise with Plate and Ladle 27.00
#33 Oyster Cocktail 4 oz...........................10.00
#548 Plate 6"..4.00
#549 Plate 7"..5.00
#550 Plate 8"..6.00
#221 Salad Bowl 10½" 12.00
#397 Saucer..3.00
#8 Sherbet/Champagne 6 oz. 10.00
#11 Sherbet 6 oz. 8.00
#681 Sugar, Footed 5.00
#567 Torte Plate 14" 16.00
#72 Water, Footed 9 oz............................14.00
#26 Wine 3 oz. 14.00

SOMETHING BLUE Design #685

Blown lead glass stemware
Platinum band on blue bowl/crystal base
See Glamour Pattern
1973 – Custom order by 1982

#31 Brandy 4½ oz.....................................14.50
#25 Claret 7½ oz.......................................14.50
#11 Sherbet/Champagne 8½ oz...............12.00

#2 Goblet 12 oz. 16.50
#63 Luncheon Goblet/Ice Tea 14 oz. 15.00
#26 Tulip Wine 7 oz..................................16.50

SOMMELIER COLLECTION Combined Lines

Crystal blown lead glass stemware
1970 – 1973

#6115/34 Continental 9½ oz. 6" 15.00
#6116/35 Grande 14 oz. 6¾"....................15.00
#6117/36 Vin Blanc 8½ oz. 7" 15.00
#6118/37 Sherry 3½ oz. 5⅝"....................14.50
#6119/38 Tulip 9 oz. 8" 15.00

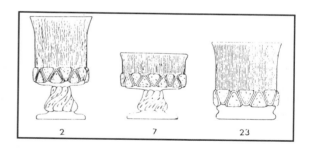

SORRENTO Pattern #2832

Hand molded stemware
See page 54 for color photos
Blue, Green, Brown, Plum
1972 – Late 1970's

#2 Goblet 9 oz. 6" 11.00
#63 Luncheon Goblet/Ice Tea 13 oz. 6¾" ..10.00
#23 Double Old Fashioned 10 oz. 4"..........8.00
#7 Sherbet 6½ oz. 3⅝" 7.00
#64 Tumbler/Highball 11 oz. 5⅝" 7.50
#26 Wine 6½ oz. 5" 10.00
#550 Plate 8"..6.00

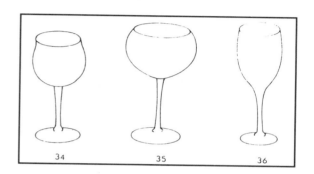

SPHERE Pattern #6121

Blown stemware
See page 60 for color photo
Gray Mist Bowl with Crystal Base; Green Mist
   Bowl with Crystal Base; Terra Bowl with
   Crystal Base
1970 – 1974
Line Matchings only after 1973

#2 Goblet 14 oz. 5⅜"................................12.00
#63 Luncheon Goblet/Ice Tea 14 oz. 5⅞"..11.00
#11 Sherbet 9 oz. 4½".............................8.00
#26 Wine 7 oz. 4⅜" 12.00

SPLENDOR Pattern #6124

Blown lead glass stemware
1972
Line Matchings Only after 1974

#2 Goblet 10½ oz. 5⅞" 15.00
#63 Luncheon Goblet/Ice Tea 14 oz. 6⅜"..14.00
#11 Sherbet/Champagne 9 oz. 5⅛"...........11.00
#26 Wine 7 oz. 6" 14.00
#549 Plate 7"..5.00
#550 Plate 8"..6.00

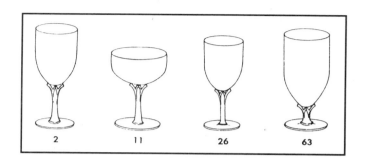

SPLENDOR Pattern #6131

Blown lead glass stemware
See pages 55 and 62 for color photos
Blue, Rust
1980's line

#2 Goblet 11 oz. 6½".................................7.00
#11 Dessert/Champagne 9 oz. 4½".............7.00

#27 Claret 7 oz. 5½" 8.00
#63 Luncheon Goblet/Ice Tea 14 oz. 6½"....8.00

SUN-RAY Pattern #2510

See page 20 for color photo
See also Glacier
Crystal; Azure, Green, Amber, Topaz 1935 –
   1938; Gold Tint 1938 – 1940; Ruby in
   selected items 1935 – 1940
All colors so difficult to find that pricing is for
   Crystal only
1935 – 1944

Ashtray, square...5.00
Ashtray, Individual.....................................6.00
Almond, Individual, Footed........................7.00
Bon Bon..10.00
Bon Bon, 3 Toed...11.00
Bowl, Handled 12.00
Bowl 13"...20.00
Butter with Cover 6"...................................25.00
Candlestick 3".................................pair 18.00
Candlestick 5½"...............................pair 12.00
Candlestick Duo...............................pair 22.00
Candelabra, 2 light 45.00
Candy Jar with Cover 25.00
Celery, Handled 10"...................................12.50
Cheese with Cover 6"..................................30.00

Cigarette Box with Cover 20.00
Cigarette Box with Cover, oblong 4½"........20.00
Claret 4½ oz. 8.00
Coaster 5.00
Cocktail, Footed 4 oz. 8.00
Comport..12.00
Condiment Tray 8½"...................................18.00

☙ SUN-RAY Pattern #2510 Cont. ☙

Cream, Footed...8.00
Cream, Individual...7.00
Cup..5.00
Decanter with Stopper 18 oz....................30.00
Decanter with Stopper, oblong 26 oz.........36.00
Decanter Holder (oblong tray) for Rye,
  Bourbon, Gin.......................................100.00
Dessert, Frozen 8.00
Fruit 5"...6.00
Fruit Cocktail 3½ oz. 7.00
Goblet 9 oz..10.00
Ice Bucket, Chrome Handle 25.00
Ice Bucket, No Handle 22.00
Jelly...10.00
Jug, 2 quart..60.00
Jug, Ice Lip...60.00
Mustard with Cover and Spoon 28.00
Mayonnaise with Plate and Ladle.............25.00
Nappy, Handled..12.00
Nappy, Flared 9½".....................................15.00
Nappy, Handled, Footed 15.00
Nappy, Handled, square 15.00
Nappy, Handled, three-cornered 15.00
Old Fashioned 6 oz...................................10.00
Oil with Stopper 3 oz. 26.00
Pitcher, pint 32.00
Pickle, Handled 6"......................................9.00
Plate 6" 6.00
Plate 7" 7.00
Plate 8" 8.00
Plate 9" 12.00
Relish, 2 part 10.00
Relish, 3 part 12.00
Relish, 4 part 14.00
Salad Bowl 12" 16.00
Salt Dip..6.00
Sandwich Plate 12"..................................18.00
Saucer 2.00
Shaker 4" ....pair 18.00
Shaker, Individual 2¼" ....pair 18.00
Sherbet 5½ oz...6.00
Soup, Onion with Cover............................25.00
Soup, Cream 12.00
Soup, Cream Plate.....................................6.00
Sugar, Footed..8.00
Sugar, Individual..6.00
Sweetmeat, Divided, Handled 10.00
Torte Plate 11"..25.00

Torte Plate 15".......................................30.00
Torte Plate 16".......................................33.00
Tray for Sugar and Cream 12.00
Tray, square 10"......................................15.00
Tray, oblong 10½".....................................15.00
Tray for Cheese or Butter 15.00
Tray, Handled oval 16.00
Tumbler, Footed 13 oz.............................12.00
Tumbler, Footed 9 oz...............................10.00
Tumbler, Footed 5 oz.................................9.00
Tumbler 5 oz...7.00
Tumbler 9 oz...8.00
Tumbler 13 oz...10.00
Whiskey 2 oz...6.00
Vase, Crimped 6".....................................14.00
Vase 7"...15.00
Vase Footed Square 9".............................16.00
Vase, Rose Bowl 3½".................................15.00
Vase, Rose Bowl 5" 20.00
Vase, Sweetpea.......................................22.00

SYDNEY Pattern #1333

Crystal pressed glass
1905 – 1913

Butter, Covered	35.00
Cabaret 9½"	15.00
Celery Tray	12.00
Champagne	15.00
Comport 4½"	8.00
Comport 8"	9.00
Comport 9"	12.00
Comport, Belled 8"	9.00
Comport, Belled 9"	12.00
Comport, Cupped 9"	12.00
Cream	16.00
Custard	10.00
Decanter, quart, Ground or Drop Stopper	35.00
Decanter, quart, Ground and Polished Stopper	40.00
Ice Cream	8.00
Molasses Can, Tin or Nickel Top	35.00
Nappy, round 4"	6.00
Nappy, round 4½"	6.00
Nappy, square 4½"	6.00
Nappy, Handled 5"	7.00
Nappy, round 6"	8.00
Nappy, square 8"	20.00
Pickle Dish 7"	14.00
Pickle Dish 8"	16.00
Pitcher, ½ gallon	45.00
Pitcher, 3 pint	35.00
Plate 6"	4.00
Salad 9"	8.00
Shaker, Blown	12.00
Shaker, Pressed	10.00
Spoon	18.00
Sweetmeat	12.00
Sugar, Covered	26.00
Tray 5x7"	15.00
Tumbler	15.00
Whiskey	10.00

SYLVAN Pattern #1119

Pressed glass
Crystal and Crystal with Gold Decoration
1902 – 1906

Almond	6.00
Bon Bon, 3 Cornered	8.00
Butter, Covered	57.50
Cabaret 8½"	10.00
Cabaret 9½"	12.00
Cabaret 11"	14.00
Cabaret 14"	16.00
Celery, Tall	27.50
Celery Tray	20.00
Chow Chow Jar with Ground Stopper	25.00
Cracker Jar	50.00
Cracker Jar and Cover	58.00
Cream	21.00
Cream, Individual	23.00
Cologne, Cut Stopper, 1 oz.	30.00
Cologne, Cut Stopper, 2 oz	35.00
Cologne, Cut Stopper, 4 oz.	50.00
Regular Comport 4"	7.00
Regular Comport 4½"	7.00
Regular Comport 6"	8.00
Regular Comport 7"	8.50
Regular Comport 8"	9.00
Regular Comport 10"	10.00
Flared Comport 4"	7.00
Flared Comport 4½"	7.00
Flared Comport 6"	8.00
Flared Comport 7"	8.50
Flared Comport 8"	9.00
Flared Comport 10"	15.00
Belled Comport 4½"	7.00
Belled Comport 6"	8.00
Belled Comport 7"	8.50

SYLVAN Pattern #1119 Cont.

Belled Comport 8" 9.00
Belled Comport 10" 12.00
Cupped Comport 10" 15.00
Finger Bowl 13.00
Ice Cream 6.00
Jelly Stand 4½" 12.00
Jelly Stand 5" 14.00
Jelly Stand, Flared 4½" 12.00
Jelly Stand, Flared 5" 14.00
Lemonade 15.00
Nappy, Handled 5" 10.00
Olive, Square 8.00
Olive, 3 Cornered 8.00
Pitcher ½ gallon 70.00
Plate 6" 4.00
Punch Bowl 40.00
Punch Bowl with Foot 50.00
Rose Bowl, Medium 15.00
Rose Bowl, Large 20.00
Sponge Cup 15.00

Spoon 15.00
Sugar, Covered 26.50
Sugar, Three Handled 28.00
Sugar, Three Handled, Covered 30.00
Sugar Sifter, Silver Plated Top 25.00
Syrup 12 oz. 35.00
Syrup 5 oz. 30.00
Shakers, Silver Plated or
   Nickel Tops 15.00
Tankard, ½ gallon 90.00
Toothpick 22.00
Tray oval 7" 10.00
Tray oval 9" 12.00
Tray oval 11" 14.00
Tray oval 13" 18.00
Tumbler, Ice Tea 20.00
Tumbler, Table 12.00
Tumbler, Wine 14.00
Tumbler, Whiskey 10.00
Vinegar 50.00

SYMPHONY Pattern #6065

**Crystal blown lead glass stemware
1956 – 1968**

#21 Cocktail/Wine 4 oz. 4⅝" 13.00
#29 Cordial 1 oz. 3⅛" 20.00
#2 Goblet 11 oz. 6⅛" 14.00
#63 Ice Tea, Footed 12 oz. 6⅜" 12.00
#88 Juice, Footed 6 oz. 4⅞" 10.00
#7 Sherbet 7½ oz. 4¾" 8.00
#495 Dessert/Finger Bowl 6.00
#549 Plate 7" 5.00
#550 Plate 8" 6.00

TEA ROOM Pattern #2222

**Re-issue of Colonial
Crystal, Green, Amber, Mother of Pearl;
   Selected items in Rose, Azure, Ebony, Wisteria, Topaz
1928 – 1933**

Bottle, Water 50.00
Bowl, Deep (3 Styles) 10½" 20.00

Bowl, Deep (2 Styles) 12" 23.00
Candlestick 4" ....pair 30.00
Cigarette Box with Cover, large 27.00
Cigarette Box with Cover, small 23.00

❦ TEA ROOM Pattern #2222 Cont. ❦

Cigarette Urn with Holder.........................18.00
Cigarette Set: 4 Ashtrays.....................set 35.00
Coaster 5.00
Claret...14.00
Cocktail..15.00
Comport 7"..16.00
Cream, Individual.....................................9.00
Decanter, quart.......................................38.00
Finger Bowl with Underplate....................10.00
Fruit Cocktail 3 oz....................................9.00
Goblet...15.00
Ice Bucket...45.00
Ice Tea 14 oz...14.00
Jelly 16.00
Jug..50.00
Oil 4 oz..35.00
Oil 6 oz..43.00

Oyster Cocktail and Liner Set...................14.00
Parfait 5 oz..15.00
Shaker with Glass Top....................pair 40.00
Shaker, Footed pair.................................25.00
Shaker, (Three Styles)......................pair 22.00
High Sherbet 4½ oz..................................12.00
Low Sherbet 4½ oz...................................12.00
Low Sherbet 3 oz.....................................12.00
Sherbet 6½ oz..11.00
Sugar, Covered..16.00
Sugar, Pail...26.00
Tumbler, Footed 2½ oz...............................8.00
Tumbler 5 oz..10.00
Tumbler 8 oz..11.00
Tumbler 9 oz..12.00
Tumbler 13 oz..14.00
Whipped Cream Pail.................................36.00

❦ TENDERNESS Design #691 ❦

Blown lead glass stemware
Platinum Band on Green Mist Bowl with Crystal Base
See Princess Pattern
1972 – 1978

#2 Goblet 8½ oz...10.00
#63 Luncheon Goblet/Ice Tea 11½ oz. 8.00

#11 Sherbet 7½ oz. 6.00
#26 Wine 5½ oz. 10.00
#549 Plate 7" Green Mist Decorated 5.00

❦ TROUSSEAU Design #642 ❦

Blown lead glass
Crystal with platinum band on bowl
See page 56 for color photo
See Fascination Pattern
1958 – 1979

#224 Bowl, Footed 10"..............................15.00
#27 Claret/Wine 4 oz. 5⅛"........................13.50
#25 Large Claret 8 oz...............................15.00
#20 Cocktail 4 oz. 4⅜" 8.00
#29 Cordial 1 oz. 3½"................................16.00
#679 Cream, Footed 8.00
#63 Ice Tea, Footed 13½ oz. 5½" 12.00
#88 Juice, Footed 5 oz. 4¼" 11.00

#2 Goblet 10 oz. 6¾"................................15.00
#11 Sherbet 7 oz. 4¾"...............................10.00
#495 Dessert/Finger Bowl..........................6.00
#549 Plate 7"..5.00
#550 Plate 8"..6.00
#620 Relish, 2 part......................................9.00
#643 Relish, 4 part....................................12.50
#644 Relish, 5 part....................................16.00
#681 Sugar, Footed 7.50

⊷⊜ TUXEDO Pattern #1578 ⊜⊷

Crystal pressed glass
See page 20 for color photo
1908 – 1910

Banana Jar	20.00
Biscuit Jar	20.00
Bon Bon, Footed	10.00
Bowl, Deep 4½"	6.00
Bowl, Deep 5"	8.00
Bowl, Deep 7"	10.00
Butter, Covered	50.00
Celery, Tall	26.00
Celery, Tray	14.00
Comport 4½"	8.00
Comport 7"	16.00
Comport 8"	20.00
Comport, square 8"	20.00
Cracker Jar, Footed	40.00
Cracker Jar, Footed, Covered	55.00
Cream	22.00
Cream, Footed Hotel	22.00
Crushed Fruit	25.00
Crushed Fruit & Cover	35.00
Crushed Fruit Spoon	20.00
Custard	8.00
Finger Bowl	10.00
Fruit Bowl	15.00
Jelly Stand 4½"	8.00
Molasses Can, Nickel or Britannia or Silver Plate Top	45.00
Nappy, Handled 5"	8.00
Nut Bowl, Footed	15.00
Nut Bowl, Two Handled	18.00
Oil, Drop Stopper 6 oz.	20.00
Oil, Ground Stopper 6 oz.	28.00
Oil, Cut Stopper 6 oz.	35.00
Oil, Drop Stopper 4 oz.	16.00
Oil, Ground Stopper 4 oz.	18.00
Oil, Cut Stopper 4 oz.	30.00
Olive Dish	12.00
Orange Bowl	15.00
Pickle Dish	12.00
Pickle Jar and Cover	35.00
Pitcher, ½ gallon	65.00
Plate 12"	10.00
Rose Bowl, Footed	15.00
Salt, Footed, Individual	10.00
Shaker, Nickel or Silver Plate or Glass or Non Corrosive Tops	18.00
Straw Jar	85.00
Straw Jar and Cover	115.00
Sugar and Cover	25.00
Sugar, 2 Handled, Open	18.00
Sugar, Footed, Hotel	18.00
Sundae	8.00
Tankard, ½ gallon	110.00
Toothpick	20.00
Tumbler, Ice Tea	20.00
Tumbler, Table	18.00
Tumbler, Wine	14.00
Vase 8"	30.00
Vase 10"	45.00

⊷⊜ VALENCIA Pattern #205 ⊜⊷

Crystal pressed glass
Late 1800s Line

Bowl, Open, High Foot 7"	30.00
Bowl, Open, Low Foot 7"	28.00
Bowl, Covered, High Foot 7"	45.00
Bowl, Covered, Low Foot 7"	40.00
Bowl, Open, High Foot 8"	35.00
Bowl, Open, Low Foot 8"	32.00
Bowl, Covered, High Foot 8"	48.00
Bowl, Covered, Low Foot 8"	45.00
Bowl 7"	15.00
Bowl 8"	17.00
Bowl 9"	20.00
Butter, Covered	28.00
Celery, Tall	26.00
Comport	26.00
Cream	15.00

⤝⇒ VALENCIA Pattern #205 Cont. ⇐⤞

Cream, Individual.....................................12.00
Cruet Set...75.00
Finger Bowl 12.00
Jug, ½ gallon..80.00
Jug/Tankard...75.00
Molasses Can 65.00
Mustard 30.00
Nappy 4½"..12.00

Nut Bowl 15.00
Oil 40.00
Salver 9"...35.00
Salver 10"...42.00
Shaker 20.00
Spoon...15.00
Sugar, Covered 12.50
Tumbler 15.00

⤝⇒ VENTURE Pattern #6114 ⇐⤞

**Crystal Bowl with Gray Mist Base
1969 – 1971**

#31 Brandy 3½ oz. 3½" 13.00
#2 Goblet 14 oz. 6⅞".................................15.00
#7 Sherbet 9 oz. 2⅞".................................12.00
#26 Wine 8 oz. 5½"....................................13.00
#549 Plate 7"...5.00

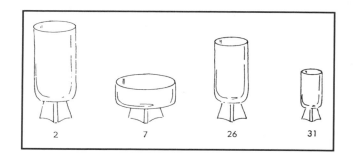

⤝⇒ VERMEIL Design #661 ⇐⤞

**Crystal blown lead glass
Gold band on bowl
See Silhouette Pattern
1965 – 1978**

#224 Bowl, Footed 10"...............................17.00
#31 Brandy 3 oz. 14.00
#25 Claret 7½ oz.......................................15.00
#681 Cream, Footed 10.00
#2 Goblet 10 oz. 16.00
#63 Luncheon Goblet/Ice Tea 14 oz. 15.00
#11 Sherbet/Champagne 8 oz. 12.00

#679 Sugar, Footed 10.00
#26 Tulip Wine 5½ oz. 15.00
#620 Relish, 2 part....................................11.50
#643 Relish, 4 part....................................15.00
#644 Relish, 5 part....................................21.00
#495 Dessert/Finger Bowl..........................6.00
#549 Plate 7"...5.00
#550 Plate 8"...6.00

⤝⇒ VERONA Pattern #200 ⇐⤞

**Crystal pressed glass
Very Early 1900s Line**

Butter and Cover.....................................35.00
Bowl, open 6" 12.00
Bowl, open 7" 14.00

Bowl, open 8" 16.00
Bowl, covered 6" 25.00
Bowl, covered 7" 26.00
Bowl, covered 8" 30.00

VERONA Pattern #200 Cont.

Celery, Tall	20.00	Jelly 5"	12.00
Comport 4"	12.00	Jug, ½ gallon	50.00
Comport, open 6"	12.00	Molasses Can	40.00
Comport, open 7"	14.00	Mustard with Bail	15.00
Comport, open 8"	16.00	Nappy 4"	8.00
Comport, Covered 6"	20.00	Nappy 4½"	8.00
Comport, Covered 7"	22.00	Oil, Cut Stopper 10 oz.	25.00
Comport, Covered 8"	25.00	Oil, 10 oz.	20.00
Cream	7.50	Salver 8"	25.00
Cream Tank	25.00	Salver 9"	26.00
Cruet Set (Tray, Oil, 2 Shakers)	45.00	Salver 10"	28.00
Custard, Handled	6.00	Shakers	pair 12.00
Custard Plate	4.00	Spoon	15.00
Finger Bowl	6.00	Sugar, Covered	12.50
Goblet	14.00	Tumbler	15.00

VERSAILLES Design #683 or #6113

Crystal blown glass stemware
Gold decorated stem
1969 – 1972
Do not confuse with Versailles Etching #278

#31 Brandy 2½ oz. 3⅞" 15.00
#25 Claret 9 oz. 6" 14.00
#2 Goblet 14 oz. 6⅞" 16.00
#63 Luncheon Goblet/Ice Tea 15 oz. 6¼" ..14.00
#11 Sherbet 10 oz. 5¾" 11.00
#26 Wine 8 oz. 6⅜" 15.00
#549 Plate 7" Not Decorated 5.00

VESPER Pattern #6086

Crystal blown glass stemware
Note: Do not confuse with earlier etched line
1959 – 1965

#29 Cordial 1¼ oz. 3³⁄₁₆" 12.50
#27 Cocktail/Wine 5½ oz. 4⅞" 7.00
#2 Goblet 11¾ oz. 6⅜" 10.00
#63 Ice Tea, Footed 13 oz. 6³⁄₁₆" 12.00
#88 Juice, Footed 5½ oz. 4½" 9.50
#11 Sherbet 7½ oz. 4⅞" 7.00
#549 Plate 7" 5.00
#550 Plate 8" 6.00

☞ VICTORIA Pattern #183 ☜

Pressed glass
See page 20 for color photo
Crystal and Crystal with Satin Finish
Believed to be first produced line. However
   Cascade Line was first advertised.
Late 1800s

Bowl 8"	30.00
Bowl 9"	48.00
Butter and Cover	100.00
Canoe	20.00
Celery, Tall	47.00
Celery, Tray	27.00
Cigar Holder	50.00
Cruet Set (2 shakers, Oil, Mustard)	100.00
Cream	35.00
Cream Tank, Individual	25.00
Cup and Saucer	45.00
Custard, Handled	10.00
Custard Plate	6.00
Finger Bowl	12.50
Flower Bowl, Large	25.00
Flower Bowl, Individual	15.00
Ice Cream Saucer	12.50
Jug, Round ½ gallon	95.00
Lamp	270.00

Mustard and Bail	25.00
Molasses Can	68.00
Molasses Can, Individual	45.00
Napkin Ring	10.00
Nappy 4½"	12.50
Nappy 5"	13.00
Nappy 9"	28.00
Nappy 10"	30.00
Nappy 3 Cornered	40.00
Nut Bowl	20.00
Oil 10 oz.	75.00
Olive, Handled	15.00
Pickle Caster	130.00
Pickle Jar and Cover	50.00
Shaker	25.00
Shot Glass	100.00
Spoon	30.00
Sugar with Cover	50.00
Toothpick	45.00
Tumbler	35.00
Water Bottle	110.00

☞ VICTORIA Pattern #6068½ ☜

Crystal blown lead glass stemware
Narrow Rib Optic
See also Puritan Pattern
1957 – 1971

#2 Goblet 10 oz. 5¾"	7.00
#11 Sherbet 6½ oz. 4⅝"	6.00
#27 Wine/Cocktail 4½ oz. 4½"	6.00
#29 Cordial 1¼ oz. 3"	10.00
#63 Luncheon Goblet/Ice Tea 13 oz. 5⅞"	8.00
#88 Footed Juice 5 oz. 4½"	7.00
#549 Plate 7"	5.00

⇒ VICTORIA Design #696 ⇐

Crystal with platinum band on bowl
Based on Wilma Pattern
1965 – 1985

#8 Champagne/High Sherbet 6 oz. 5⅝" 11.00
#25 Claret 4½ oz. 6" 14.00
#27 Claret 6½ oz. 6½" 14.00
#84 Continental Champagne 5 oz. 8⅛" 18.00
#21 Cocktail 3½ oz. 5¼"...........................11.00
#29 Cordial ¾ oz. 3⅞" 21.00
#2 Goblet 10 oz. 7⅝"................................18.00

#63 Luncheon Goblet/Ice Tea
   13 oz. 5⅞".......................................17.00
#11 Low Sherbet 6 oz. 4⅜".......................11.00
#33 Oyster Cocktail 4 oz. 3⅝" 12.00
#72 Water, Footed 10 oz. 5⅜"....................16.00
#35 Magnum Wine, 16 oz. 7¼"..................15.00
#549 Plate 7"...5.00
#550 Plate 8"...6.00

⇒ VICTORIAN Pattern #4024 ⇐

Crystal, Crystal Base with Regal Blue Bowl,
Crystal Base with Burgundy Bowl, Crystal
Base Empire with Green Bowl. Selected
items made in Ruby.
Do not confuse with very early Victoria Pat-
tern #183 or the later Victoria Pattern
#6068½ and Victoria Design #696
1934 – 1943
Add 30% for colors

Cocktail 4 oz. 10.00
Claret/Wine 3½ oz.....................................13.00
Compote 5" 15.00
Cordial 1 oz. 16.00
Goblet 11 oz. 14.00

Goblet 10 oz. 14.00
Oyster Cocktail 4 oz. 9.00
Rhine Wine 3½ oz. 12.00
Saucer Champagne 6½ oz..........................11.00
Sherbet 5½ oz..8.00
Sherry 2 oz...11.50
Tumbler, Footed 1½ oz. 10.00
Tumbler, Footed 5 oz...................................12.00
Tumbler, Footed 8 oz...................................13.00
Tumbler, footed 12 oz..................................13.50

⇒ VIRGINIA Pattern #2977 ⇐

Hand molded stemware and giftware
See page 56 for color photo
Green, Dark Blue, Light Blue, Brown, Peach
Crystal, Gray
1978 – 1985

#319 Candlestick 6" ....pair 20.00
#171 Compote, Footed............................15.00
#2 Goblet 10 oz. 7¼"...............................5.00
#63 Luncheon Goblet/Ice Tea 13 oz. 6⅞"....5.00
#11 Sherbet 7 oz. 5⅛".............................4.50

#550 Plate 8"...6.00
Plate 10" 8.00
#761 Vase 6" 8.00
Vase 7"...8.00
#27 Wine 6 oz. 6¹⁄₁₆" 7.00

VIRGINIA Pattern #1467

Crystal pressed glass
1906 – 1915
*Items in lead crystal 1974 – 1978

Almond, Individual 6.00
Bon Bon, Heart, Spade, Club, or Diamond
   Shape..8.00
Bon Bon, square 8.00
Bowl, Deep, Footed 8".............................25.00
Bowl, Deep, Footed 9".............................30.00
Bowl, Deep, Footed, Bell Shape 8" 25.00
Bowl, Deep, Footed, Bell Shape 9" 30.00
Bowl, Shallow, Footed 7" 18.00
Bowl, Shallow, Footed 8" 20.00
Bowl, Shallow, Footed 9" 22.00
Butter, Covered 50.00
Celery Tray..16.50
Comport, unfinished 4½" 6.00
Comport 4½" 8.00
Comport 8"..15.00
Comport 9"..18.00
Cream 15.00
Cream, Hotel 12.00
Custard...8.00
Finger Bowl..10.00
Hostess Server with Spoon 15.00
Ice Jug, ½ gallon....................................65.00
Jelly Bowl..10.00
Molasses Can (2 Styles) 40.00
Nappy 4½"..6.00
Nappy 5" 6.00
*Nappy 6½" shallow 4.00
Nappy 6" 8.00
Nappy 7" 10.00
Nappy 8" 14.00
Nappy 9" 16.00
Nappy, Handled 4½" 8.00
Nappy, Handled 5" 10.00
Oil 8 oz...50.00
Olive, 3 Cornered 15.00

Plate 8" 8.00
*Pickle Dish 8" 12.00
*Pickle Dish 8½" 8.00
Pitcher, ½ gallon....................................65.00
Punch Bowl 16"..35.00
Punch Bowl & Foot 16"..............................50.00
Salt, Individual......................................10.00
Shakers (2 Styles)............................pair 16.50
Salver 9"...20.00
Salver 10"...25.00
Salver 11"...30.00
Spoon...18.00
Spoon Tray...12.00
Sugar, Covered.......................................25.00
Sugar, Hotel 15.00
*Sweetmeat 4.00
Toothpick..16.00
Tumbler 16.00
Water Bottle 65.00
Wine 12.00

⇥ VISION Pattern #3008 Morgantown ⇤

Blown lead glass stemware
Crystal, Ebony, Midnight Blue, Nutmeg, White
1972 – 1973

#25 Claret 8 oz. 6".....................................14.00
#29 Cordial 2 oz. 3⅝"..............................15.00
#2 Goblet 12 oz. 7⅛".................................14.00
#63 Ice Tea 13 oz. 6⅝"...........................14.00
#11 Sherbet 11 oz. 5¾"..........................12.00
#26 Tulip Wine 7 oz. 6⅜".........................15.00

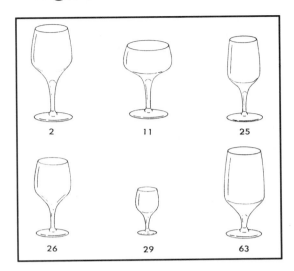

⇥ VOGUE Pattern #2106 ⇤

Crystal pressed glass
See page 20 for color photo
1916 – 1929

Ashtray 8.00	Cream 10.00
Banana Split 8.00	Cream, Hotel 8.00
Banana Split, Footed 10.00	Cream, Individual......................8.00
Bon Bon, Footed 5½" 16.00	Custard...................................5.00
Bowl, Low Footed 5½" 16.00	Egg 15.00
Bowl, Low Footed, Covered 18.00	Finger Bowl (2 Styles) 8.00
Bowl, Low Footed, Crimped 6" ...14.00	Finger Bowl Plate 6" 6.00
Bowl, oval 8" 12.00	Finger Bowl Plate 6¼" 6.00
Bowl, oval 9" 14.00	Fruit Bowl...............................15.00
Bowl, oval 10" 16.00	Goblet 9.00
Buffet Tray 10.00	Honey Jar 15.00
Butter, Covered 30.00	Honey Jar, Covered 20.00
Butter, Individual.....................10.00	Ice Cream.................................8.00
Butter, oval 25.00	Ice Tea Tumbler, Straight 13 oz. ...8.00
Butter, oval, covered................30.00	Ice Tumbler, Flared 13 oz. 8.00
Candle, Handled........................12.00	Ice Tea Tumbler, 15 oz. 10.00
Celery Dip 10.00	Ice Tea Plate 4¾" 4.00
Celery, Tall...............................12.00	Ice Tub...................................20.00
Celery Tray................................9.00	Ice Tub Plate 9" 6.00
Cheese and Plate 22.00	Jelly, High Footed 4" 10.00
Cigar Jar, Covered....................25.00	Jelly, High Footed, covered 4" 15.00
Cigarette Box, Covered Large ...25.00	Jelly, High Footed, 4¾" 12.00
Cigarette Box, Covered small 20.00	Jelly, High Footed, Covered 4¾" ...20.00
Coaster 3⅜"...............................4.00	Jug, quart 20.00
Coca-Cola.................................10.00	Jug, 3 quart 25.00

Jug, 3 quart, covered.................................30.00
Jug, ½ gallon 30.00
Jug, ½ gallon, covered 35.00
Lemon Dish, Flared 5 to 6" 12.00
Lemon Dish, Covered 18.00
Lemonade, Footed, Handled 12 oz. 14.00
Match Box, covered 15.00
Molasses Can, Nickel or Silver Top 30.00
Molasses Can Plate 5" 5.00
Mug 8.00
Mustard, Covered 20.00
Mustard, Covered, Spoon 25.00
Mustard, Covered 5 oz...............................15.00
Nappy 3¾" 5.00
Nappy 4¼" 6.00
Nappy (2 styles) 4¾" 6.00
Nappy 5¼" 7.00
Nappy 6¾" 8.00
Nappy 7¾" 9.00
Nappy 8¾" 10.00
Nappy, 2 Handled, Crimped 5½" 8.00
Nappy, Crimped 6½" 9.00
Nappy, Crimped 7½" 10.00
Nappy, Handled, Flared 5".........................7.00
Nappy, Handled, Covered 4½"....................8.00
Nappy, Shallow 5½".....................................7.00
Nappy, Shallow 7¼".....................................8.00
Nasturtium Vase 12.00
Nut Bowl, square 4½" 8.00
Oil, Drop Stopper 4 oz. 20.00
Oil, Drop Stopper 6 oz. 22.00
Oil, Ground Stopper 4 oz. 25.00
Oil, Ground Stopper 6 oz. 28.00
Olive Dish 5⅝" 12.00
Parfait 6 oz. (2 styles) 8.00
Pear or Pickle Dish 15.00
Pickle Dish 8" 12.00
Preserve, 2 Handled, Covered 40.00
Punch Bowl..50.00
Punch Bowl with Foot................................60.00
Punch Bowl with High Foot 65.00
Relish Dish...10.00
Relish Dish, Partitioned.............................12.00
Salt Dip...8.00
Sauce Bowl 8.00

Sauce Bowl Plate.......................................4.00
Sauce Ladle...15.00
Shaker, Nickel or Glass Top......................13.00
Sherbet 3 oz. 4.00
Sherbet, Low 5 oz.......................................5.00
Sherbet, High Footed 5 oz..........................6.00
Soda, Footed 4 oz.......................................6.00
Soda, Footed 6 oz 8.00
Soda, Footed 8 oz 10.00
Soda, Footed 10 oz 12.00
Soda, Footed 12 oz 12.00
Spoon...15.00
Sugar, Covered (2 styles) 15.00
Sugar, Individual, Covered 15.00
Sugar Sifter..18.00
Sugar, Hotel, covered 16.00
Sugar Server 25.00
Sundae 4 oz. 6.00
Syrup, Metal Handle...................................30.00
Toothpick, Handled 14.00
Tray 10" 10.00
Tub, Small 8.00
Tumbler, Table, Flared 8.00
Tumbler, Table, Straight..............................8.00
Tumbler, 5 oz. 6.00
Tumbler, 8 oz. 7.00
Tumbler, 10 oz. 8.00
Tumbler, 12 oz. 10.00
Vase 9"..13.00

VOGUE Pattern #6099

Blown lead glass stemware
Solid Crystal and Gold Tint Bowl with Crystal Base
1961 – 1976
Line Matchings only in 1974. Custom orders in 1981.

#29 Cordial 1 oz. 3 9/16" 18.00
#2 Goblet 11 oz. 6 7/8" 15.00
#88 Juice, Footed 5 1/2 oz. 4 7/8" 12.00
#63 Luncheon Goblet/Ice Tea 14 oz. 6 5/8" ..13.00
#11 Sherbet 6 1/2 oz. 5 1/16" 10.00
#27 Wine/Cocktail 4 1/2 oz. 5 5/16" 12.00
#495 Dessert/Finger Bowl 6.00
#549 Plate 7" 5.00
#550 Plate 8" 6.00

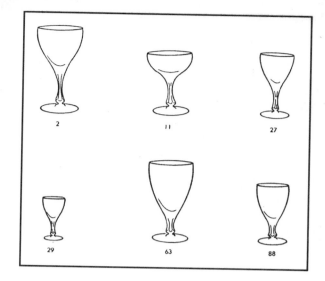

WEDDING BELLS Pattern #789

Crystal pressed glass
Some items decorated in Ruby or Gold
1900 – 1903

Berry Bowl 7" 25.00
Berry Bowl 8" 26.00
Berry Bowl 9" 30.00
Bowl, Oval 9" 21.00
Butter, Covered 88.00
Celery, Tall 38.00
Celery Tray 20.00
Cream 30.00
Custard 12.50
Decanter, Quart 120.00
Finger Bowl 12.50
Jug 105.00
Nappy 4 1/2" 9.00
Pickle/Olive Dish 15.00
Punch Bowl 200.00

Punch Bowl Foot 100.00
Shaker, Large, Nickel Top 17.50
Shaker, Small, Nickel Top 21.00
Shaker, Small, Silver Plated Top 25.00
Spooner 30.00
Sugar, Covered 45.00
Syrup, Nickel Top 65.00
Syrup, Regular Top 60.00
Tankard 105.00
Toothpick 28.00
Tumbler 18.00
Vinegar/Oil 55.00
Water Bottle 70.00
Whiskey 60.00
Wine ....

⊷ **WEDDING RING Design #626** ⊶

Crystal with platinum band on bowl
See page 64 for color photo
Combination pattern
See Courtship #6051½ for stems
#4185, 2364, 2666, 2785 for table items
1953 – 1982 Custom orders only after 1982

#2364/195 Bowl, Salad 9" 20.00
#2364/224 Bowl, Footed 10" 15.00
#2324/315 Candlestick 4" ....pair 22.00
#6051½/27 Claret/Wine 4 oz. 4½" 19.00
#6051½/20 Cocktail 4¼ oz. 3⅞" 11.00
#6051½/29 Cordial 1¼ oz. 3⅛" 22.00
#2785/681 Cream, Footed 3½" 11.00
#2666/668 Cream, Individual 11.00
#2666/396 Cup 7.50
#6951½/2 Goblet 10½ oz. 6³⁄₁₆" 15.00
#6051½/60 Ice Tea, Footed 12¼ oz. 3⅛" ...22.00

#6051⅛/8 Juice, Footed 5 oz. 4" 13.00
#2364/477 Mayonnaise with Plate and
   Ladle 28.00
#6051½/33 Oyster Cocktail 4¾ oz. 3¾" 9.00
#2785/620 Relish, 2 part 10.00
#2785/643 Relish, 4 part 12.50
#2785/644 Relish, 5 part 16.00
#2666/397 Saucer 3.00
#6051½/4 Sherbet 6½ oz. 4⅜" 10.00
#2785/679 Sugar 2⅝" 10.00
#2666/687 Sugar, Individual 10.00
#2666/686 Tray for Individual Sugar and
   Cream 11.00

⊷ **WESTCHESTER Pattern #6012** ⊶

Crystal blown lead glass stemware
See page 58 for color photo
Crystal or Crystal Base with Colored Bowl:
  Ruby, Empire Green, Burgundy, Regal Blue
1936 – 1970

Brandy 1 oz. 15.00
#8 Champagne (High Sherbet) 5½ oz. 5" ...11.00
#25 Claret 4½ oz. 5¾": 15.00
#21 Cocktail 3 oz. 4⅝" 13.00
#29 Cordial 1 oz. 3½" 17.00
Creme de Menthe 2 oz. 12.50
#2 Goblet 10 oz. 6⅞" 15.00
#88 Juice, Footed 5 oz. 4¼" 11.00
#60 Luncheon Goblet/Ice Tea 14 oz. 5¾" ..15.00
#11 Low Sherbet 5½ oz. 4" 10.50
#33 Oyster Cocktail 4 oz. 3½" 10.00
Rhine Wine 4½ oz. 15.00
Sherry 2 oz. 15.00
#26 Wine 3 oz. 4⅝" 15.00
#72 Water, Footed 10 oz. 5⅜" 21.00
#495 Dessert/Finger Bowl.........................6.00
#548 Plate 7" 5.00
#550 Plate 8" 6.00

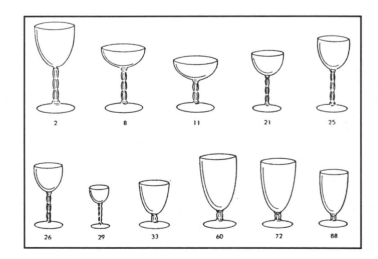

⊶ WILMA Pattern #6016 ⊷

Blown lead glass stemware
16 Rib Regular Optic
See page 57 for color photo
Crystal or Azure Bowl with Crystal Base
Custom Orders: Pink Bowl with Crystal Base
1965 – 1985

#8 Champagne/High Sherbet 6 oz. 5⅝" 11.00
#25 Claret 4½ oz. 6" 14.00
#27 Claret 6½ oz. 6½" 14.00
#84 Continental Champagne 5 oz. 8⅛" 18.00
#21 Cocktail 3½ oz. 5¼"............................11.00
#29 Cordial ¾ oz. 3⅞".............................21.00
#2 Goblet 10 oz. 7⅝".................................18.00

#88 Juice, Footed 5 oz. 4⅝" 12.00
#63 Luncheon Goblet/Ice Tea 13 oz. 5⅞" ..17.00
#11 Low Sherbet 6 oz. 4⅜".........................11.00
#33 Oyster Cocktail 4 oz. 3⅝" 12.00
#72 Water, Footed 10 oz. 5⅜".....................16.00
#35 Magnum Wine 16 oz. 7¼"....................15.00
#549 Plate 7"..5.00
#550 Plate 8"..6.00

⊶ WIMBLEDON Pattern #6126, WI02 ⊷

Crystal blown lead glass stemware
See page 57 for color photo
See Corsage Plum and Gazebo
Late 1970's – 1982

#11 Dessert/Champagne 9 oz. 5⅝"............9.00
#2 Goblet 12 oz. 7"....................................13.00

#63 Luncheon Goblet/Ice Tea 13 oz. 6" 13.00
#26 Wine 7 oz. 5¾" 12.00

⊶ WINDSOR Pattern #6049 ⊷

Blown lead glass stemware
Crystal
1952 – 1965

#25 Claret 5 oz. 5⅝" 9.00
#21 Cocktail 4 oz. 4⅞".................................7.00
#29 Cordial 1¼ oz. 3½" 12.00
#2 Goblet 11¼ oz. 7".................................8.00
#63 Ice Tea, Footed 15¼ oz. 6¼" 10.00
#88 Juice, Footed 5¾ oz. 4⅞".....................6.00
#8 Sherbet/Champagne 7¼ oz. 5¼" 8.00
#11 Low Sherbet 7¼ oz. 4⅜".......................6.00
#33 Oyster Cocktail 4½ oz. 4" 6.50
#18 Parfait 6¾ oz. 6".................................8.50
#26 Wine 4 oz. 5⅛" 10.00
#485 Dessert/Finger Bowl...........................6.00
#549 Plate 7"..5.00
#550 Plate 8"..6.00

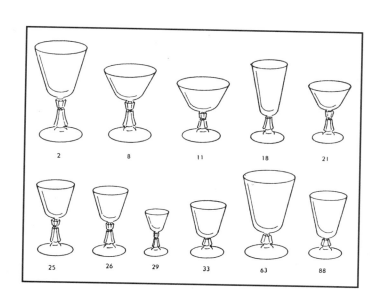

WISTAR Pattern #2620

Crystal
1941 – 1944

Bon Bon, 3 Toed	12.50
Candlestick 4"	pair 25.00
Celery 9½"	13.50
Cream, Footed	12.00
Fruit Bowl 13"	19.00
Goblet 9 oz.	17.00
Lily Pond 12"	29.00
Mayonnaise with Plate and Ladle	27.00
Nappy, Regular, Handled	8.00
Nappy, Flared, Handled	8.00
Nappy, Square	8.50
Nappy, Handled, 3 Cornered	9.00
Nut Bowl, 3 Toed	16.00

Plate 7"	5.00
Salad Bowl 10"	21.00
High Sherbet 6 oz.	9.00
Sugar, Footed	7.00
Torte Plate 14"	17.50
Tricorne, 3 Toed	14.00
Tumbler 5 oz.	10.00
Tumbler 12 oz.	13.00

WOODLAND Pattern #2921

Hnad molded stemware and giftware
See page 58 for color photo
Crystal, Blue, Brown, Green
Late 1970's Pattern
Custom Order by 1981

#517 Bowl 7"	12.00
#317 Candlesticks	pair 18.00
#2 Goblet 9½ oz. 6¹³⁄₁₆"	6.50
#448 Jelly, Footed	10.00
#63 Luncheon Goblet/Ice Tea	
14½ oz. 6¹¹⁄₁₆"	7.50
#505 Nappy & Cover 5"	10.00

#506 Nappy 5"	5.00
#554 Serving Plate 10"	10.00
#653 Shakers	pair 15.00
#7 Sherbet 8 oz. 5¼"	5.00
#659 Sugar	7.00
Vase, Bud	10.00
#26 Wine 6½ oz. 5¹³⁄₁₆"	6.50

YORK Pattern #1118

Crystal pressed glass
See page 20 for color photo
1902 – 1904

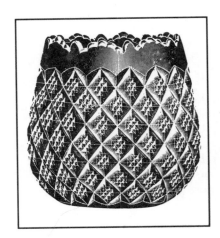

Berry Bowl 4½"	5.00
Berry Bowl 8"	17.50
Butter, Covered	55.00
Custard	8.00
Cream	22.50
Shaker (2 Styles) Nickel or	
Silver Tops	each 10.00
Spoon	25.00
Sugar, Covered	30.00
Syrup, Silver Plated Handle & Top	30.00

Giftware

Fostoria's extensive gift lines are rooted in the dinnerware and casual dinnerware lines. Many items in those lines were lifted and became part of the general gift selections. Decanter sets, Smoking Sets, Candy Jar Assortments, Cheese Sets, Salad Sets, Bowl Collections, Vase Assortments and more, made for a rich and varied gift offering. Casual dinnerware lines, with fewer strictly dinnerware items provided coordinated gift items, for those who would choose a theme-oriented gift from retail registrations. Heirloom, Sonata and Contour are typical of that practice. Frequently, when a line was reduced to "matching service only" and not available as a complete line, parts of the line still appeared in sets and collections. A favored item often found a second life.

From the first, however, Fostoria offered individual gift items not intended to be part of a regular line. Wonderful candelabra, bowls, figurines and other unusual gift items added to Line items resulted in a broad, ever changing gift line unsurpassed by any in the glass industry. This extensive production combined with Fostoria's extended production time add to the challenges which have only recently come to the attention of the collecting world.

As before indicated, the gift selections presented here conform to the limits of plain or self detailed decoration. That position has not always been possible to maintain, but it remains the general guideline for this discussion. Beyond these limitations, however, there exists another important source of gift items; the lunch time whimsey, creative work of employees who were free to design items for themselves on their free time. Often, with a small batch of colored glass left from regular production, a worker would pour it into a mold of his choice, sometimes creating rare and unlisted items/colors. These small gift items, never part of company production, may still be considered as Fostoria Glass, of course. Many rarities, prototypes and morgue items started life as lunch time projects. With no listings, but with identity certain, most of these are rare, all are treasures. Confidence in the seller is fundamental to the acquisition of these rare items.

One of the least recognized gift items from early gift production are Fostoria's Bubble Balls, intended for use in containers as decorative alternatives for floral arrangements. Identifying Fostoria's Bubble Balls is difficult but size, Fostoria's known colors, and a smoothed pontil mark will eliminate the Mexican balls which had flooded the 1930's gift market. Look, also, for the good quality of glass which has become our standard measurement. These listings come from company catalogs in 1935 as well as *House Beautiful* half page advertisements in 1934 and 1935.

Glass fruit, another early item to be used in table decorations is rare and confusing when compared to fruit produced by other glass houses. Our listing is from Fostoria's 1935 catalog and includes: Grapes, Oranges, Bananas, Pears, Peaches, and Apples. All were made in Ruby, Burgundy, Empire Green, and Silver except the Peach and Pear which were not produced in Green. As you examine glass fruit, look for Fostoria's colors as well as the smoothed pontil mark. Seldom seen, all items are rare. Do not confuse these older items with the beautiful solid red apples which were never a part of the fruit line, but made at the factory as lunch hour whimsies. These later red apples were Moundsville favorites for a time, but the secret was too good to keep and they have since traveled to all parts of the country.

Glass animals were an important part of the gift ware line. They were first called Table Ornaments and we find several groupings appearing at various times. The first listing, a Penguin, Pelican, Seal and Polar Bear were made in Crystal, Topaz and Silver Mist and dated from 1935 to 1943. The Horse bookend dated 1939 – 1958 was first made in Crystal with Silver Mist added shortly. The Elephant bookend was produced from 1939 to 1943, introduced in Crystal with Silver Mist added a year later. Also included in the figural bookend line was an elegant Eagle made in Silver Mist in 1939. It was offered the next year in crystal. The most elusive of the bookends, the Owl, was made in 1943 only and was confined to crystal. Much later, in 1970 – 1980 they were reproduced in Ebony.

Standing and reclining Colts as well as Deer were early additions to the animal line. They were included in the years 1940 – 1943 and were, again, made in Crystal and Silver Mist. In the 1970's they were privately commissioned and sold in blue and you should expect to see them in that color. The Deer and several sleighs were reissued in 1950 in Milk Glass. A Santa seemed important and one was added in 1955. He was 9½" tall and is as hard to find as the jolly old elf himself. In 1950 the animal line expanded with the introduction of the Chanti-cleer which came in Crystal or Ebony and an Ebony with gold decoration. A few sightings of a Milk Glass Chanticleer have been reported. A Duck family, including a mother and three ducklings, walking, heads up or heads back, two Squirrels who either ran or stood and a Goldfish in either a horizontal or vertical posi-tion as well as a Seahorse all continued in crys-tal until 1958 with the exception of the Goldfish which was dropped from the line in 1957. It remains the rarity of the Fostoria animals. In 1965 the Duck family and the Squirrels were reintroduced, this time in Amber, Olive Green and Cobalt Blue as well as a Mist treatment of these colors. The original crystal remains more sought-after. By 1971, new, more abstract ani-mals joined Fostoria's ark. These animals were confusingly called "Whimsies" and are, indeed whimsical, amorphic and altogether different from what had come before. They were pro-duced in Crystal, Lemon and Olive as well as a Mist of these colors. Of such recent production, these may be the "sleepers" of the animal line. All were out of production by 1973. This group included a Stork, Cat, Dolphin, Frog, Ladybug, Baby Rabbit and Mother Rabbit. Before we leave all these animals we should be aware that such small items were natural objects for the Lunch time projects we have discussed. All possibilities exist and one should not be overly surprised if a pink Rabbit comes your way. Take very good care of him.

Other figurals in production early and late are several different Madonnas, a Sacred Heart and a Saint Francis, all elegant glass artistry. They were made in Crystal and Silver Mist. A tiny 4" Madonna in Silver Mist, believed to have been sold only at company outlet stores, will be found in addition to these. Also of interest to fig-ural collectors are the Chinese Lute and Lotus Figures as well as a Chinese bookend, often referred to as Buddha. All of these, in Ebony with gold decoration, date from 1953. Crystal, Silver Mist and plain Ebony were soon added.

A late 1977 Art Glass line designed by James Carpenter was short lived, but is of so much interest that it deserves special mention. Called by the various names of Impromptu, Impressions, Interpretations and Images, these four designer lines are lovely vase collections. The shapes are as shown here, but they are one-of-a-kind because of the creative effort involved in their coloration. The process used involved molten crystal poured over bits of col-ored glass which melted and swirled into ethe-real abstract designs. The unpredictable design was different in each item. The touch of color was a light touch and each artist was allowed complete freedom in his artistry, achieving an understated end of day effect. Stretch glass, Verre De Soie, White Carnival are all terms which may suggest the treatments used in these groupings. The original 1977 – 1978 sales orders show the shape line drawings and colors in which one might expect to find them. Unifor-mity was not the standard except for the shapes which we believe are limited to those shown here. Be aware, however, that there was a good bit of experimentation and prototype production with these vases. Do not feel that your findings must be limited to these selections. Each item was a unique creation, an expression of color limited only by the glass artist himself. As con-ceived, each item was to have had a polished bottom, signed and dated by the artist. You will find most to be so. Many, however, left as back stock when the line was dropped, have rough bottoms, and are not perfectly finished and unsigned. Once again, shape identification is primary and will be our best guide for authenti-cation. Knowing the story behind this produc-tion adds to the value which collectors have placed upon this late, wonderful gift line.

Of course, these details only skim the sur-face of Fostoria's gift line and we may never really know all we would like to know about it. We intend to return to the subject, however, for it is a wonderful world of fine quality glass, beautifully designed and includes some of the most elegant glass in home furnishings.

AMERICAN MILESTONES SERIES #555

Crystal
1971 – 1976

Betsy Ross (Old Glory) Plate 10½" 12.50
Star Spangled Banner 10½" 12.50
Washington Crossing the Delaware 10½" ..12.50
Spirit of '76 10½" 12.50
Shrine of Democracy 10½" 12.50
One Nation Under God 10½" 12.50
Francis Scott Key 10½" 12.50

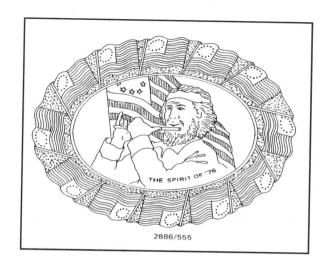

2886/555

ANIMALS AND FIGURALS

See pages 18, 19, and 21 for color photos

ANIMALS
Group 1
#2531 Pelican 3⅞"x4½" Crystal/Silver Mist
    (add 40% for topaz)..............................55.00
#2531 Seal 3⅞"x4½" Crystal/Silver Mist
    (add 40% for topaz)..............................55.00
#2531 Penguin 4⅝" Crystal/Silver Mist
    (add 40% for topaz)..............................50.00
#253 Polar Bear 4⅝"x4" Crystal/Silver Mist
    (add 40% for topaz)..............................50.00
#2589 Reclining Colt 2½" x 2¾" 30.00
#2589 Standing Colt 3⅞" x 2½" 35.00
Blue Colt..40.00
#2589 Deer 2⅜" x 2" Sitting/Standing
    Crystal 35.00
    Silver Mist 40.00
    Milk Glass 50.00
Sleigh 3"...30.00
Sleigh 4¼" 35.00
Sleigh 6" 40.00
Santa 350.00
#2564 Rearing Horse Bookend 5¼x7"
    Crystal/Silver Mist 55.00
#2615 Owl Bookend 7½" Crystal.............150.00
    Ebony..200.00
#2595 Eagle Bookend 7½"x5" 85.00
#2580 Elephant Bookend 6¼"x7¼ Crystal/
    Silver Mist 82.00
#2601 Lyre Bookend 7"x5½" 55.00
Chanticleer..185.00

2631/702   2631/703

2632/404 2632/405 2632/406 2632/407

304   357   410

420   452   527

627   628

⚹ ANIMALS AND FIGURALS Cont. ⚹

Ebony 275.00
Seahorse 100.00
Goldfish Horizontal 125.00
Goldfish Vertical 125.00

Group 2
Clear Amber & Olive: Silver Mist Colors of
   Amber, Olive, Crystal
#702 Sitting Squirrel 3⅛" 25.00
#703 Running Squirrel 2⅝" 25.00
#404 Mama Duck 4" 22.00
#405 Duckling, Head Back 2½" 15.00
#406 Duckling, Walking 2⅜" 15.00
#407 Duckling, Head Down 1" 15.00
#408 Four Duckling Set 45.00
Add 50% for Cobalt on Squirrel, Duckling Items
Add 25% for Crystal on Squirrel, Duckling Items

Group 3
Clear Crystal, Lemon, Olive Green: Silver Mist,
   Silver Mist Colors of Lemon and Olive Green
#304 Stork 2" 20.00
#357 Cat 3¾" 20.00
#410 Dolphin 4¾" 25.00
#420 Frog 1⅞" 20.00
#452 Lady Bug 1¼" 18.00
#527 Owl 2¾" 20.00
#627 Baby Rabbit 1¼" 15.00
#628 Mama Rabbit 2⅛" 20.00

FIGURALS
#466 Chinese Lotus 12¼" Crystal 125.00

Silver Mist 200.00

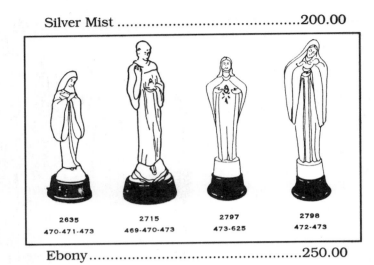

2635
470-471-473

2715
469-470-473

2797
473-625

2798
472-473

Ebony 250.00

#467 Chinese Lute 12¼" Crystal 125.00
   Silver Mist 200.00
   Ebony 250.00
Chinese Bookend 150.00
#472 Mermaid 10⅛" 120.00
#2653/471 Madonna 10" Crystal 35.00
   Silver Mist 60.00
#473 Lighted base for Madonna 15.00
Madonna 11¼" Silver Mist with Base 80.00
#469 Saint Francis 13½" Crystal 125.00
   Silver Mist 250.00
#2797/473 Sacred Heart 13½" 125.00
#2798/473 Madonna and Child 13½"
   Crystal 85.00

⚹ ARISTOCRAT COLLECTION ⚹

Crystal
1971 – Late 1970's

#2843/583 Three Piece Tidbit Set 20.00
#2843/870 Nappy (boxed set of
   four) 5½" 20.00
#1505/899 On the Rocks (boxed set
   of four) 9 oz. 20.00

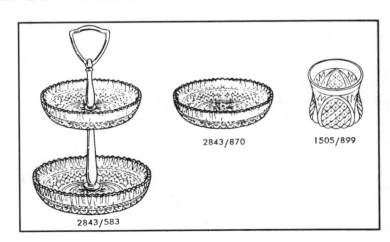

2843/870

1505/899

2843/583

⇒ ARLINGTON Pattern #2684 ⇐

Handmade milk glass
Do not confuse with early Arlington Decoration
1960's Line

#119 Ashtray 7" 12.00
#182 Lace Bowl 7"x11½".............................35.00
#919 Compote, Belled 8"x9⅝" 30.00
#918 Compote, Square 9½"........................30.00
#917 Compote, Flared 8" 30.00
#915 Compote and Cover 11½"..................35.00
#528 Oil and Stopper 5 oz. 6⅝"...............125.00

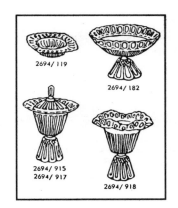

⇒ ART GLASS ⇐

Impressions, Interpretations, Images, and
** Impromptu**
See page 22 for color photos

Values on these late art glass lines depend
upon size and complexity of design. Cased items
may go as high as $250.00, other types begin at
about $100.00 and reach as high as $200.00.
Expect these rare, one-of-a-kind examples to
increase in the near future.

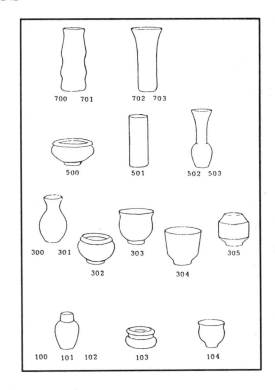

⇒ ARTISAN Pattern #2703 ⇐

Crystal, Marine, Amethyst
1961 – 1964

#174 Bowl, 3 Cornered 12".......................15.00
#189 Bowl, Oblong 14¾"............................20.00
#191 Buffet Plate, Square 13"...................20.00

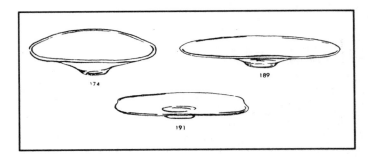

ASPEN BARWARE #AS02

Lead crystal
See page 63 for color photo
1970's – 1985

#23 Double Old Fashioned 11 oz. 6.00
#64 Highball 13 oz. 8.00

BENNINGTON Pattern #BE04

24% Lead Crystal Barware
1970 – 1985

#64 Highball 12 oz. 5½" 8.00

#23 Double Old Fashioned 10 oz. 3¾".........8.00

BERRY Pattern #2712

Handmade Milk Glass
1961 – 1965
Do not confuse with Berry Etching

#179 Bowl 8" 16.00
#180 Bowl, Cupped 7½" 16.00
#355 Bowl, Shallow 6½" 15.00
#354 Candy with Cover 4¾"x6¼" 25.00
#449 Dessert 4½" 9.00
#688 Cream, Individual 4" 9.00
#311 Flora-Candle 2⁵⁄₁₆" 12.00
#592 Jelly, Footed 3¼" 10.00
#450 Nappy, Oblong 4½" 9.00
#452 Nappy, 3 Cornered, 4½" 9.00
#687 Sugar, Individual 3⅝" 9.00
#697 Tray for Sugar and Cream 10.00
#799 Vase, Bud 8" 15.00

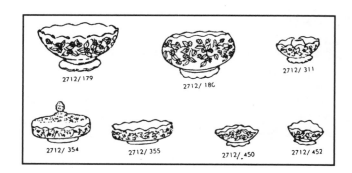

BETSY ROSS Pattern #2620

Handmade Milk Glass
1961 – 1965

#241 Basket 11½x4⅝" 32.50
#192 Bowl, Cupped 8½" 22.00
#216 Bowl, Flared 10½" 26.00
#314 Candlestick 3" ....pair 25.00
#64 Ice Tea 12 oz. 15.00
#2 Goblet 9 oz. 6" 12.00
#502 Nappy, Handled, Square 4" 11.00
#8 Sherbet 4 oz. 4" 10.00

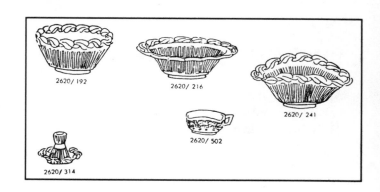

BICENTENNIAL MUG

Crystal, Amber
1974 – 1976

#2493/705 Mug 15 oz. 20.00

BUBBLE BALLS

See page 21 for color photo
**Bubble Balls were advertised in 1934 – 35
issues of *House Beautiful* magazine.**
**Crystal, Empire Green, Ruby, Regal Blue,
Burgundy**
**Burgundy, Ruby, and Regal Blue should be val-
ued at 25% above Empire Green. Crystal
should be valued at 50% above listed figures.**

EMPIRE GREEN
#4129 2½" 8.50
#4126 4" 15.00
#4126 5" 17.00
#4126 6" 20.00
#4126 7" 25.00
#4126 8" 30.00
#4126 9" 42.00

SILVER MIST
#4116 4" 15.00
#4116 5" 16.00

#4116 6" 18.00
#4116 7" 20.00
#4116 8" 30.00
#4116 9" 45.00

GOLDEN SWIRL
#4116 4" 17.00
#4116 5" 18.00
#4116 6" 20.00
#4116 7" 20.00

Ebony 4" 35.00

MOTHER OF PEARL OPALESCENT
#4116 4" 13.00
#4116 5" 15.00
#4116 6" 17.00
#4116 7" 18.00

CASUAL FLAIR Pattern #4180

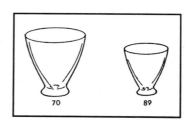

Crystal, Harvest Yellow, Sky Blue, Fawn
Late 1950's – 1962

#89 Juice 7 oz. 4" 5.00
#70 Tumbler 12 oz. 4½" 6.00

❧ CATALINA Pattern #6046 ❧

Crystal or Crystal Stem with Cinnamon Bowl 1951 – 1955

Sherbert/Old Fashioned 3".........................3.00
Juice/Cocktail 3¼" 4.00

Water Tumbler/Scotch & Soda 4⅜" 5.00
Ice Tea/Highball 5"......................................4.00
Dessert/Finger Bowl 2¼" 4.00

❧ CENTENNIAL II COLLECTION ❧

Lead Crystal in Crystal, Cobalt Blue, Ruby Introduced in 1970. Some items continued until 1985

#1121/219 LOUISE Pattern
Footed Compote 9" Ruby, Crystal..........25.00
#1229/676 FRISCO Pattern High
Covered Candy Jar 6¾" Crystal..............26.00
#1300/217 DRAPE Pattern Footed Fruit
Bowl 10½" Cobalt Blue........................ 90.00
751 Vase 4½" Crystal............................20.00
#1497/521 CRESAP Pattern Bowl 8½"
Crystal 20.00
#1605/601 SHERWOOD Pattern
Square Vase 7¾" Cobalt Blue 18.00
#1641/630 SOVEREIGN Pattern Round
Salver 10" Ruby, Crystal 35.00
#1704/517 ROSBY Pattern Bowl 7½"
Crystal 10.00
#1704/554 Serving Plate Crystal 12.00
#1704/360 Relish Tray 10¼" Crystal 11.00
#1704/676 Sugar & Cover 7" Crystal 13.50
#1704/680 Cream 5" Crystal...................11.00
#1704/592 Footed Preserve 3½" Crystal ...10.00
#1704/499 Handled Nappy 4¾"
Crystal 10.00
#1704/501 3 Cornered Nappy 4½"
Crystal 11.00
#1827/801 RAMBLER Pattern Footed
Vase 9" Ruby 30.00
#1827/211 Salad Bowl 10½" Ruby 30.00
#1827/451 Square Footed Preserve 3½"
Crystal 15.00
#1827/499 Handled Nappy 4¾" Crystal....14.00
#1827/501 5" 3 Cornered Handled Nappy
Crystal 14.00
#1913/127 FLEMISH Basket 11" Crystal..35.00
#2860/2 PANELLED DIAMOND POINT
Pattern Goblet 10½" 12.00
#2860/7 Dessert/Champagne 7 oz.
Crystal 9.00
#2860/26 Wine 6½ oz. Crystal.................11.00

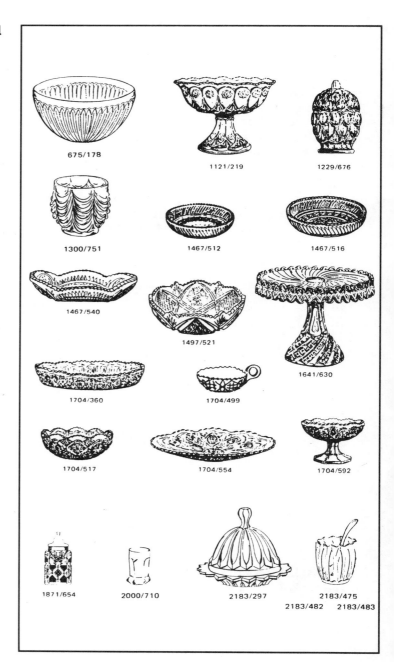

675/178

1121/219

1229/676

1300/751

1467/512

1467/516

1467/540

1497/521

1641/630

1704/360

1704/499

1704/517

1704/554

1704/592

1871/654

2000/710

2183/297

2183/475
2183/482   2183/483

↜ CENTENNIAL II COLLECTION Cont. ↝

#2860/63 Luncheon Goblet/Ice Tea 13 oz.
  Crystal 11.00
#2869/550 Salad Plate 8" Crystal...............8.00
#2681/23 ASPEN Pattern Double Old Fash-
  ioned 11 oz. Crystal 8.00
#2681/64 Highball 13 oz. Crystal...............8.00
#2862/23 STOWE Pattern Double Old Fash-
  ioned 11 oz. Crystal 6.00
#2862/64 Highball 13 oz. Crystal...............7.00
#675/178 Round Serving Bowl 8" Crystal..12.00
#1871/654 BRILLIANT Pattern Shaker
  with Chrome Top Crystal ....pair 10.00
#2000/710 Toothpick Holder 2¾" Crystal ...8.00
#2183/297 COLONIAL PRISM Pattern Covered
  Server 6" Crystal...................................28.00
#2183/475 Marmalade 3¾" Crystal with
  Stainless Steel Ladle 20.00
#2183/506 Nappy 5" Crystal 8.00
#2377/76 Tumbler 8½ oz. Crystal 8.00
#2377/354 Candy Box & Cover Crystal 25.00
#2377/355 Snack Bowl 5⅜" Crystal 10.00
#2377/454 Quart Pitcher Crystal 25.00
#2377/785 Vase 8" Crystal 10.00
#2521/327 Bird Candle Holder 12.00
#2710/687 DAISY AND BUTTON Pattern
  Individual Sugar 3"...............................10.00
#2710/688 Individual Cream 3" 10.00
#2538/543 Placecard Holder/Ashtray
  Crystal 5.00
#2752/120 Ashtray 8" Crystal................10.00
#2828/111 Ashtray 6" Crystal..................8.00
#2828/757 Vase 6" Crystal 10.00
#2864/123 Ashtray 5½" Crystal 8.00
#2864/145 Ashtray 3" Set of 4 Crystal 14.00
#2864/147 Ashtray 2¾" Set of 4 Crystal ...14.00
#2864/148 Ashtray 3⅛" Set of 4 Crystal ...14.00
#2864/327 Candle B 2½" 5.00
#2864/380 Wine Coaster 5½" Crystal 3.00
#2865/377 Coaster A 3½" Set of 4
  Crystal...13.50
#2865/378 Coaster B 3½" Set of 4
  Crystal 13.50

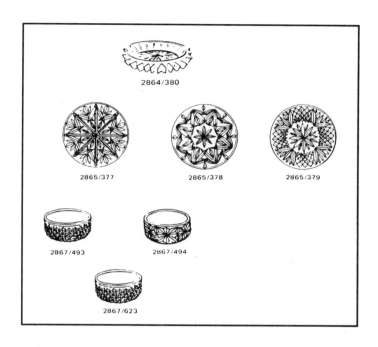

#2867/379 Coaster C 3½" Set of 4
  Crystal 13.50
#2867/493 Napkin Ring A Set of 4
  Crystal 10.00
#2867/494 Napkin Ring B Set of 4
  Crystal 10.00
#2867/623 Salt Dip 2" Set of 4 Crystal.....10.00
#2885/2 STRATTON Pattern Goblet 10 oz.
  Crystal 10.00
#2885/11 Dessert/Champagne 7 oz.
  Crystal 7.00
#2885/26 Wine 5 oz. Crystal....................9.00
#2885/63 Luncheon Goblet/Ice Tea 12 oz.
  Crystal 8.00
#2885/23 Double Old Fashioned 10 oz.
  Crystal 7.00
#2885/64 Highball 12 oz. Crystal...............7.00
#2883/761 Footed Vase 6" 7.50

↜ COLONIAL PRISM Pattern #CO13 ↝

Crystal
See page 34 for color photo
1978 – 1982

#212 Bowl 10"...16.50
#506 Bowl 5"..9.00
#568 Torte Plate 14".................................22.50
#649 Shaker with Chrome Top ....pair 16.00

#297 Covered Server 24.00
#687 Sugar 12.50
#688 Cream 10.00
#620 Relish, 2 Part...................................12.00

⊷ CONGO Pattern #4162 ⊶

Modern Primitive Tumbler Line
Amberina, Marine, Pink, Smoke
Early 1960's – 1965

#58 Beverage/Water 14 oz. 5" 4.00
#41 Cooler/Ice Tea 21 oz. 6¾" 5.00
#84 Juice 6 oz. 3¾" 5.00
#495 Dessert 8.00
#549 Salad/Dessert Plate 7⅞" 8.00

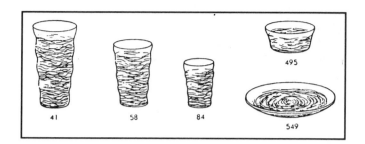

⊷ COVENTRY Pattern #2834 ⊶

Crystal and Honey Gold
Late 1960's – 1973
Selected items became part of Group International Gift Line

#135 Bon Bon 11.00
#191 Bowl 8" 15.00
#195 Bowl 9" 18.00
#300 Butter with Cover 8" 20.00
#680 Cream 3⅞" 10.00

#540 Pickle Dish 8" 10.00
#560 Plate, Serving 12" 12.00
#620 Relish, 2 part 8" 16.00
#624 Relish, 4 part 11⅛" 17.00
#651 Shakers 2¾" ....pair 15.00
#677 Sugar 3⅝" 11.00
#567 Torte Plate 14" 21.00

⊷ CROWN COLLECTION ⊶

Crystal, Gold, Royal Blue, Ruby
Late 1950's – 1965

Windsor Crown #2749
#386 Footed Chalice & Cover 8½" 78.00
#388 Footed Chalice 6¾" 62.00
#676 Covered Candy, 5½" 45.00
#677 Candy 3¾" 22.00
#133 Bottle and Stopper 4¾" 48.00
#314 Candleholder 3½" 38.00

Hapsburg Crown #2750
#386 Footed Chalice & Cover 9¼" 78.00
#388 Footed Chalice 7¼" 62.00
#676 Candy & Cover 5¾" 45.00
#677 Candy 3¾" 22.00

Navarre Crown #2751
#195 Bowl 9" 68.00
#198 Bowl & Cover 9" 125.00
#199 Footed Bowl 9" 75.00
#203 Footed Bowl & Cover 9" 150.00
Luxembourg Crown #2766
#311 Trindle Candle Bowl 7¼" 68.00

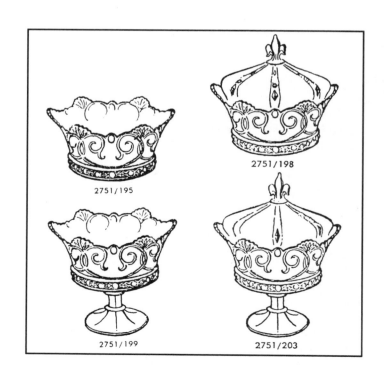

2751/195

2751/198

2751/199

2751/203

⊱ CRYSTAL WEDDING ASSORTMENT ⊰

See Old English Pattern #1460
Crystal pressed glass gold decorated
1906 – 1908

Butter, Covered 55.00	Pitcher ½ gallon 50.00
Cream 28.00	Spoon......................................28.00
Nappy 4½" 10.00	Sugar, Covered......................................32.00
Nappy 8" 30.00	Tumbler 16.00

⊱ DAISY AND BUTTON Pattern #2710 ⊰

Handmade Milk Glass
1950's – 1965

#300 Butter and Cover 9½"......................25.00
#688 Cream, Individual 3½" 10.00
#501 Nappy, Handled, 3 Cornered 3".........9.00
#502 Nappy, Handled, square 4¾" 10.00
#687 Sugar, Individual 3"........................15.00
#697 Tray for Sugar and Cream 9¼"..........8.50

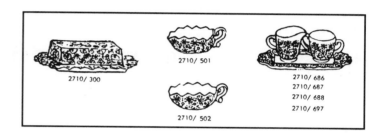

⊱ DAWN Pattern #2670 ⊰

Terrace Tumbler Line
Crystal and Honey
Early 1960's Pattern. Appeared last in 1965.

#495 Dessert Bowl 6 oz. 1⅞".......................5.00
#61 Ice Tea 12½ oz. 5" 6.00
#89 Juice 5 oz. 3½" 4.00
#73 Water 10½ oz. 3¾" 5.00

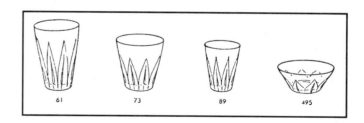

⊱ DUSK Pattern #2671 ⊰

Terrace Tumbler Line
Crystal and Honey
Early 1960 Pattern. Appeared last in 1965.

#495 Dessert Bowl 6 oz. 2"..........................5.00
#61 Ice Tea 13½ oz. 5" 6.00
#89 Juice 5 oz. 3⅝" 4.00
#73 Water 10 oz. 3⅝".................................5.00

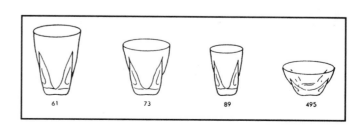

➤➤ DECORATOR COLLECTION ➤➤

Silver Mist 100.00
Madonna, Silver Mist 4" 10.00

All Teal Green, Lavender and Ruby
1964

#2424/179 Petal Bowl, Footed 6¾" 15.00
#2424/795 Basket, Footed 10" 25.00
#2497/787 Flying Fish 8" 35.00
#2517/135 Handled Bon Bon 5" 8.00
#2560/767 Ruffled Vase 6" 10.00
#2666/807 Pitcher Vase 10".....................25.00
#2692/388 Comport, Footed 6½" 18.00
#2700/152 Hanky Bowl 6" 10.00
#2718/828 Bud Vase, Footed 12"............12.00

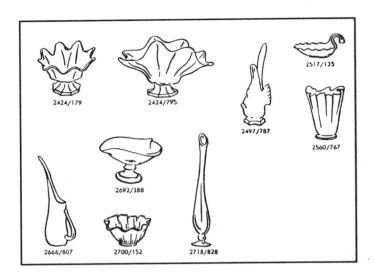

➤➤ DIAMOND SUNBURST Pattern #2711 ➤➤

Handmade Milk Glass
1961 – 1965

#679 Sugar 3⅜" 10.00
#680 Cream 4¼" 8.00

➤➤ EBONY GLASS ITEMS ➤➤

#774 Vase 7½" 20.00
#168 Round Bowl 7"................................10.00
#801 Vase 9" 22.00
#830 Vase 13" 25.00
#779 Vase 7½" 35.00
#543 Place Card Holder...........................5.00
#374 Covered Cigarette Box 5½"x4½" 22.00
#316 Candlestick 4½" 16.50
#195 Salad Bowl 9" 15.00
#311 Flora-Candle 2⅜"h 6"d 18.00
#477 Mayonnaise with Plate and Ladle 25.00
#478 Mayonnaise 5⅜" 13.00
#120 Ashtray 9" 12.00
#313 Candlestick 2½" 15.00
#373 Cigarette Holder 2¾" 10.00
#459 Hurricane Lamp, Complete 11¾"......40.00
#291 Bubble Ball 4" 22.00
#751 Snack Bowl 3⅞" 10.00

⟜ FAIRLANE BARWARE Pattern #FA03 ⟞

See page 63 for color photo
1970's – 1985

#23 Double Old Fashioned 11 oz. 3½".........6.00
#64 Highball 14 oz. 5½"............................5.00

⟜ FLAME Pattern #2545 ⟞

Crystal
Azure, Gold Tint 1944
1936 – 1944
Add 60% for Azure, 30% for Gold Tint

Bowl, oval 12½" 30.00
Candy Box with Cover, oval ½1b.............30.00
Candlestick 2" ....pair 22.00
Candlestick 4½"..............................pair 30.00
Candlestick Duo..............................pair 45.00
Candlelabra, 2 light, Prisms 80.00
Lustre ....pair 45.00
Sauce Boat......................................15.00
Tray, Lunch, Handled 12".......................25.00
Tray, Sauce Boat................................12.00
Vase 10"...25.00

⟜ FRUIT ⟞

1935
These rare fruit items seem not to have wide distribution as several who helped with pricing said they were not even aware of production. Almost as one they added, "WOW!" Those who have seen/bought/sold them valued these at about $35.00 each.

Grapes
Oranges
Bananas
Pears
Peaches
Apples

⟜ GARDEN CENTER ITEMS ⟞

#834/70 Jenny Lind Pitcher Silver Mist,
  Amber Silver Mist, Milk Glass 80.00
#1121/389 Compote Silver Mist, Amber
  Silver Mist, Milk Glass 25.00
#2364/197 Lily Pond 9" Crystal, Silver
  Mist...20.00
#2364/251 Lily Pond 12" Crystal, Silver
  Mist...25.00

169

GARDEN CENTER ITEMS Cont.

#2638/220 Oblong Bowl 10½" Crystal 20.00
#2666/189 Oval Bowl 8¼" 15.00
#2692/234 Fruit Bowl Silver Mist,
    Amethyst Silver Mist..............................15.00
#2692/760 Handled Urn 6" Silver Mist.....28.00
#2692/828 Handled Urn 12" Silver Mist...45.00
#2693/162 Franklin Urn & Cover Silver
    Mist, Milk Glass..70.00
#2703/189 Oblong Bowl 10¼" Amethyst
    Silver Mist, Silver Mist, Spruce 20.00
#2724/779 Goblet Vase Amber Silver Mist,
    Silver Mist, Spruce 7½" 18.00
#2725/761 Handled Urn Silver Mist,
    Spruce Silver Mist 4⅜" 25.00
#4152/751 Vase Bowl Silver Mist, Spruce
    Silver Mist 3⅞" 10.00
#4166/151 Footed Bowl Silver Mist 5"......12.50
#4166/199 Footed Bowl Silver Mist, Spruce
    Silver Mist 6¼" 17.50

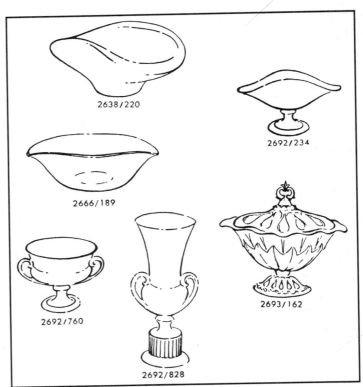

GIFTWARE LINE #2470

Rose, Green 1933 – 1942
Wisteria, Topaz 1933 – 1938
Gold Tint 1938 – 1942
Selected items in Ruby 1935 – 1939
Selected items in Regal Blue, Burgundy,
   Empire Green 1933 – 1942
1933 – 1942

Bon Bon...10.00
Bowl, 7"..12.00
Bowl, Footed 10½" 22.00
Bowl, Footed 12" 25.00
Candlestick (2 styles) 5½" 22.00
Comport (2 styles) 6" 22.00
Cake Plate, Handled 10" 18.00

Lemon Dish..12.00
Relish, 3 Part 18.50
Relish, 4 Part 20.00
Service Dish 9" 12.00
Sweetmeat, Handled 6"............................10.00
Tray, Round 9¾".......................................20.00
Vase, 8"..12.00
Vase, 10"..15.00
Vase, 11½" 18.00

GLACIER #2807

**Crystal hand molded
Late production**

#112 Small Ashtray 3¾" 5.00
#113 Medium Ashtray 5½"..........................6.50
#114 Large Ashtray 8¾"............................10.00
#377 Cigarette Lighter, Gold or Silver 10.00

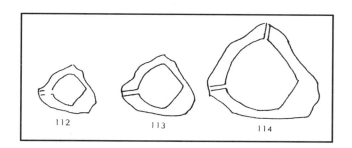

GRAPE LEAF Pattern #2513

**Crystal, Regal Blue, Burgundy, Empire Green
1935 – 1942**

Almond, Individual.....................................5.00
Candy Jar with Cover..............................20.00
Mayonnaise with Plate and Ladle..............20.00
Mint Dish, Handled 4" 10.00
Plate, Salad 7"...8.00
Preserve, Handled 5" 8.00
Relish, 2 Part 10.00
Relish, 3 Part 12.00

HAWAIIAN Pattern #2737

**Amber with Brown Accent Color
Amber with Peacock Blue Accent Color
1961 – 1964**

#106 Appetizer Set (#568 Cracker Plate
    and #478 Sauce Dish, Amber only) 45.00
#126 Basket 9"..33.00
#179 Ruffled Bowl 8" 26.00
#188 Ruffled Bowl 9" 35.00
#208 Deep Bowl 8" 30.00
#239 Shallow Bowl 11½"............................37.50
#266 Oval Bowl 15" 42.50
#369 Cheese and Cracker Set (#568 Cracker
    Plate and #266 Walnut Cheese Block)....60.00
#394 Shrimp and Dip Set (#248 Shrimp
    Bowl, Footed Dip, Amber only) 65.00
#415 Flower Float 8" 37.50
#500 Handled Candy 8"............................30.00
#567 Torte Plate 14" 45.00
#767 Ruffled Vase 6¾"..............................37.00
#807 Pitcher Vase 8⅞"..............................42.50

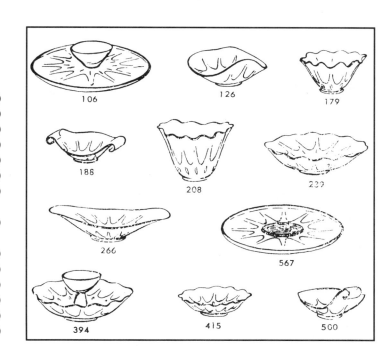

HEIRLOOM Miscellaneous Pattern #5056

Made in Yellow, Blue, Pink, Green, Opal, Bittersweet (Orange), Limited amount Ruby
1959 – 1970
Note: Do not confuse with later Heirloom Etched design

#2720/126 Basket 12"		40.00
#2729/135 Bon Bon 7"		26.00
#2727/155 Bowl, Square 6"		28.00
#2727/152 Bowl, Hanky 6"		28.00
#2720/168 Bowl, Crinkle 6½"		34.00
#2720/191 Bowl, Star 8½"		35.00
#2720/202 Bowl, Square 9"		35.00
#2183/168 Bowl 7"		30.00
#1515/208 Bowl, Deep 10"		38.00
#2729/540 Bowl, Oval		38.00
#2727/239 Bowl, Crimped 11"		39.00
#2727/231 Bowl, Shallow 11"		34.00
#1515/270 Bowl, Oblong 15"		60.00
#2730/319 Candlestick 6"	pair	55.00
#2726/311 Candleholder 3½"	pair	46.00
#2183/311 Flora-Candle 3⅞"	pair	48.00
#1515/311 Candle Vase 10"		42.00
#1570/255 Centerpiece 12"		42.00
#1515/279 Centerpiece Oval 16"		50.00
#2730/364 Epergne Small		92.00
#1515/634 Epergne Large		135.00
#2730/254 Epergne 12"		50.00
#2720/170 Florette Square 5⅜"		32.00
#2183/415 Flower Float 10"		36.00
#2728/807 Pitcher Vase 9"		80.00
#2727/550 Plate 8"		25.00
#2727/557 Plate 11"		38.00
#2570/575 Plate 17"		48.00
#2728/751 Vase Handled 4½"		39.00
#1229/757 Bud 6"		18.00
#2730/319 Vase Epergne 7"		50.00
#1515/312 Epergne 9"		45.00
#2728/827 Vase, Winged 11"		50.00
#1002/827 Vase 11"		42.00
#1002/834 Vase 18"		80.00
#1002/834 Vase 20"		100.00
#1002/834 Vase 24"		130.00

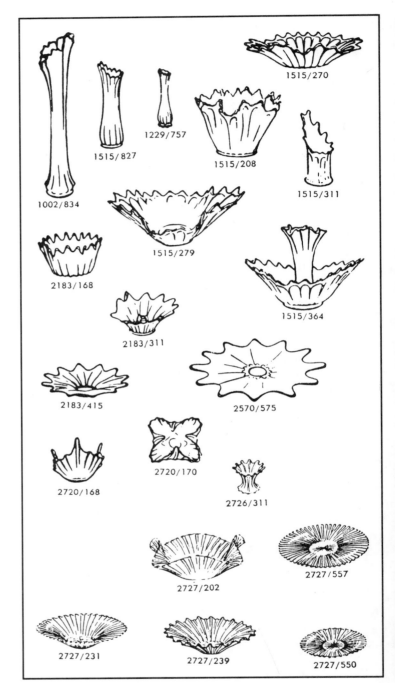

1002/834
1515/827
1229/757
1515/208
1515/270
1515/311
2183/168
1515/279
2183/311
1515/364
2183/415
2570/575
2720/168
2720/170
2726/311
2727/202
2727/557
2727/231
2727/239
2727/550

HENRY FORD MUSEUM COLLECTION

Flint Glass Crystal, Olive Green, Copper Blue and Silver Mist as indicated
1963 – 1970
Note: Argus #2770, Exeter #6109 stems and #2860 Panelled Diamond Point items also included in Henry Ford Collection

#2776/327 Candlestick 9" Crystal, Olive, Blue 35.00
#2777/327 Rebecca Candlestick 9¾" Olive, Blue, Silver Mist ....pair 150.00
#2777/388 Rebecca Ribbon Compote 12¾" Silver Mist, Olive, Blue 150.00
#2778/347 Four Petal Candy and Cover 8" Crystal, Olive, Blue.........................33.00
#2779/219 Pressed Block/Footed Bowl 10½" Crystal, Olive, Blue 47.50
#2780/388 Dolphin Ribbon Compote 8" Silver Mist, Green Silver Mist, Blue Silver Mist 35.00
#2786/803 Sandwich Draped Footed Vase 9" Crystal, Green, Blue 30.00
#2787/387 Ribbon Covered Compote 6½" Crystal, Blue, Green 35.00
#2788/389 Plume Compote Crystal, Green, Blue 18.00
#2790/818 Footed Tulip Vase 10" Crystal, Blue, Green 27.50
#2973/105 Strawberry Diamond Salt 3¼" Crystal, Blue, Green..........................9.00

2776/327   2777/327   2777/388

2778/347   2779/219   2780/388

2786/803   2787/387

HOLLY AND RUBY HO02

See page 38 for color photo
Ruby
1978 – 1982

#567 Torte Plate 14".............................32.50
#506 Nappy 5" 15.00
#211 Bowl 10".......................................27.50
#584 Divided Party Server with 2 Ladles...20.00
#549 Plate 7"...12.50

#315 Candlestick 4½"............................16.50
#312 Bird Candle Holders ....each 15.00
#762 Bud Vase 6" (Colony) 25.00
#682 Sugar (Colony)..............................22.50
#682 Cream (Colony)..............................22.50

⚒ HOMESPUN Pattern #4183 ⚒

Gold, Moss Green, Teal Blue
Late 1950's – Discontinued after 1965

#84 Juice/Old Fashioned 9 oz. 3⁵⁄₁₆" 10.00
#64 Water/Scotch & Soda 11½ oz. 4" 12.00
#58 Ice Tea/Highball 15 oz. 5¹¹⁄₁₆" 14.00

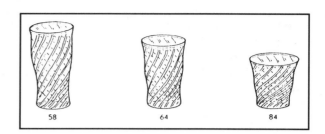

⚒ INCA Pattern #4163 ⚒

Modern Primitive Tumbler Line
Early 1960's – 1965

#58 Beverage 14 oz. 5½" 6.00
#41 Cooler 21 oz. 6¾" 8.00
#495 Dessert 12 oz...................................5.00
#84 Juice 6 oz. 3¾" 5.00
#549 Salad/Dessert Plate 7⅜" 8.00

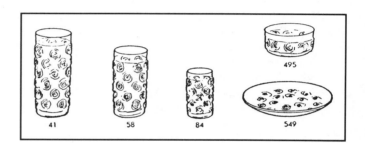

⚒ JENNY LIND Pattern ⚒

Handmade Milk Glass
White, Pink, Blue
1961 – 1965
Add 35% – 50% for colors

#842 Cologne Flask with Stopper 10¾" ...100.00
#385 Tray for Comb and Brush 11½"........55.00
#287 Glove Box with Cover 10⅜" 70.00
#276 Handkerchief Box with Cover 5½" 60.00
#293 Jewel Box with Cover 6"..................42.00
#281 Pin Box with Cover 5" 42.00
#544 Pin Tray 6" 25.00
#454 Pitcher 8¼" 95.00
#587 Pomade with Cover 2⅛"...................40.00
#580 Puff with Cover 3⅛".........................44.00
#70 Tumbler 4½" 35.00

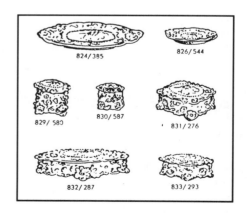

JEWELERY

Late Production

Rose Pendant 15.00

Cameo Pendant 15.00
Heart Pendant 15.00

KARNAK Pattern #4161

Modern Primitive Tumbler Line
Smoke, Pink, Marine, Amber
1961 – 1965

#58 Beverage/Water 14 oz. 5" 8.00
#41 Cooler 21 oz. 6¾" 7.00
#84 Juice 6 oz. 3¾" 5.00
#495 Dessert Bowl 12 oz. 8.00
#549 Salad/Dessert Plate 7⅜" 8.00

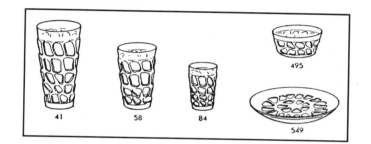

LEXINGTON Pattern #2449

Olive Green, Brown, Yellow
1974 – 1979

#199 Bowl, Footed 8"................................12.50
#224 Bowl, Footed, Flared 10" 12.00
#319 Candleholder 6".......................pair 20.00
#681 Cream, Footed 4" 8.00
#421 Fruit 5"...7.00
#622 Relish, 3 part, Round......................10.00
#679 Sugar, Footed 3½".............................7.00
#758 Vase 6" 11.00

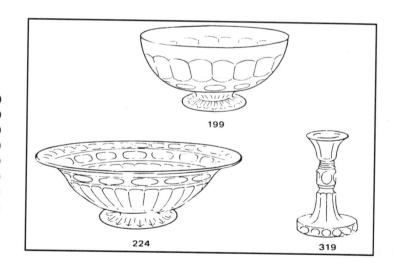

MAH JONGG SET

Very Rare

All enamels 27.50

MONROE Pattern #2694

Handmade Milk Glass
1950s – 1965

#234 Bowl, Banana 10¾"..........................50.00
#217 Bowl, Shallow Fruit 10½"................42.00
#250 Bowl, Fruit 10" 50.00
#630 Salver 11¼".....................................44.00

2678/ 250

MYRIAD Pattern #2592

See page 20 for color photo
Crystal
1941 – 1945

Ashtray, oblong 4" 10.00
Ashtray, Individual...................................5.00
Bowl 8½" 20.00
Bowl, Console...40.00
Bowl, Fruit 11" 25.00
Candlestick 4" ....pair 26.00

Candlestick, Double 30.00
Candy Box with Cover 5½".......................20.00
Cigarette Box with Cover, oblong 8" 22.00
Lily Pond 10½"...18.00
Salver 12" 34.00
Vase, Flared 9" 30.00

NEEDLEPOINT Pattern #4184

See page 48 for color photo
Gold, Moss Green, Teal Blue
Discontinued after 1965
Late 1950's

#84 Juice/Old Fashioned 8 oz. 3¹/₁₆" 10.00
#64 Water/Scotch & Soda 12¼ oz. 4½" 12.00
#58 Ice Tea/Highball 16½ oz. 5½" 14.00

58   64   84

OUR AMERICAN STATES PLATES

Crystal
1972 – 1976

#2850 Pennsylvania 15.00
#2851 Texas..15.00
#2852 Massachusetts.............................15.00
#2853 Florida...15.00
#2854 Hawaii 15.00
#2871 Michigan 10½" 15.00
West Virginia..15.00
#2838 Ohio 15.00
#2845 California 15.00
#2846 New York......................................15.00

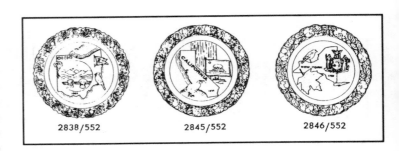

2838/552   2845/552   2846/552

⊷⊸ PANELLED DIAMOND POINT Pattern #2860 ⊷⊸

Lead Crystal
Unit in Centennial II Collection
1973

#7 Dessert/Champagne 7 oz. 4⅝" 10.00
#2 Goblet 10½ oz. 6½" 12.00
#63 Luncheon Goblet/Ice Tea 13 oz. 6⁵⁄₁₆" .12.00
#26 Wine 6½ oz. 5½" 10.00

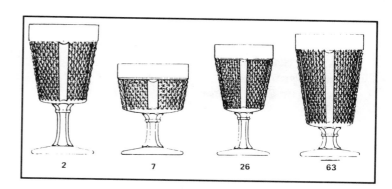

⊷⊸ RANDOLPH Pattern #2675 ⊷⊸

Handmade Milk Glass
1961 – 1965

#250 Bowl, Footed, Shallow 10" 27.00
#307 Buffet Plate, Footed 12½" 23.00
#319 Candleholder 6" ....pair 16.00
#312 Candleholder 1½" ....pair 13.00
#681 Cream, Footed 3⅝" 12.00
#409 Egg Cup 4½" 14.00
#153 Nappy, Square 6" 13.00
#512 Nappy 6" 12.00
#511 Nappy, Oblong 5" 10.00
#520 Nappy, Cupped 5⅜" 12.00
#513 Preserve with Cover, Footed 5⅝".......25.00
#652 Plate 9" 10.00
#654 Shaker with chrome top 3½" .....pair 15.00
#676 Sugar, Footed with Cover 5¾" 18.00

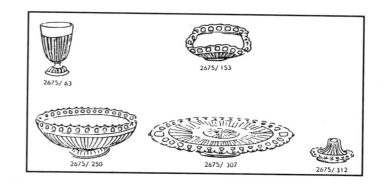

⊷⊸ ROULETTE Pattern #2739 ⊷⊸

Ebony with Crystal, Ruby with Crystal
1968

#208 Star Bowl 10" 15.00
#231 Quadrangle Bowl 11" 15.00
#248 Tricorn Bowl 12" 15.00
#266 Oval Centerpiece.............................18.00
#767 Petal Vase 7" 12.00
#785 Basket Vase 8" 18.00
#792 Trident Vase 8½" 18.00
#832 Flame Vase 15" 18.00
#316 Candlestick, Crystal only 9.00

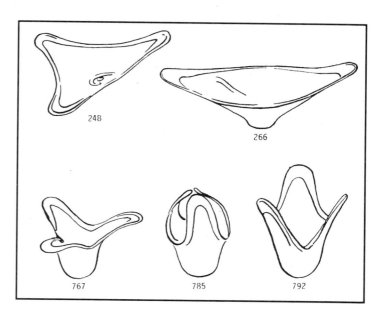

☞ SCULPTURE Pattern ☜

Mixed number line
Lead Crystal
Crystal or Grey Mist
1961 – 1970

#2570/795 Basket 5½"h, 8"w, 17"l 33.00
#2741/279 Bowl, Lineal 4¼"h, 5½"w,
    18"l 27.00
#2741/266 4 Bowl, oval 6½"h, 6⅝"w,
    14"l 25.00
#2743/179 Bowl, Petal 10¾"d 31.00
#2745/183 Bowl, Trindle 8½"d 27.00
#2742/311 Candleholder 3½"h.........pair 30.00
#2756/168 Cosmic 8½" 27.00
#2740/415 Float 2⅜"h, 7"w, 14¼"l...........32.00
#2745/208 Ruffle Bowl 5¾" x 5¾" 30.00
#2740/168 Spire Bowl 5½"h, 6"w, 8"l 23.00
#2744/174 Tricorn 5⅝"h, 13½"w 25.00
#2740/1126 Oblong 3¼"h, 4½"w, 13"l.......26.00
#2570/189 Shell 7¼"h, 9½"w, 14"l...........32.00
#2745/758 Florette Vase 8¼"h 19.00
#2741/755 Vase, Pinch 6"h, 3"w, 11½"l....29.00
#2743/767 Vase, Star 7¼"h.....................27.00
#2744/830 Vase, Swung 12½"h...............44.00

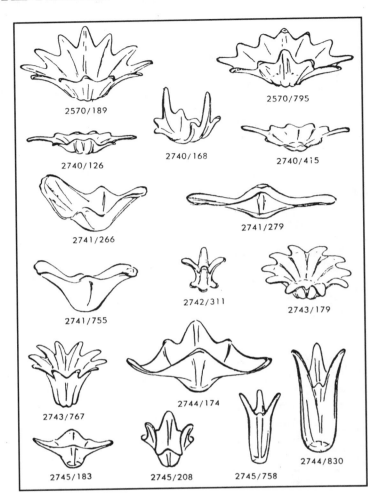

☞ SEASCAPE Pattern #2685 ☜

Blue, Green, Pink, Opalescent
1954 – 1958

Bowl 8"...28.00	Mint Tray 7½"......................................25.00
Bowl, Footed 8¾" 46.00	Preserve, Handled 6½" 22.00
Bowl, Square 8¾" 36.00	Relish, 2 part 9" 32.00
Bowl 11½" 42.00	Relish, 3 part 11¾" 44.00
Bowl, Pansy 4½" 22.00	Salad Bowl 10"....................................45.00
Buffet Plate 14" 55.00	Salver 12"...45.00
Candleholder 4½" ....single 20.00	Sugar 2⅞"...20.00
Cream 3⅜"..20.00	Sugar, Individual................................30.00
Cream, Individual..............................30.00	Tray for Sugar and Cream 20.00
Mayonnaise with Plate and Ladle.............58.00	Tray, oval 7½"......................................24.00

SEA SHELLS Pattern #2825 and #2844

Crystal, Copper Blue, Green
1971 – 1973

#2825/201 Small Shell 9½" 12.00
#2825/259 Medium Shell 13" 14.00
#2825/280 Large Shell 18" 20.00
#2825/172 Rolled Edge Bowl 7" 12.50
#2825/193 Rolled Edge Bowl 8½" 15.00
#2825/317 Flared Candlestick 3½" 15.00
#2844/172 Rolled Edge Bowl 7" 12.50
#2844/175 Shallow Bowl 7½" 12.50
#2844/208 Flared Edge Bowl 10" 15.00
#2844/231 Flared Edge Bowl 11" 16.50
#2844/257 Rolled Edge Bowl 12½" 20.00
#2844/275 Rolled Edge Bowl 15" 29.00
#2844/311 Flora Candlestick 15.00
#2844/575 Torte Plate 17" 20.00
#2844/751 Vase 4" 10.00
#2844/758 Vase 8" 12.50

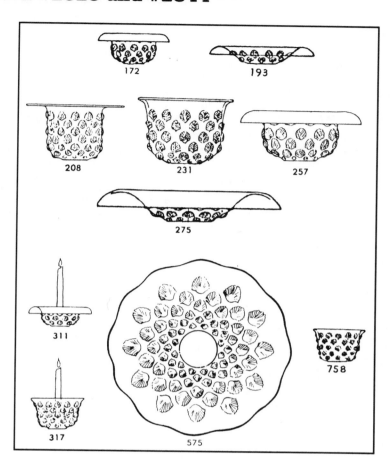

SERENDIPITY

Crystal
1972 – Late 1970's

2842/311 Individual Candleholder 8.00
2842/539 Paperweight 10.00
2842/337 Candleholder 9½" 12.00
2842/124 Ashtray 9½" 12.00
2856/539 Paperweight A 6" 9.00
2856/545 Paperweight B 6" 9.00
2856/546 Paperweight C 6" 9.00
2856/547 Paperweight D 6" 9.00
2857/124 Ashtray 10" 12.00
2857/117 Ashtray B 7" 8.00
2856/118 Ashtray C 7" 8.00
2858/152 Crimp 5" 8.00
2858/178 Crimp 8" 10.00
2858/207 Crimp 10" 12.00
2842/112 Ashtray/Candleholder 2" 5.00

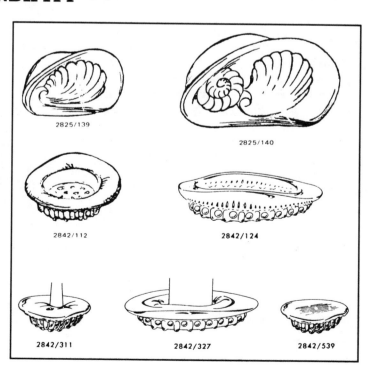

SERENDIPITY Cont.

2856/139 Small Shell Bookend 3¾" ..pair 13.50
2856/140 Large Shell Bookend 5¾"...pair 16.50
2856/141 Bookend E 5"..........................15.00
2866/313 Candleholder 2" 5.00
2866/315 Candleholder 4" 5.00
2866/319 Candleholder 6" 8.00
2868/545 Family Paperweight
   Mother 5½"...................................9.00
2868/546 Family Paperweight
   Father 5½"....................................9.00
2842/311 Individual Candleholder............5.00
2842/327 Candleholder 9½"....................15.00
2856/139 Bookend A 5".........................15.00
2856/140 Bookend B 5".........................15.00

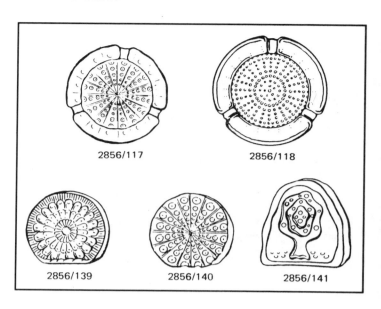

2856/117   2856/118

2856/139   2856/140   2856/141

SHANTUNG Pattern #2795

Part of Group International Gift Line
Fern Green/Tangerine, Mayan Blue/Fern
  Green
1967 – 1968

#250 Bowl, 12" Fern Green Bowl/Tangerine Base,
  Mayan Blue Bowl/Fern Green Base...........25.00
#284 Bowl 16" Fern Green Bowl/Tangerine
  Base, Mayan Blue Bowl/Fern Green Base ..30.00
#325 Candleholder 8" Fern Green,
  Mayan Blue, Tangerine..................pair 20.00
#330 Candleholder 12" Fern Green,
  Mayan Blue, Tangerine..................pair 25.00
#833 Candle/Vase 18" Fern Green/
  Tangerine, Mayan Blue/Tangerine
  ....pair 30.00
#835 Candle/Vase 22" Fern Green/
  Tangerine, Mayan Blue/Fern Green
  Base ....pair 45.00

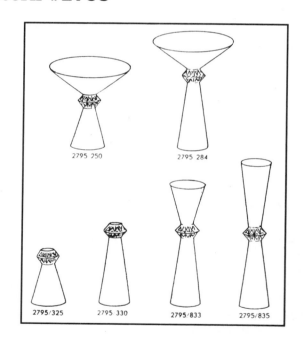

2795 250   2795 284

2795/325   2795 330   2795/833   2795/835

SHELL ACCESSORIES

#2803/380 Shell Coaster Crystal, Black
  Pearl, Lemon Twist 7.50
#2823/421 Shell Dessert 5⅞" Crystal
  Luster, Black Pearl Luster, Lemon Twist
  Luster 7.50

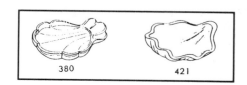

380   421

⋙ SIERRA Pattern #2816 ⋘

Crystal
1979 – 1982

#110 Ashtray 4½" 4.00
#111 Ashtray 5½" 5.00
#178 Accent Bowl 8" 8.00
#219 Footed Centerpiece 10" 12.00
#325 Candle/Pedestal 8" 12.00
#630 Footed Server 11½" 15.00
#645 Tri-Server 6½" 10.00
#757 Flora-Vase 6" 12.00
#768 Footed Urn 7" 15.00

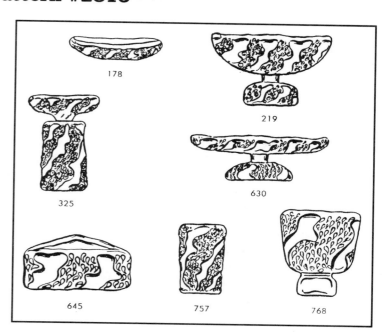

⋙ SILVER MIST ⋘

Glass from several lines treated in an acid, resulting in a frosted finish much like old camphor glass. This listing remains open-ended as the treatment could be and was used on various items in several different lines. The process left open possibilities for lunchtime projects and not all Silver Mist can be said to have been documented. Consider this as a representative, but incomplete listing.

#2419 Ashtray 10.00
#2520 Ashtray..10.00
#2457 Ashtray..18.00
#2534 Ashtray..15.00
#2494 Bitters Bottle 15.00
#2517 Bon Bon 18.00
#2536 Bowl, Handled 9" 20.00
#2484 Bowl, Handled 10" 28.00
#4024 Bowl, Footed 10" 25.00
#2535 Candlestick 5½" ....pair 20.00
#4024 Candlestick 6" ....pair 20.00
#2472 Candlestick, Duo ....pair 25.00
#2496 Candlestick, Duo ....pair 30.00
#2484 Candlestick 2 Light.....................39.00
#2484½ Candlesticks with drips 3½"..pair 40.00
#2496 Candlesticks, Trindle 36.50
#4099 Candy Jar with Cover 26.50
Cigarette Box with Cover 22.00

Claret 3½ oz. 6.00
#4115 Cocktail, Footed 4 oz. 6.00
#2518 Cocktail Shaker, Gold Top 25.00
#2518½ Cocktail Shaker, Gold Top..........25.00
#2525 Cocktail Shaker, Gold Top 25.00
#2525½ Cocktail Shaker, Gold Top 20.00
#2519 Cologne with Stopper....................30.00
#4024 Cordial 11.00
#2494 Cordial Bottle 25.00
#2429 Cordial Tray..................................20.00
#249½ Cream 28.00
#2494 Decanter.......................................25.00
#2518 Decanter.......................................32.00
#2502 Decanter with Stopper 35.00
#2492 Fish Canape 15.00
#4024 Goblet 11 oz. 15.00
#4014½ Goblet 10 oz. 8.00
#2518 Jug...42.50
#2517 Lemon Dish 8.00
#2440 Mayonnaise, 2 part 6½" 15.00
#2513 Mayonnaise with Ladle 22.00
#2538 Nappy 11".....................................16.00
#2538 Nappy 6"...6.00
#2538 Nappy 4½".......................................6.00
Old Fashioned, Sham Bottom 7 oz..............6.00
Oyster Cocktail 4 oz. 7.00

Pelican 55.00
Penguin..55.00
#2519 Puff with Cover 25.00
Plate 6" 4.00
Plate 7" 5.00
Plate 8" 7.00
Polar Bear 55.00
#2513 Preserve, Handled 5"...................15.00
#2440 Relish, 2 part Handled...................15.00
#2440 Relish, 3 part Handled...................15.00
#2419 Relish, 4 part................................12.00
#2419 Relish, 5 part................................15.00
#2513 Relish, 2 part................................12.00
#2513 Relish, 3 part................................14.00
#4024 Rhine Wine 3½ oz............................8.00
#4024 Saucer Champagne 6 oz. 8.00
#2440 Sauce Dish, oval 6½" 4.00
Seal..55.00
#2497 Seafood Cocktail...........................35.00
#4024 Sherbet 5½ oz.................................8.00
#2497 Sugar 28.00
#2517 Sweetmeat......................................8.00
#2440 Tray, oval 8½".................................20.00
#2518 Tumbler 10 oz. 8.00
#4024 Tumbler, Footed 5 oz. 8.00
#4024 Tumbler, Footed 8 oz. 9.00

#4024 Tumbler, Footed 12 oz. 11.00
#701 Tumbler, Sham Bottom 10 oz. 6.00
#701 Tumbler, Sham Bottom 12 oz. 6.00
#2404 Vase 6"..25.00
#2428 Vase 9"..26.00
#2428 Vase 13"...27.00
#2489 Vase 5½"...23.00
#2522 Vase 8"..28.00
#2523 Vase 6½"...24.00
#4103 Vase 4"..15.00
#4110 Vase 7½"...24.00
#4129 Vase/Bubble Ball 2½".....................16.00
#4116 Vase/Bubble Ball 4".......................16.00
#4116 Vase/Bubble Ball 5".......................20.00
#4116 Vase/Bubble Ball 6".......................26.00
#4116 Vase/Bubble Ball 7".......................30.00
#4116 Vase/Bubble Ball 8".......................34.00
#4116 Vase/Bubble Ball 9".......................40.00
#5088 Vase, Bud 8"..................................18.00
#5091 Vase, Bud 6½" 18.00
#887 Whiskey, Optic 1¾ oz.........................6.00
#2518 Whiskey 2 oz. 4.00
#2502 Whiskey 4.00
#2404 Whiskey, Footed 5.00
#2518 Wine 5 oz..6.00
#2503 Wine Jug 25.00

⇒ SMOKING ACCESSORY SELECTION ⇐

See page 21 for color photo of Mardi Gras Cigarette Box

Mardi Gras Cigarette Box 15.00
#2550½/107 3 Piece Ashtray Set in all Crystal,
  all Blue, or all Amber, also available in
  Blue and Crystal or Crystal, Blue and
  Amber. As Set......................................15.00
#2550/112 Small Ashtray 3⅛" from #107
  set 4.00
#2550/113 Medium Ashtray 4¼" from #107
  set 5.00
#2550/114 Large Ashtray 5½" from #107
  set 6.00
#2609/115 Oblong Ashtray 4½" Crystal......5.00
#2618/374 Covered Cigarette Box 5½"
  Crystal 16.00
#2618/115 Oblong Ashtray 4½" 5.00
#2622/113 Round Ashtray 4½" Crystal 6.00

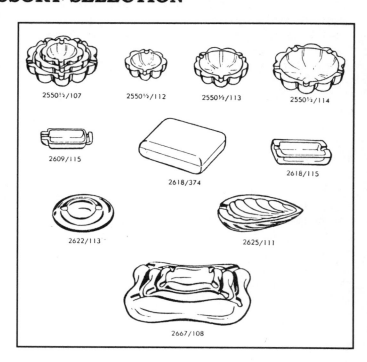

2550½/107   2550½/112   2550½/113   2550½/114

2609/115   2618/374   2618/115

2622/113   2625/111

2667/108

#2625/111 Round Ashtray 6½" Crystal 7.00

#2667/108 3 Piece Ashtray Set Crystal 30.00

#2667/111 Small Ashtray 5" from #108 set
Crystal 8.00

#2667/119 Medium Ashtray 7" from #108 set
Crystal 10.00

#2667/120 Large Ashtray 9" from #108 set
Crystal 12.00

#2667/120 Large Ashtray 9" from #108 set
Ebony..20.00

#2731/374 Covered Cigarette Box
5¾" x 4½" Crystal..................................20.00

#2731/114 Round Ashtray 7½" Crystal,
Amber, Blue, Green 12.00

#2731/115 Oblong Ashtray 4" Crystal........9.00

#2731/123 Ashtray 5" Crystal....................7.00

#2746/118 Footed Ashtray 6" Ruby Mist
and Green Textured..............................18.00

#2747/107 2 Piece Ashtray Set Crystal,
Amber, Green 14.00

#2747/111 Square Ashtray 4½" from #107
set Crystal, Amber, Green.......................7.00

#2747/119 Square Ashtray 6" from #107
set Crystal, Amber, Green.......................9.00

#2747/113 Morton Ashtray 3" Amber Mist,
Pink Mist..15.00

#2752/120 Round Ashtray 8" Crystal........8.00

#2752/374 Oblong Covered Cigarette Box
6¼" x 4¼" Crystal..................................20.00

#2753/108 3 Piece Ashtray Set Crystal,
Brown, Gold 20.00

#2753/111 Small Ashtray 5½" from #108
set Crystal, Brown, Gold 5.00

#2753/119 Medium Ashtray 7½" from #108
set Crystal, Brown, Gold.........................7.00

#2753/124 Large Ashtray 10½" from #108
set Crystal Brown, Gold...........................8.00

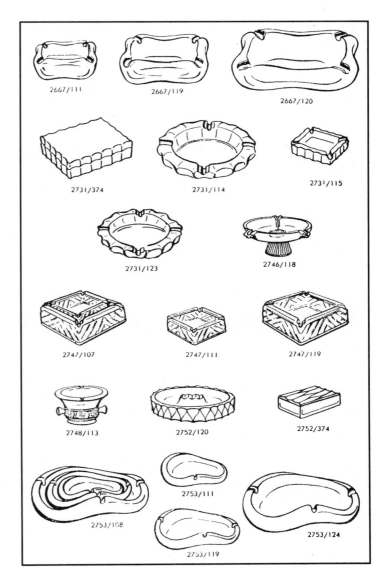

183

SONATA Pattern #2364

Crystal
1940 – 1973

Almond, Individual	6.00
#249 Bowl, Flared 12"	15.00
#421 Baked Apple 6"	8.00
#332 Candlesticks Duo	pair 26.00
Candy Box with Cover	20.00
Celery 11"	12.00
Cheese, Footed	9.00
Cheese and Cracker	33.00
Comport 6"	12.00
Comport 8"	25.00
Cracker Plate	14.00
#549 Crescent Salad 7¼"	11.00
Fruit 5"	7.00
#259 Fruit Bowl 13"	15.00
#197 Lily Pond 9"	15.00
#251 Lily Pond 12"	22.00
Mayonnaise with Plate and Ladle	27.50
Mayonnaise, 2 part, 2 ladles	15.00
Pickle Dish 8"	8.00
#620 Relish, 2 Part	16.00
#622 Relish, 3 Part	15.00
#195 Salad Bowl 9"	14.00
#221 Salad Bowl 10½"	17.00
#557 Sandwich Plate 11"	17.00
Sauce Dish, oval	10.00
#393 Rim Soup 8"	18.00
#655 Shaker, Chrome Top	pair 14.50
#567 Torte Plate 14"	19.00
#573 Torte Plate 16"	22.00
#723 Handled Serving Tray 11¼"	25.00

SPOOL Pattern #2550

Crystal, Azure, Gold Tint
1938 – 1944

Ashtray, Individual 3⅛"	4.50
Ashtray, Round 3¼"	5.00
Ashtray, Large 5½"	7.00
Bowl, Straight Sides 8"	16.50
Bowl, Flared 9½"	20.00
Bowl, oval 11"	30.00

Buffet Plate 14"	25.00
Candlestick 3"	pair 16.00
Centerpiece	15.00
Cigarette Box with Cover, oblong	30.00
Cigarette Box with Cover, round 3½"	32.00
Comport 6"	15.00

⊷⊷ SPOOL Pattern #2550 Cont. ⊷⊷

Decanter with Stopper, quart 33.00
Mayonnaise with Plate and Ladle.............27.00
Nappy 6½" 12.50
Plate 13"..20.00
Sweetmeat...8.00

Vase, Straight 5½" 14.00
Vase, Flared 5" 13.00
Vase, Flared 6" 19.00
Vase, Straight 6" 18.00
#2518 Whiskey 1½ oz. 6.00

⊷⊷ STANDISH Pattern #4132 ⊷⊷

Crystal blown lead glass tumblers
See page 63 for color photo
Early 1940's – 1985

#23 Double Old Fashioned 13 oz. 3⅝".........5.00
#64 Highball 14 oz. 4⅞" 4.00
#22 Old Fashioned 7½ oz............................4.00
#73 Scotch & Soda 9 oz. 4⅝".........5.00
#100 Whiskey 1½ oz. 2⅛" 4.00
#89 Whiskey Sour 5 oz. 3⅝" 4.00

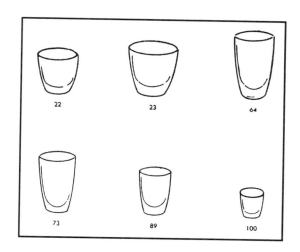

⊷⊷ STARLIGHT Pattern #ST07 ⊷⊷

Crystal giftware
Late 1980's

#179 Bowl 8"...12.00
#344 Candy Box, Covered 20.00
#686 Sugar and Cream with Tray............25.00

#255 Tray 12" x 6"....................................15.00
#560 Serving Tray 12" 15.00
#810 Vase 12.00

⊷⊷ STOWE Pattern ⊷⊷

Crystal barware
1980 – 1985

#23 Double Old Fashioned 11 oz. 4"..........5.00

#64 Highball 13 oz. 5⅛"..............................5.00

⊰⊸ STRATTON Pattern #2885 ⊸⊱

Lead Crystal
See page 63 for color photo
Late 1970's – 1985

#433 Bowl 6"..............................15.00
#380 Coaster.................................3.59
#22 Dessert/Champagne 7 oz. 5¼"...........8.00
#2 Goblet 10 oz. 6½"....................11.00
#63 Luncheon Goblet/Ice Tea 12 oz. 6⅝"..16.50

#23 Double Old Fashioned 10 oz. 3⅞"........7.00
#64 Highball 12 oz. 5½"....................8.00
#26 Wine 5 oz. 5½"........................11.00
#433 Ice Tub 4½" x 6"....................20.00
#550 Plate 8"...............................6.00

⊰⊸ TABLE CHARMS ⊸⊱

Late 1950's – 1965

#312 Peg Vase 8" Crystal or Pink.............16.00
#334 Trindle Candle Arm 2¼" x 7½"
  Crystal 23.50
#460 Flora-Candle/Snack Bowl 5"
  Crystal or Pink 5.00
#364 Table Charms Set #1 10" x 11"........90.00
  #334 Trindle Candle Arm Crystal
  #312 Peg Vase Crystal or Pink
  #460 3 Flora-Candle/Snack Bowls Crystal
   or Pink
#364 Table Charms Set #2 10" x 9" 75.00
  #334 Trindle Candle Arm Crystal
  #312 3 Peg Vases Crystal or Pink
  #460 Flora-Candle/Snack Bowl Crystal
   or Pink
#364 Table Charms Set #3 10" x 11" 70.00
  #334 Trindle Candle Arm Crystal
  #460 3 Flora-Candle/Snack Bowls
  Crystal or Pink
#364 Table Charms Set #4 10" x 9" 70.00
  #334 Trindle Candle Arm crystal
  #312 3 Peg Vases Crystal or Pink

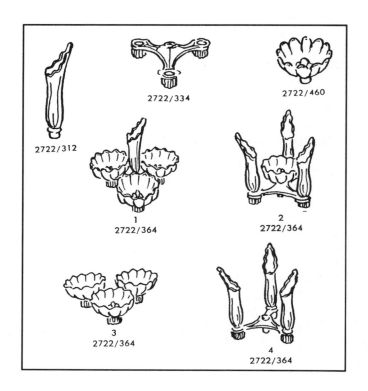

⊰⊸ TIARA Pattern #6044 ⊸⊱

Crystal blown glass
1951 – Late 1950's
Note: Do not confuse with Tiara Cutting
  #903

Bowl, Dessert/Finger Bowl........................6.00
Cocktail/Juice 3¼"....................................3.50
Ice Tea/Highball 5⅞" 3.50
Sherbet/Old Fashioned 3¼" 3.50
Water/Scotch & Soda 4⅝" 3.50

TRANSITION Pattern #2936

Lead crystal barware
See pages 55 and 63 for color photos
Late 1970's – 1985

#123 Ashtray 5.00
#179 Bowl, Serving 8" 11.50
#554 Buffet Plate 11" 8.00
#319 Candleholder..................................12.00
#665 Chip and Dip (11" Buffet Plate with
   5" Salad Plate) 15.00

#686 Cream and Sugar......................set 10.00
#23 Double Old Fashioned
   12 oz. 4⅛"...5.00
#63 Highball 12 oz. 5⅝".........................5.00
#894 Plate, Salad/Dessert 5" 5.00
#372 Wine/Juice 7 oz. 5" 4.00

VINTAGE Pattern #2713

Handmade Milk Glass
1961 – 1965

#179 Berry Bowl 8" 13.00
#499 Berry Dessert 4½".............................6.00
#183 Bowl, Crimped 8".............................16.00
#300 Butter with Cover, oblong 8¼" 15.00
#311 Candleholder/Leaf 1⁹⁄₁₆" ....pair 15.00
#315 Candleholder 4" 14.00
#347 Candy Jar with Cover 6³⁄₁₆"...............19.00
#688 Cream, Individual 3⅞" 7.00
#2 Goblet 11 oz. 6¼" 8.00
#63 Ice Tea, Footed 13 oz. 6¼"..................8.00
#500 Nappy, Crimped 4" 7.00
#502 Nappy, Square 4" 7.00
#550 Plate 8" 6.00
#348 Planter 11.00
#653 Shaker 3½".............................pair 11.00
#11 Sherbet 7½ oz. 4¾" 6.00
#687 Sugar, Individual 3⅜" 9.00
#697 Tray for Sugar and Cream 7⅝"..........7.00
#720 Leaf Tray 8⅜"..................................12.50

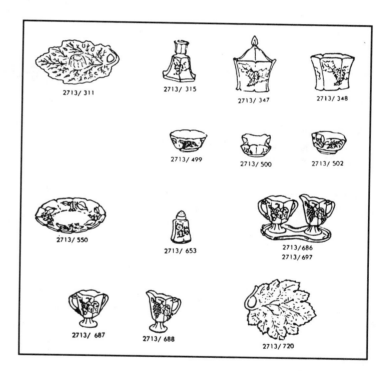

⊶⊸ **WINBURN Pattern #1704** ⊸⊶

Handmade Milk Glass
1961 – 1965

#297 Butter & Cover, 8¼".........................40.00
#680 Cream 4½"......................................11.00
#450 Jelly, oblong 4"...............................12.50
#451 Jelly, Square 3⅛"............................12.50
#452 Jelly, 3 Cornered 3⅛"......................12.50
#457 Jug/Ice Lip ½ gallon 8"...................42.00
#501 Nappy, Handled, 3 Cornered.............8.00
#502 Nappy, Handled, square 8.00
#528 Oil with Stopper 6 oz. 6¼"..............30.00
#605 Punch Bowl 16" 2¾ gallon 175.00
#606 Punch Bowl, Foot 16" x 7¼"............30.00
#15 Punch Cup 5½ oz. 6.00

1704/457

#676 Sugar with Cover 6⅞" 10.00
#76 Water Tumbler 7 oz. 4⅜"....................11.00

⊶⊸ **YORK BARWARE Y001** ⊸⊶

Crystal
See page 63 for color photo
Do not confuse with York Pattern #1118
1970's – 1985

#23 Double Old Fashioned ....8.00   #64 Highball 6.00

188

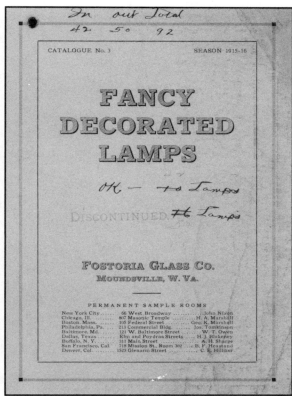

In out Total
42 50 92

CATALOGUE No. 3   SEASON 1915-16

FANCY DECORATED LAMPS

OK — to Lamps

DISCONTINUED. *# Lamps*

FOSTORIA GLASS CO.
MOUNDSVILLE, W. VA.

PERMANENT SAMPLE ROOMS

New York City .... 66 West Broadway .... John Nixon
Chicago, Ill. .... 807 Masonic Temple ...... H. A. Marshall
Boston, Mass. .... 105 Federal Street ...... Geo. K. Marshall
Philadelphia, Pa. ..... 213 Commercial Bldg. ... Jos. Tomkinson
Baltimore, Md. .... 121 W. Baltimore Street ..... W. T. Owen
Dallas, Texas .... Elm and Poydras Streets ... H. J. Blakeney
Buffalo, N. Y. .... 311 Main Street .... A. H. Sharpe
San Francisco, Cal. ... 718 Mission St., Room 302 ... B. F. Heastand
Denver, Col. .... 1523 Glenarm Street .... C. E. Hilliker

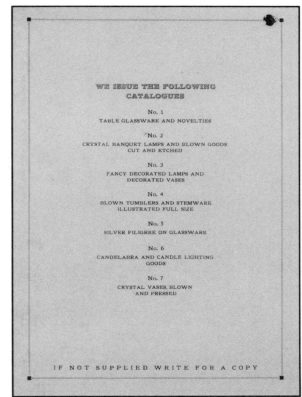

WE ISSUE THE FOLLOWING
CATALOGUES

No. 1
TABLE GLASSWARE AND NOVELTIES

No. 2
CRYSTAL BANQUET LAMPS AND BLOWN GOODS
CUT AND ETCHED

No. 3
FANCY DECORATED LAMPS AND
DECORATED VASES

No. 4
BLOWN TUMBLERS AND STEMWARE
ILLUSTRATED FULL SIZE

No. 5
SILVER FILIGREE ON GLASSWARE

No. 6
CANDELABRA AND CANDLE LIGHTING
GOODS

No. 7
CRYSTAL VASES, BLOWN
AND PRESSED

IF NOT SUPPLIED WRITE FOR A COPY

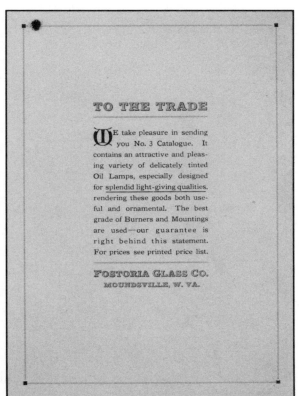

TO THE TRADE

WE take pleasure in sending you No. 3 Catalogue. It contains an attractive and pleasing variety of delicately tinted Oil Lamps, especially designed for splendid light-giving qualities, rendering these goods both useful and ornamental. The best grade of Burners and Mountings are used—our guarantee is right behind this statement. For prices see printed price list.

FOSTORIA GLASS CO.
MOUNDSVILLE, W. VA.

FURNISHED IN THREE DECORATIONS
Two Decorations Shown

RIO
Height 18 inches, Globe 7 inches
Dec. A, Rose, Ruby and Yellow Tints

RIO
Height 18 inches, Shade 7 inches
Dec. B, Poppy, Green and Yellow Tints

RIO
Dec. C, Wild Rose, Black and Green Tints

FURNISHED IN THREE DECORATIONS
Two Decorations Shown

FOX
Height 16 inches, Globe 7½ inches
Dec. A, Rose, Ruby and Yellow Tints

FOX
Height 16 inches, Globe 7½ inches
Dec. B, Wild Lily, Green and Yellow Tints

FOX
Dec. C, Poppy, Russian Green and Yellow
Tints

FURNISHED IN THREE DECORATIONS
Two Decorations Shown

ROSE
Height 18 inches, Globe 7½ inches
Dec. B, Rose, Green and Yellow Tints

ROSE
Height 18 inches, Shade 7 inches
Dec. C, Rose, Brown and Yellow Tints

ROSE
Dec. A, Rose, Ruby and Yellow Tints

FURNISHED IN THREE DECORATIONS
Two Decorations Shown

IOWA
Height 18½ inches, Globe 8 inches
Dec. A, Christmas Flower, Ruby, Yellow
and Blue Tints

IOWA
Height 18½ inches, Globe 8 inches
Dec. B, Poppy, Black, Green and Yellow
Tints

IOWA
Dec. C, Rose, Dark Blue, Green and
Yellow Tints

190

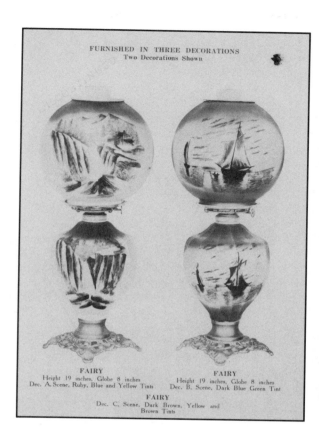

FURNISHED IN THREE DECORATIONS
Two Decorations Shown

FAIRY
Height 19 inches, Globe 8 inches
Dec. A, Scene, Ruby, Blue and Yellow Tints

FAIRY
Height 19 inches, Globe 8 inches
Dec. B, Scene, Dark Blue Green Tint

FAIRY
Dec. C, Scene, Dark Brown, Yellow and
Brown Tints

FURNISHED IN THREE DECORATIONS
Two Decorations Shown

DIXIE
Height 19 inches, Shade 10 inches
Dec. A, Rose, Ruby, Ivory and Carmine
Tints

DIXIE
Height 20½ inches, Globe 9 inches
Dec. B, Rose, Green and Yellow Tints

DIXIE
Dec. C, Hollyhock, Black, Green and
Orange Tints

FURNISHED IN THREE DECORATIONS
Two Decorations Shown

ANTLER
Height 20 inches, Shade 10 inches
Dec. A, Scene, Ruby, Blue and Yellow
Tints

ANTLER
Height 21½ inches, Globe 9 inches
Dec. C, Scene, Yellow, Brown and Ivory
Tints

ANTLER
Dec. B, Scene, Olive Green, Blue and
Yellow Tints

FURNISHED IN THREE DECORATIONS
Two Decorations Shown

BLAIR
Height 21 inches, Globe 9 inches
Dec. A, Peony, Ruby and Yellow Tints

BLAIR
Height 21 inches, Globe 9 inches
Dec. B, Chrysanthemum, Green and Yellow
Tints

BLAIR
Dec. C, Rose, Black, Green and Yellow
Tints

FURNISHED IN TWO DECORATIONS

HURON
Height 20½ inches, Shade 10 inches
Dec. A, Wild Rose, Brown and Yellow
Tints

HURON
Height 22 inches, Globe 9 inches
Dec. B, Roses, Green and Yellow Tints

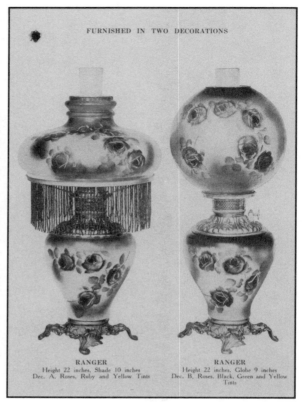

FURNISHED IN TWO DECORATIONS

RANGER
Height 22 inches, Shade 10 inches
Dec. A, Roses, Ruby and Yellow Tints

RANGER
Height 22 inches, Globe 9 inches
Dec. B, Roses, Black, Green and Yellow
Tints

FURNISHED IN TWO DECORATIONS

SUNBEAM
Height 26 inches, Globe 9 inches
Dec. A, Carnation, Mahogany and Yellow
Tints

SUNBEAM
Height 26 inches, Shade 10 inches
Dec. B, Roses, Black, Green and Yellow
Tints

FURNISHED IN TWO DECORATIONS

BEACON
Height 23 inches, Globe 10 inches
Dec. A, Wild Rose, Ruby and Yellow
Tints

BEACON
Height 23 inches, Globe 10 inches
Dec. B, Dahlia, Green and Yellow Tints

FURNISHED IN THREE DECORATIONS
Two Decorations Shown

ELWOOD
Height 25 inches, Shade 10 inches
Dec. A, Rose, Ruby, Yellow and Carmine
Tints

ELWOOD
Height 25 inches, Globe 10 inches
Dec. C, Hollyhock, Black, Green, Yellow
and Orange Tints

ELWOOD
Dec. B, Poppy and Daisy, Green, Carmine
and Yellow Tints

FURNISHED IN THREE DECORATIONS
Two Decorations Shown

BRISTOL
Height 25½ inches, Globe 10 inches
Dec. A, Peony, Ruby and Ivory Tints

BRISTOL
Height 25½ inches, Globe 10 inches
Dec. B, Roses, Black, Green and Yellow
Tints

BRISTOL
Dec. C, Stencil Rose, Brown, Green and
Yellow Tints

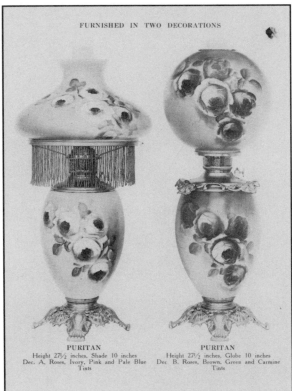

FURNISHED IN TWO DECORATIONS

PURITAN
Height 27½ inches, Shade 10 inches
Dec. A, Roses, Ivory, Pink and Pale Blue
Tints

PURITAN
Height 27½ inches, Globe 10 inches
Dec. B, Roses, Brown, Green and Carmine
Tints

FURNISHED IN THREE DECORATIONS
Two Decorations Shown

LONOKE
Height 25 inches, Globe 10 inches
Dec. A, Anemone, Pink, Blue and Ivory
Tints

LONOKE
Height 25 inches, Globe 10 inches
Dec. B, Orchid, Apple Green, Ivory and
Carmine Tints

LONOKE
Dec. C, Roses, Black, Green, Yellow and
Pink Tints

193

FURNISHED IN TWO DECORATIONS

WAVERLY
Height 25 inches, Shade 10 inches
Dec. A, Roses, Apple Green, Carmine and
Blue Tints

WAVERLY
Height 25 inches, Globe 10 inches
Dec. B, Roses, Brown Green, Yellow and
Blue Tints

FURNISHED IN TWO DECORATIONS

LINCOLN
Height 28½ inches, Globe 11 inches
Dec. A, Peony, Ruby, Pink, Yellow and
Malachite Green Tints

LINCOLN
Height 28½ inches, Shade 12 inches
Dec. B, Roses, Dark Ivory and Variegated
Tints

FURNISHED IN TWO DECORATIONS

STURGEON
Height 25 inches, Globe 11 inches
Dec. A, Rose, Pink, Yellow, Ivory and
Blue Tints

STURGEON
Height 25 inches, Globe 11 inches
Dec. B, Poppy, Dark Brown, Brown Green,
Dark Ivory and Apple Green Tints

FURNISHED IN TWO DECORATIONS

ALETHEA
Height 28 inches, Globe 11 inches
Dec. A, Anemone, Ruby Tint

ALETHEA
Height 28 inches, Globe 11 inches
Dec. B, Rose and Apple Blossoms, Apple
Green, Ivory, Blue and Pink Tints

FURNISHED IN TWO DECORATIONS

GEORGIAN
Height 26½ inches, Globe 11 inches
Dec. A, Hydrangea, Light Ivory, Pink, Blue
and Yellow Tints

GEORGIAN
Height 26½ inches, Shade 12 inches
Dec. B, Yellow and Pink Rose, Black, Dark
Green and Pink Tints

FURNISHED IN TWO DECORATIONS

LAFAYETTE
Height 29 inches, Globe 11 inches
Dec. A, Orchid, Brown Monotone

LAFAYETTE
Height 29 inches, Globe 11 inches
Dec. B, Poppy, Green Monotone

FURNISHED IN TWO DECORATIONS

DULUTH
Height 26½ inches, Globe 12 inches
Dec. A, Carnation, Variegated Tints

DULUTH
Height 26½ inches, Globe 11 inches
Dec. B, Poppy, Black, Dark Green and
Pink Tints

FURNISHED IN TWO DECORATIONS

PACIFIC
Height 31½ inches, Globe 12 inches
Dec. A, Rose, Ruby Tint

PACIFIC
Height 31½ inches, Globe 12 inches
Dec. B, Hollyhock, Olive Green, Yellow
and Orange Tints

MAGNOLIA
Height 30½ inches, Globe 12 inches
Dec. A, Peony, Brown, Ruby, Yellow and
Pale Blue Tints

MAGNOLIA
Height 30½ inches, Globe 12 inches
Dec. B, Chrysanthemum, Dark Ivory and
Variegated Tints

PALISADE
Height 33 inches, Globe 12 inches
Dec. A, Rose and Daisy, Dark Ivory, Green
Carmine and Blue Tints

PALISADE
Height 33 inches, Globe 12 inches
Dec. B, Wild Rose, Black, Dark Green,
Yellow and Pink Tints

See price list page 7

Dec. A

Dec. B

Dec. C

No. 339 LAMPS

See price list page 7

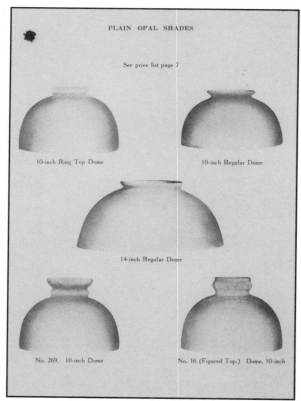

10-inch Ring Top Dome

10-inch Regular Dome

14-inch Regular Dome

No. 269. 10-inch Dome

No. 16 (Figured Top.) Dome, 10-inch

By Ye Candlelight, Fostoria Glass Co. Catalogue #6

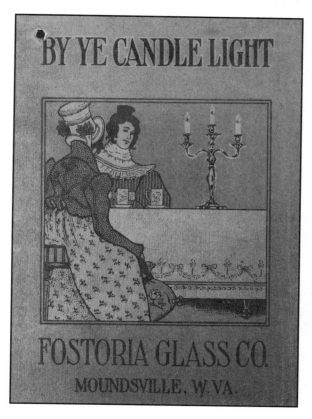

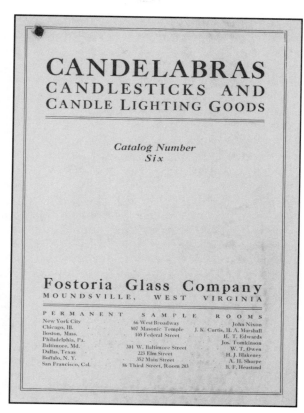

CANDELABRAS
CANDLESTICKS AND
CANDLE LIGHTING GOODS

Catalog Number
Six

Fostoria Glass Company
MOUNDSVILLE, WEST VIRGINIA

PERMANENT SAMPLE ROOMS

New York City ..... 66 West Broadway ..... John Nixon
Chicago, Ill. ..... 807 Masonic Temple ..... J. K. Curtis, H. A. Marshall
Boston, Mass. ..... 165 Federal Street ..... H. T. Edwards
Philadelphia, Pa. ..... Jos. Tomkinson
Baltimore, Md. ..... 304 W. Baltimore Street ..... W. T. Owen
Dallas, Texas ..... 223 Elm Street ..... H. J. Blakeney
Buffalo, N. Y. ..... 352 Main Street ..... A. H. Sharpe
San Francisco, Cal. ..... 86 Third Street, Room 203 ..... B. F. Heastand

WE take pleasure in handing you our Catalog No. 6 of Candle-lighting goods. For neatness in design and brilliancy of glass these goods are unsurpassed. Our aim is to please you, no matter how fastidious the taste, and we cordially invite your order, which will have our careful and prompt attention.

Goods priced by the single piece; or single article complete in this Catalog only.

Respectfully,

Fostoria Glass Co.

November 1st, 1909

MADE OF BRILLIANT CRYSTAL GLASS

FOSTORIA GLASS COMPANY
MOUNDSVILLE, W. VA.

No. 25. 5-Light Candelabra
With Spearhead Prisms
Height 24 inches, Spread 18 inches
Diameter of Base 8½ inches
Price as illustrated $13.50   Price Standard Etched $16.00

FOSTORIA GLASS COMPANY
MOUNDSVILLE, W. VA.

No. 25½ 5-Light Candelabra Etched
With Spearhead Prisms and Eight Colonial Prisms
Height 27 inches. Spread 18 inches
Diameter of Base 8½ inches
Price as illustrated $18.00   Price without Etching $15.50

FOSTORIA GLASS COMPANY
MOUNDSVILLE, W. VA.

No. 17 5-Light Candelabra
With U Drop Prisms
Height 23 inches. Spread 15 inches
Diameter of Base 8 inches
Price as illustrated $10.25

FOSTORIA GLASS COMPANY
MOUNDSVILLE, W. VA.

No. 18 4-Light Candelabra
With U Drop Prisms
Height 21 inches. Spread 12 inches
Diameter of Base 8 inches
Price as illustrated $7.60

FOSTORIA GLASS COMPANY
MOUNDSVILLE, W. VA.

No. 24 4-Light Candelabra
With Spearhead Prisms
Height 21 inches. Spread 14 inches
Diameter of Base 8½ inches
Price as illustrated $7.75

No. 23 3-Light Candelabra
With Spearhead Prisms
Height 22 inches. Spread 15 inches
Diameter of Base 6½ inches
Price as illustrated $6.60

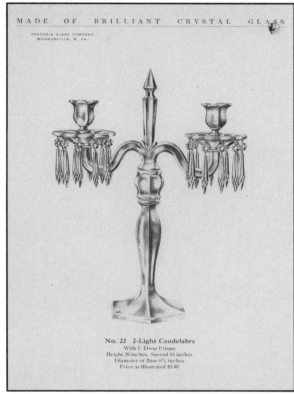

No. 22 2-Light Candelabra
With U Drop Prisms
Height 20 inches. Spread 15 inches
Diameter of Base 6½ inches
Price as illustrated $5.00

No. 21 Lustre Candlestick
With Spearhead Prisms
Height 12½ in. Diameter of Base 5½ in.
Price as illustrated $2.00

No. 4 Lustre Candlestick
With U Drop Prisms
Height 10 inches. Diameter of Base 5 inches
Price as illustrated $1.00

No. 35 5-Light Candelabra
Height 26 inches. Spread 18 inches. Diameter of Base 8 inches
With Fostoria Candle Lamps complete with Candles, Shades and U Drop Prisms
This Candelabra is complete, ready to light
Price as illustrated $10.50

No. 34   4-Light Candelabra
Height 25 inches. Spread 14 inches. Base 6½ inches
With Fostoria Candle Lamps complete with Candles, Shades and U Drop Prisms
This Candelabra is complete, ready to light
Price as illustrated $7.75

No. 33   3-Light Candelabra
Height 25 inches. Spread 15 inches. Base 6½ inches
With Fostoria Candle Lamps complete with Candles, Shades and U Drop Prisms
This Candelabra is complete, ready to light
Price as illustrated $7.00

No. 32   2-Light Candelabra
Height 20 inches. Spread 15 inches. Base 6½ inches
With Fostoria Candle Lamps complete with Candles, Shades and U Drop Prisms
This Candelabra is complete, ready to light
Price as illustrated $5.25

No. 3   7-Light Banquet Candelabra
With U Drop Prisms
Height 30 inches. Spread 20 inches
Diameter of Base 8 inches
Price as illustrated $20.00. One Vase extra included

FOSTORIA GLASS COMPANY
MOUNDSVILLE, W. VA.

No. 7   5 Light Candelabra
With U Drop Prisms
Height 23 inches. Spread 15 inches
Diameter of Base 7 inches
Price as illustrated $10.25. One Vase extra included

FOSTORIA GLASS COMPANY
MOUNDSVILLE, W. VA.

No. 5A   2-Light Candelabra
With U Drop Prisms
Height 16 inches. Spread 14 inches
Diameter of Base 6 inches
Price as illustrated $5.60

FOSTORIA GLASS COMPANY
MOUNDSVILLE, W. VA.

No. 15   2-Light Candelabra
With U Drop Prisms
Height 13 inches. Spread 14 inches
Diameter of Base 7 inches
Price as illustrated $4.25

FOSTORIA GLASS COMPANY
MOUNDSVILLE, W. VA.

No. 1   4-Light Candelabra
With U Drop Prisms
Height 21 inches. Spread 12 inches
Diameter of Base 6 inches
Price as illustrated $6.75. One Vase extra included

FOSTORIA GLASS COMPANY
MOUNDSVILLE, W. VA.

No. 13 5-Light Candelabra
With U Drop Prisms
Height 18 inches. Spread 15 inches
Diameter of Base 7 inches
Price as illustrated $9.35, One Vase extra included

FOSTORIA GLASS COMPANY
MOUNDSVILLE, W. VA.

Fostoria Candle Lamps

No. 1639 Candle Lamp Complete
Height 13½ inches
With Spearhead Prisms, Shade and Candle all
ready to light
Price as illustrated $2.00 each
By the pair $3.75

No. 1490 Candle Lamp Complete
Height 13½ inches
With Shade and Candle all ready to light
Price as illustrated $1.50 each
By the pair $2.75

Extra Candle used exclusively with Fostoria Candle Lamps, 5 cents each

FOSTORIA GLASS COMPANY
MOUNDSVILLE, W. VA.

No. 1513 No Handle
15 cents each

No. 1513 Handled
25 cents each

No. 1612 5-inch Christmas Candle
10 cents each

No. 26 Candle Lamp
With Shade and Candle
40 cents each

No. 1666 Handled
25 cents each

FOSTORIA GLASS COMPANY
MOUNDSVILLE, W. VA.

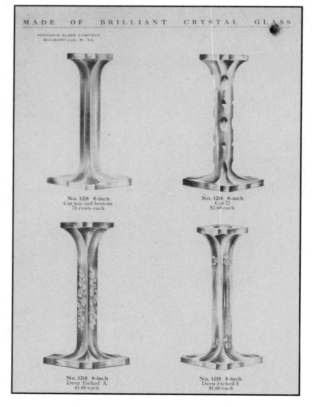

No. 1218 8-inch
Cut top and bottom
75 cents each

No. 1218 8-inch
Cut 72
$2.60 each

No. 1218 8-inch
Deep Etched A
$1.00 each

No. 1218 8-inch
Deep Etched E
$1.00 each

202

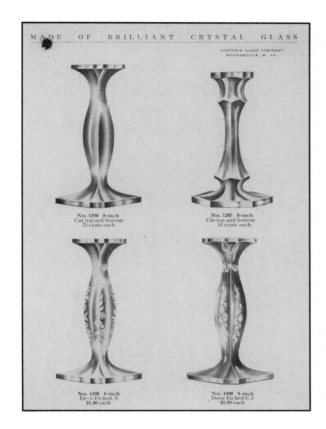

FOSTORIA GLASS COMPANY
MOUNDSVILLE, W. VA.

No. 1490 8-inch
Cut top and bottom
75 cents each

No. 1205 8-inch
Cut top and bottom
75 cents each

No. 1490 8-inch
De-o Etched A
$1.00 each

No. 1490 8-inch
Deep Etched C-2
$1.00 each

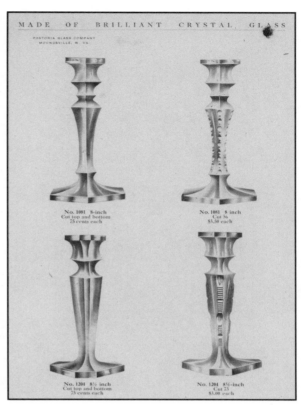

FOSTORIA GLASS COMPANY
MOUNDSVILLE, W. VA.

No. 1081 8-inch
Cut top and bottom
75 cents each

No. 1081 8 inch
Cut 56
$3.50 each

No. 1204 8½ inch
Cut top and bottom
75 cents each

No. 1204 8½-inch
Cut 73
$5.00 each

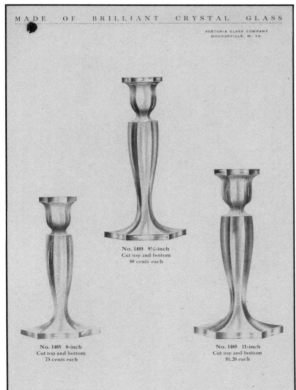

FOSTORIA GLASS COMPANY
MOUNDSVILLE, W. VA.

No. 1485 9½-inch
Cut top and bottom
80 cents each

No. 1485 8-inch
Cut top and bottom
75 cents each

No. 1485 11-inch
Cut top and bottom
$1.20 each

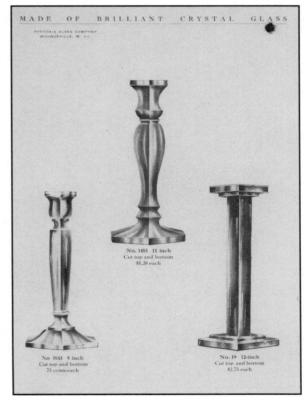

FOSTORIA GLASS COMPANY
MOUNDSVILLE, W. VA.

No. 1453 11 inch
Cut top and bottom
$1.20 each

No. 1643 9 inch
Cut top and bottom
75 cents each

No. 19 12-inch
Cut top and bottom
$2.75 each

203

FOSTORIA GLASS COMPANY
MOUNDSVILLE, W. VA.

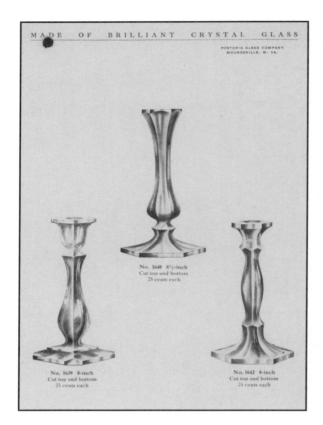

No. 1640 8½-inch
Cut top and bottom
75 cents each

No. 1639 8-inch
Cut top and bottom
75 cents each

No. 1642 8-inch
Cut top and bottom
75 cents each

FOSTORIA GLASS COMPANY
MOUNDSVILLE, W. VA.

No. 1064 8-inch
75 cents each

No. 161 7 inch
15 cents each

No. 112 9 inch
55 cents each

No. 1103 9½-inch
25 cents each

FOSTORIA GLASS COMPANY
MOUNDSVILLE, W. VA.

No. 1103 Lustre
Height 14½ inches
$1.75 each

No. 1103 Lustre
Height 18½ inches
$2.25 each

No. 1103 Lustre
Height 22½ inches
$3.50 each

FOSTORIA GLASS COMPANY
MOUNDSVILLE, W. VA.

Matchings on Articles Illustrated in this Catalog

U Drop
Prism

Candle Lamp Chimney

Spearhead
Prism

Candle Lamp Pot

Bobache

Candleholder

Candle Lamp Base
with Peg

No. 26 Candle Lamp
without Shade

Candle Lamp Base
without Peg

The Gray Printing Co., Fostoria, Ohio

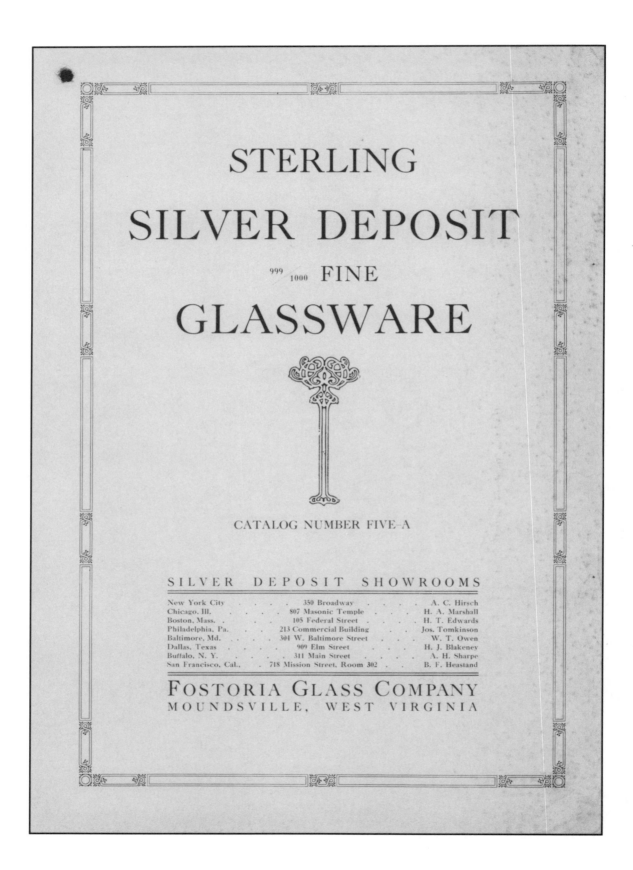

STERLING
SILVER DEPOSIT
$\frac{999}{1000}$ FINE
GLASSWARE

CATALOG NUMBER FIVE-A

SILVER DEPOSIT SHOWROOMS

New York City	350 Broadway		A. C. Hirsch
Chicago, Ill.	807 Masonic Temple		H. A. Marshall
Boston, Mass.	105 Federal Street		H. T. Edwards
Philadelphia, Pa.	213 Commercial Building		Jos. Tomkinson
Baltimore, Md.	304 W. Baltimore Street		W. T. Owen
Dallas, Texas	909 Elm Street		H. J. Blakeney
Buffalo, N. Y.	311 Main Street		A. H. Sharpe
San Francisco, Cal.,	718 Mission Street, Room 302		B. F. Heastand

FOSTORIA GLASS COMPANY
MOUNDSVILLE, WEST VIRGINIA

¶ If interested in Candle Lighting Goods, viz:—Candelabras, Candlesticks, etc., send for Catalog Number SIX.

¶ Also Catalog Number TWO showing Thin Blown Glassware in Deep Plate Etchings, Light Cuttings, etc.

Silver Deposit $\frac{999}{1000}$ Fine Glassware

WE are headquarters for glassware, and the styles shown in this catalog represent our most appropriate and effective blanks for Silver designs. Our decorations are strictly original patterns, *white inside*, the result of careful workmanship and inspection. We guarantee to maintain the excellence that has distinguished Fostoria Product for years. Every piece bears our trade mark label ⊕ a guarantee of highest grade of Sterling Silver used. Illustrations on the following pages convey an adequate idea of the splendid variety offered at most attractive prices.

All prices subject to Jeweler's Circular Key, with an additional discount of 5% for cash 30 days: 60 days net. 5% cash discount applies to goods illustrated in THIS CATALOG ONLY.

All articles priced each, and not per dozen.

Goods sold F. O. B. Moundsville, regular charge for packages.

FOSTORIA GLASS COMPANY

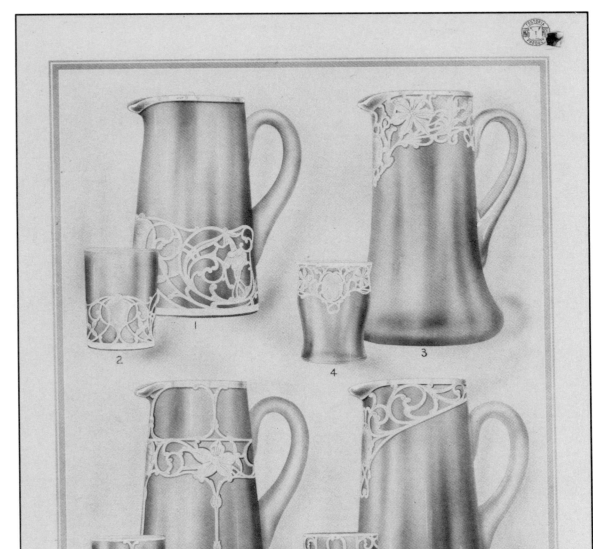

SILVER DEPOSIT WARE $\frac{999}{1000}$ FINE

Item 1 No. 3006—351, Jug, Capacity 54 oz. $9.50
" 2 No. 3820—351, Tumbler, 10 oz. 2.25
" 3 No. 3724—311, Jug, Capacity 2 quarts, Solid
                Silver Handle 8.50
· 4 No. 3858—311, Tumbler, 10 oz. 2.50

Item 5 No. 3006—350, Jug, Capacity 54 oz. $8.50
" 6 No. 3820—350, Tumbler, 10 oz. 2.00
" 7 No. 3007—314, Jug, Capacity 65 oz. 6.50
" 8 No. 3820—314, Tumbler, 10 oz. 1.60

One-third Size

6

SILVER DEPOSIT WARE $\frac{989}{1000}$ FINE

Item 9 No. 3007—332, Jug, Capacity 65 oz. . . . $ 4.00
" 10 No. 3820—332, Tumbler, 10 oz. 1.30
" 11 No. 3111—311, Optic Jug, Capacity 64 oz. 8.50
" 12 No. 3820—311, Optic Tumbler, 10 oz. . . . 2.35

Item 13 No. 3005—344, Claret Jug, Capacity 48 oz. . $18.00
" 14 No. 3889—344, 6 oz. Tumbler 4.00
" 15 No. 3005—317, Claret Jug, Capacity 48 oz.
Solid Silver Handle 18.00

One-third Size

7

SILVER DEPOSIT WARE $\frac{999}{1000}$ FINE

Item 16 No. 3787—313, Jug, Capacity 44 oz. . . . $ 6.50
" 17 No. 3056—348, Jug, Cut Star Bottom,
         Capacity 54 oz. 10.00
" 18 No. 3452—350, Jug Decanter, Capacity 33 oz. 11.00

Item 19 No. 3600—350, 2¼ oz. Tumbler . . . . . $ 1.20
" 20 No. 3452—312, Jug Decanter, Capacity 33 oz. 13.50
" 21 No. 3600—312, 2¼ oz. Tumbler 2.00

One-third Size

8

SILVER DEPOSIT WARE $\frac{999}{1000}$ FINE

Item 22 No. 3300—313, Quart Decanter $15.00	Item 26 No. 3300—352, Quart Decanter $15.00
" 23 No. 3600—313, 2¼ oz. Tumbler 1.10	" 27 No. 3793—352, H. S. Champagne 5.00
" 24 No. 3464—313, 18 oz. Decanter 10.00	" 28 No. 3600—352, 2¼ oz. Tumbler 2.25
" 25 No. 3300—313, Pint Decanter 11.00	

One-third Size

SILVER DEPOSIT WARE $\frac{999}{1000}$ FINE

Item 29	No. 3712—350, Sugar $1 00	Item 34	No. 3478—351, Cream $2.00
" 30	No. 3712—350, Cream 1.00	" 35	No. 3478—319, Sugar 2.00
" 31	No. 3712—332, Sugar 1.00	" 36	No. 3478—319, Cream 2.00
" 32	No. 3712—332, Cream 1.00	" 37	No. 3159—337, Sugar 3.00
" 33	No. 3478—351, Sugar 2.00	" 38	No. 3159—337, Cream 3.00

One-third Size

10

SILVER DEPOSIT WARE $\frac{993}{1000}$ FINE

Item 39 {	No. 3049 — 350, Cheese	$1.00
	No. 3737 — 350, Cracker Plate	1.70
" 40 {	No. 3049 — 332, Cheese	.87½
	No. 3737 — 332, Cracker Plate	.87½
" 41	No. 3842 — 332, Sherbet	1.20
" 42	No. 3842 — 350, Sherbet	1.50
" 43	No. 3842 — 310, Sherbet	3.00
" 44	No. 3863 — 332, Ind. Nut	.85

Item 45	No. 3863 — 351, Ind. Nut	$1.00
" 46	No. 3863 — 332, Fruit	1.50
" 47	No. 3863 — 350, Fruit	2.00
" 48 {	No. 3840 — 332, Sherbet	1.00
	No. 3840 — 332, Plate	1.20
" 49 {	No. 3840 — 350, Sherbet	1.50
	No. 3840 — 350, Plate, Cut Star Bottom . . .	2.00

One-third Size

11

SILVER DEPOSIT WARE $\frac{999}{1000}$ FINE

Item 153   No. 3056—404, Jug, Cut Star Bottom, Capacity 54 oz. $9.00
"   154   No. 3820—404, Tumbler, 10 oz. 1.75
"   155   No. 3005—393, Claret Jug, Capacity 48 oz.   6.00
"   156   No. 3889—393, Tumbler, 6 oz. 1.50

Item 157   No. 3005—406 Claret Jug, Capacity 48 oz. $6.00
"   158   No. 3889—406 Tumbler, 6 oz. 1.30
"   159   No. 3007—392 Jug, Capacity 65 oz. 5.00
"   160   No. 3820—392 Tumbler, 10 oz. 1.50

One-third Size

B

215

SILVER DEPOSIT WARE $\frac{999}{1000}$ FINE

Item 161   No. 3904—420, Bon Bon, Cut Star Bottom $12.00
  "   162   No. 3000—407, 8 inch Placque 8.50
            Also furnished in 6 in. size, $6.00; 7 in., 7.50
  "   163   No. 3718—408, 6 in. Ice Tub, Cut Star Bottom 9.50

Item 164   No. 3719—407, Sandwich Plate, 10½ in., Cut
                    Star Bottom $18.00
  "   165   No. 3796—410, Vase, 8½ in. 15.00
  "   184   No. 3478—419, Lavender Salt 7.50

-One-third Size

C

216

SILVER DEPOSIT WARE $^{999}_{1000}$ FINE

Item 166 No. 3478—399, Cream, Cut Star Bottom . . $3.50
  " 167 No. 3478—399, Sugar, Cut Star Bottom   3.50
  " 168 No. 3006—398, Jug, Cut Star Bottom, Capac-
            ity 54 oz.   9.00
  " 169 No. 3820—398, Tumbler, 10 oz., Cut Star   2.00
  " 170 No. 3465—398, Oil, 8 oz. Cut Star Bottom   5.50

Item 171 No. 3478—398, Cream, Cut Star Bottom . . $2.75
  " 172 No. 3478—398, Sugar, Cut Star Bottom   2.75
  " 173 No. 3719—398, Sandwich Plate, 10½ inch,
            Cut Star Bottom   9.00
  " 174 No. 3733—398, Marmalade and Cover, Cut
            Star Bottom 5.50

One-third Size

D

217

SILVER DEPOSIT WARE $\frac{999}{1000}$ FINE

Item 175   No. 3465—399, Oil, 8 oz., Cut Star Bottom $7.50
"   176   No. 3227—399, 4½ in. Nappy, Cut Star Bot.   4.50
"   177   No. 3227—399, 8 in. Nappy, Cut Star Bot.   15.00
"   178   No. 3006—399, Jug, Cut Star Bottom, Capacity 54 oz.   12.00
"   179   No. 3820—399, Tumbler, 10 oz., Cut Star Bot.   3.00

Item 180   No. 3733—399, Marmalade and Cover, Cut Star Bottom $7.50
"   181   No. 3719—399, Sandwich Plate, 10½ in., Cut Star Bottom   12.00
"   182   No. 3000—399, 7 in. Placque   7.00
"   183   No. 3281—399, 5 in. Lemon Dish, Cut Star and Engraved 4.50

One-third Size

E

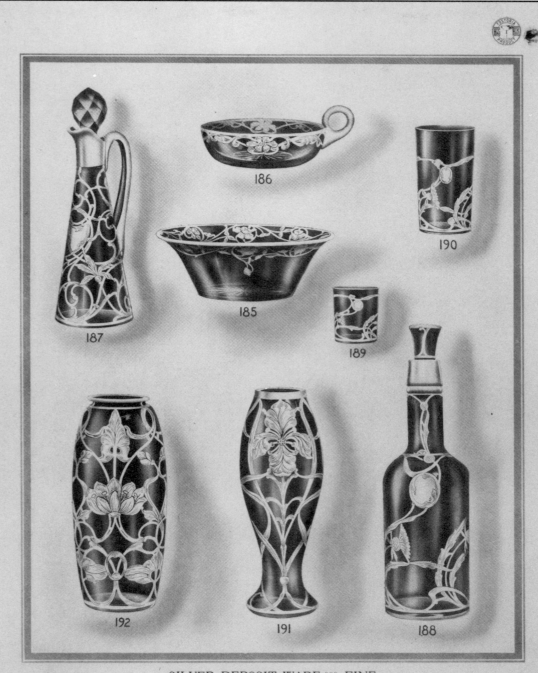

SILVER DEPOSIT WARE 999⁄1000 FINE

Item 185	No. 3848—411, 7 in. Deep Fruit, Cut Star Bot.	$6.50	Item 189	No. 3701—402, Whiskey, 2¼ oz.	$1.20
" 186	No. 3255—409, 5 in. Hld. Nappy, Cut Star Bot.	4.00	" 190	No. 3701—402, Highball, 8 oz.	2.00
" 187	No. 3894—418, 8 oz. Oil	6.50	" 191	No. 3797—417, Vase, 8½ in	8.00
" 188	No. 3319—402, Bar Bottle	6.75	" 192	No. 3895—416, Vase, 8 in.	12.50

One-third Size

F

SILVER DEPOSIT WARE 999/1000 FINE

Item 193	No. 3803—393, Tall Compote	$3.00	Item 198	No. 3432½—412, Ind. Salt	$0.25
" 194	No. 3840—370, Sherbet	1.25	" 199	No. 3666—394, Puff Box and Cover	3.50
	No. 3840—370, Sherbet Plate	1.25	" 200	No. 3725—396, 5 in. Vase	1.70
" 195	No. 3802—393, Low Deep Compote	2.50	" 201	No. 3300—403, Quart Decanter	8.50
" 196	No. 3314—413, Shaker, Sterling Silver and Pearl Top	75	" 202	No. 3600—403, Whiskey, 2¼ oz.	1.50
" 197	No. 3437—414, Shaker, Cut, Sterling Silver and Pearl Top	1.00	" 203	No. 3000—395, 7 in. Placque	4.00
				Also furnished in 8 in. size	5.00

One-third Size

G

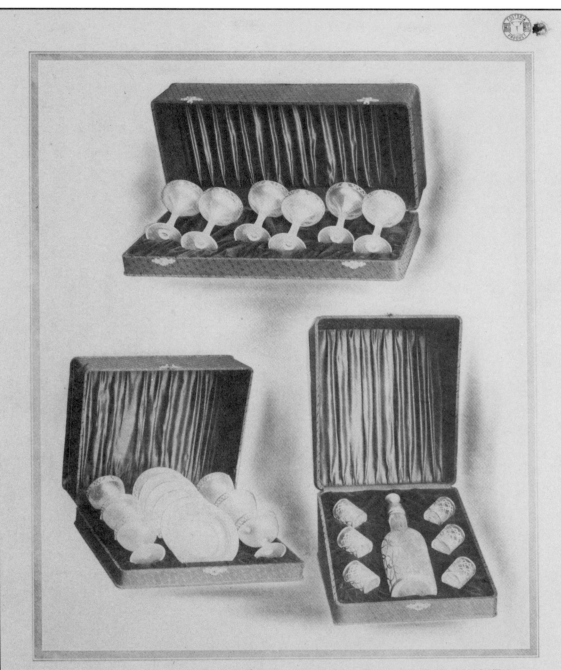

PLUSH CASES — GREEN TRIMMED, GREEN LINED — FINEST QUALITY.

Case No. 101, showing six 3840 Sherbets $4.75
Case No. 102, showing one 3478 Sugar and One Cream 3.25
Case No. 103, showing one 3319 Bottle and 6 Whiskeys 6.50
Case No. 104, showing six 3840 Sherbets and 6 Plates 6.00
Case No. 105, showing twelve 3840 Sherbets and 12 Plates 12.00
Case No. 106, showing six 3793 H. S. Champagne 6.50
Case No. 107, showing one Lemon Dish 1.75

Case No. 108, showing six 3107, Coaster $2.50
Case No. 109, showing six 3863 Fruit 5.00
Case No. 110, showing six Cheese and 6 Plates 6.00
Case No. 111, showing six 3863 Ind. Nut 2.50
Case No. 115, showing one Jug, six Tumblers 8.50
Case No. 116, showing one Bar Bottle, six Highballs and
   six Whiskies 13.00

NOTE — Be careful to order by case number. Above prices refer to *cases only.*

11

221

SILVER DEPOSIT WARE $\frac{999}{1000}$ FINE

Item 59 No. 3863—313, 2 oz. Sherry $1.70	Item 65 No. 3802 —332, Low Deep Compote . . . $3.00
" 60 No. 3009—332, 4 oz. Wine 70	" 66 No. 3802 —351, Low Deep Compote . . . 4.00
" 61 No. 3701—332, 2 oz. Liquor 65	" 67 No. 3718 —332, Nut Bowl, Cut Star Bottom 2.75
" 62 No. 3981—332, Toothpick 60	" 68 No. 3863 —313, 1 oz. Cordial 1.20
" 63 No. 3922—350, Toothpick, Cut Flute 1.00	" 69 No. 3107 —000, Coaster, Cut Star Bottom . .75
" 64 No. 3802—310, Low Deep Compote 6.00	" 70 No. 3693½—332, Coaster 1.40

One-third Size

13

SILVER DEPOSIT WARE $\frac{999}{1000}$ FINE

Item 71	No. 3697	312, Carafe	$ 9.00		Item 75	No. 3701	342, 8 oz. Highball	$ 3.50
	No. 3423	312, Tumbler	3.00		" 76	No. 3701	342, 2¼ oz. Whiskey	1.25
" 72	No. 3806	354, Water Bottle, Special Cut Neck	20.00		" 77	No. 3322	343, Liquor Bottle	12.00
" 73	No. 3558	350, Water Bottle, Cut Neck	12.00		" 78	No. 3858	343, 8 oz. Highball	4.00
" 74	No. 3319	342, Liquor Bottle Cut Neck	10.00		" 79	No. 3858	343, 3½ oz. Whiskey	1.75

One-third Size

14

80½

85

80

83

84

82

81

SILVER DEPOSIT WARE $\frac{999}{1000}$ FINE

Item 80 No. 3744–332, Whipped Biscuit, Cut Star
Bottom, Height 9 inches . . $4.75
" 80½ Whipped Biscuit, Side View
" 81 No. 3719–332, Sandwich Plate, 10½ inch,
Cut Star Bottom 4.75

Item 82 No 3719–333, Sandwich Plate 10½ inch, Cut
Star Bottom $8.50
" 83 No. 3218–320, Candle, 8 inch 5.00
" 84 No. 3218–345, Candle, 8 inch 6.00
" 85 No. 3485–321. Candle, 8 inch 6.00

About one-third Size

15

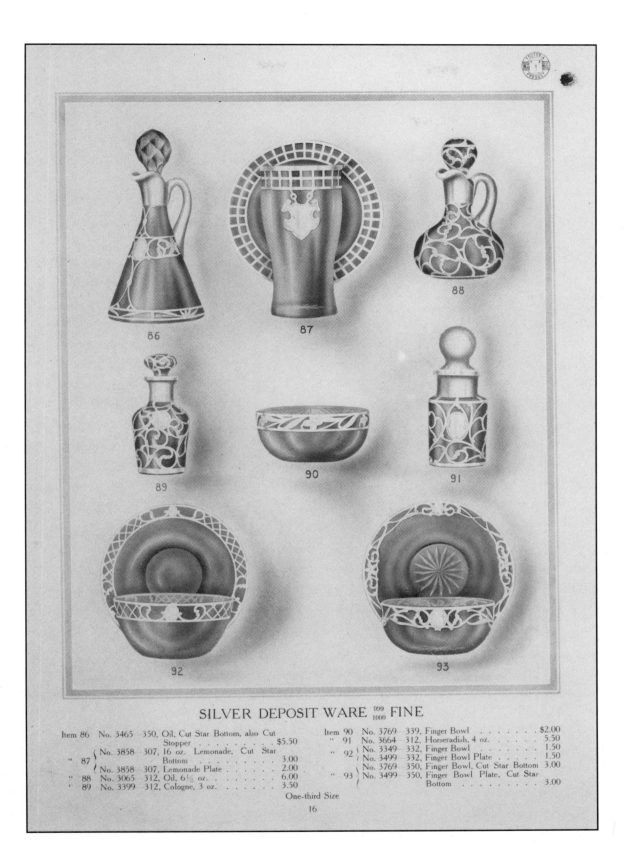

SILVER DEPOSIT WARE $\frac{999}{1000}$ FINE

Item 86	No. 3465 350, Oil, Cut Star Bottom, also Cut	
	Stopper	$5.50
" 87 {	No. 3858 307, 16 oz. Lemonade, Cut Star	
	Bottom	3.00
	No. 3858 307, Lemonade Plate	2.00
" 88	No. 3065 312, Oil, 6½ oz.	6.00
" 89	No. 3399 312, Cologne, 3 oz.	3.50

Item 90	No. 3769 339, Finger Bowl	$2.00
" 91	No. 3664 312, Horseradish, 4 oz.	5.50
" 92 {	No. 3349 332, Finger Bowl	1.50
	No. 3499 332, Finger Bowl Plate	1.50
" 93 {	No. 3769 350, Finger Bowl, Cut Star Bottom	3.00
	No. 3499 350, Finger Bowl Plate, Cut Star	
	Bottom	3.00

One-third Size

16

SILVER DEPOSIT WARE $\frac{999}{1000}$ FINE

Item 94 No. 3733—350, Marmalade and Cover, Cut
    Star Bottom . . . . $ 6.00
 " 95 No. 3733—331 Marmalade and Cover . . . 7.00
 " 96 No. 3666—347 Puff Box and Cover 6.00
 " 97 No. 3718—323 6 inch Ice Tub, Cut Star
    Bottom 10.00
 " 98 No. 3227—353, 4½ inch Nappy, Cut Star
    Bottom 3.00

Item 99 No. 3227—353, 8 inch Nappy, Cut Star
    Bottom . . . . $ 8.50
 " 100 No. 3711—346, Cigar Jar and Cover, Cut
    Star Bottom 15.00
 " 101 No. 3686—355, Cheese and Cover, Cut Star
    Bottom 12.00

One-third Size
17

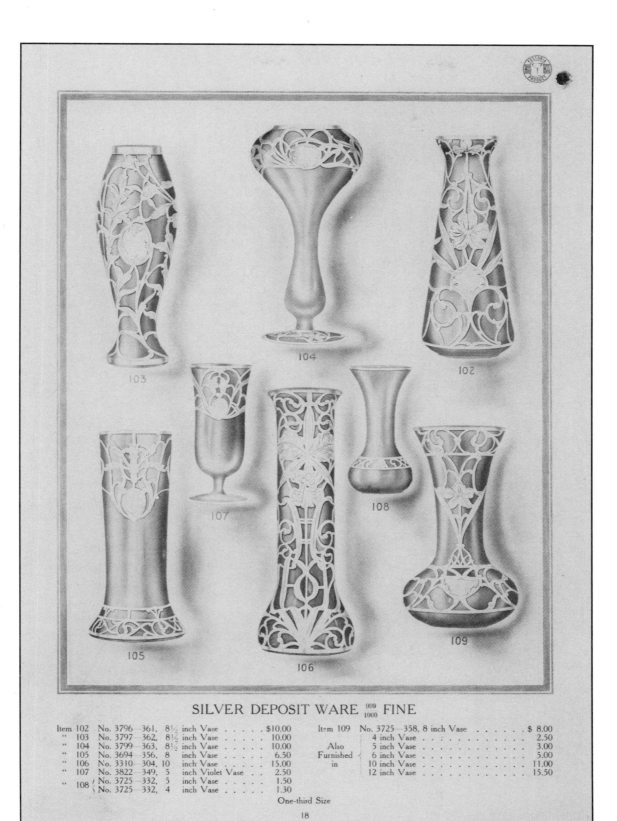

SILVER DEPOSIT WARE $\frac{999}{1000}$ FINE

Item 102	No. 3796—361,	8½ inch Vase	. . . . .	$10.00
" 103	No. 3797—362,	8½ inch Vase	. . . . .	10.00
" 104	No. 3799—363,	8½ inch Vase	. . . .	10.00
" 105	No. 3694—356,	8 inch Vase	. . . .	6.50
" 106	No. 3310—304, 10	inch Vase	. . . .	15.00
" 107	No. 3822—349,	5 inch Violet Vase	. . .	2.50
" 108	{ No. 3725—332,	5 inch Vase	. . . . .	1.50
	{ No. 3725—332,	4 inch Vase	. . . . .	1.30

Item 109	No. 3725—358, 8 inch Vase	. . . . . .	$ 8.00
	4 inch Vase	. . . .	2.50
Also	5 inch Vase	. . . .	3.00
Furnished	6 inch Vase	. . . .	5.00
in	10 inch Vase	. . . .	11.00
	12 inch Vase	. . . .	15.50

One-third Size

18

SILVER DEPOSIT WARE $\frac{999}{1000}$ FINE

Item 130 No. 3483—369, 2 oz. One Drink Decanter . $2.00
" 131 No. 3848—378, 7 in. Fruit Bowl 5.50
" 132 No. 3485—371, 8 in. Candle 3.00

Item 133 No. 3275—373, 10 in. Vase, Triangle Shape, $14.50
" 134 No. 3858—366, 10 oz. Tumbler 6.00
" 135 No. 3316—366, Jug (capacity 64 oz.) . . . 25.00

About one-third size

21

SILVER DEPOSIT WARE $\frac{999}{1000}$ FINE

Item 136   No. 3848—378, 8½ in. Flared Fruit $6.50
"   137   No. 3848—378, 8 in.   Bon Bon 6.50
"   138   No. 3848—378, 9 in.| Sandwich Plate . . . 6.50

Item 139   9 in. Plate same as Item 138 . . . . $ 6.50
Also No. 3051—378, Flower Dish 4.00
Complete Set 10.50

About one-third size

22

BIBLIOGRAPHY AND SUGGESTED READING

Fostoria Its First Fifty Years, written by Hazel Marie Weatherman and published in 1972, introduced Fostoria Glass as a collectible to today's glass students. It remains the most complete assemblage of information covering that period in Fostoria production. Mrs. Weatherman has added color and date information to the pictorial coverage of these important early lines. Her subsequent price guides add even more information, including important data on late stems.

Fostoria The Popular Years, first published in 1982 by Patrick McGrain and subsequently copyrighted by Park Avenue Publications is in its second printing and highlights production during the 1940s – 1960s. With emphasis on Fostoria's late production, it adds to the body of information which collectors find important. Up-to-date price guides have been issued. Both the book and the price guides have been available from Park Avenue Publications Ltd., Box 838, Racine, WI 53404.

Fostoria #2056 American Pattern, written in 1986 and revised in 1989 by William S. Litman, pictures and identifies all of the American pattern items known by the author. Items are numbered and measured. Dates of production are given as they could be only by one so closely connected to Fostoria's production as was the late Mr. Litman. This work is an invaluable aid to many American collectors. The Fostoria Glass Society has issued a price guide to accompany the book and they both may be ordered from the Society at P.O. Box 826, Moundsville, WV 2604.

Colony by Fostoria, written by William and Lila Litman in 1990, gives the same detailed information on the Colony line that was given in the American Book. Complete and detailed, the Colony book may also be obtained from the Fostoria Glass Society.

Coin Glass Hand Crafted by Fostoria 1958 – 1982, written by Ronald and Sunny Stinson in 1988 and copyrighted by the Fostoria Glass Society of North Texas, pictures and presents anecdotal information about the popular Coin Line made over the 24 years of Fostoria production. With so many Coin collectors, this book has an important place in Fostoria publications. It may be ordered from Ronald Stinson, 16 West Avenue C, San Angelo, TX 76903.

Facets of Fostoria, the publication mailed to members of the Fostoria Glass Society of America, has been information for collectors. In 1990 an index of *Facets* articles was compiled by Gary Schneider. Published by the Fostoria Glass Society of Southern California, this index brings order and sequence to the detailed information covered in articles and excerpts over a ten year span of publication.

Henry J. Liebmann is writing twelve accounts covering different aspects of Fostoria Glass Company production. These specialized works are informative, well documented and illustrated. They offer important data, much of which has not before been available to collectors. An up to date listing of these publications and ordering information is available from the author at 758 Colony Circle, Pittsburgh, PA 15241.

Books on Antiques and Collectibles

This is only a partial listing of the books on antiques that are available from Collector Books. All books are well illustrated and contain current values. Most of the following books are available from your local book seller, antique dealer, or public library. If you are unable to locate certain titles in your area, you may order by mail from COLLECTOR BOOKS, P.O. Box 3009, Paducah, KY 42002-3009. Customers with Visa or MasterCard may phone in orders from 8:00 – 4:00 CST, M – F – Toll Free 1-800-626-5420. Add $2.00 for postage for the first book ordered and $0.30 for each additional book. Include item number, title, and price when ordering. Allow 14 to 21 days for delivery.

BOOKS ON GLASS AND POTTERY

1810	American Art Glass, Shuman	$29.95
2016	Bedroom & Bathroom Glassware of the Depression Years	$19.95
1312	Blue & White Stoneware, McNerney	$9.95
1959	Blue Willow, 2nd Ed., Gaston	$14.95
3719	Coll. Glassware from the 40's, 50's, 60's, 2nd Ed., Florence	$19.95
3311	Collecting Yellow Ware – Id. & Value Gd., McAllister	$16.95
2352	Collector's Ency. of Akro Agate Glassware, Florence	$14.95
1373	Collector's Ency. of American Dinnerware, Cunningham	$24.95
2272	Collector's Ency. of California Pottery, Chipman	$24.95
3312	Collector's Ency. of Children's Dishes, Whitmyer	$19.95
2133	Collector's Ency. of Cookie Jars, Roerig	$24.95
3724	Collector's Ency. of Depression Glass, 11th Ed., Florence	$19.95
2209	Collector's Ency. of Fiesta, 7th Ed., Huxford	$19.95
1439	Collector's Ency. of Flow Blue China, Gaston	$19.95
1915	Collector's Ency. of Hall China, 2nd Ed., Whitmyer	$19.95
2334	Collector's Ency. of Majolica Pottery, Katz-Marks	$19.95
1358	Collector's Ency. of McCoy Pottery, Huxford	$19.95
3313	Collector's Ency. of Niloak, Gifford	$19.95
1039	Collector's Ency. of Nippon Porcelain I, Van Patten	$24.95
2089	Collector's Ency. of Nippon Porcelain II, Van Patten	$24.95
1665	Collector's Ency. of Nippon Porcelain III, Van Patten	$24.95
1447	Collector's Ency. of Noritake, 1st Series, Van Patten	$19.95
1034	Collector's Ency. of Roseville Pottery, Huxford	$19.95
1035	Collector's Ency. of Roseville Pottery, 2nd Ed., Huxford	$19.95
3314	Collector's Ency. of Van Briggle Art Pottery, Sasicki	$24.95
3433	Collector's Guide To Harker Pottery - U.S.A., Colbert	$17.95
2339	Collector's Guide to Shawnee Pottery, Vanderbilt	$19.95
1425	Cookie Jars, Westfall	$9.95
3440	Cookie Jars, Book II, Westfall	$19.95
2275	Czechoslovakian Glass & Collectibles, Barta	$16.95
3315	Elegant Glassware of the Depression Era, 5th Ed., Florence	$19.95
3318	Glass Animals of the Depression Era, Garmon & Spencer	$19.95
2024	Kitchen Glassware of the Depression Years, 4th Ed., Florence	$19.95
3322	Pocket Guide to Depression Glass, 8th Ed., Florence	$9.95
1670	Red Wing Collectibles, DePasquale	$9.95
1440	Red Wing Stoneware, DePasquale	$9.95
1958	So. Potteries Blue Ridge Dinnerware, 3rd Ed., Newbound	$14.95
3739	Standard Carnival Glass, 4th Ed., Edwards	$24.95
1848	Very Rare Glassware of the Depression Years, Florence	$24.95
2140	Very Rare Glassware of the Depression Years, Second Series	$24.95
3326	Very Rare Glassware of the Depression Years, Third Series	$24.95
3327	Watt Pottery – Identification & Value Guide, Morris	$19.95
2224	World of Salt Shakers, 2nd Ed., Lechner	$24.95

BOOKS ON DOLLS & TOYS

2079	Barbie Fashion, Vol. 1, 1959-1967, Eames	$24.95
3310	Black Dolls – 1820 - 1991 – Id. & Value Guide, Perkins	$17.95
1514	Character Toys & Collectibles, 1st Series, Longest	$19.95
1750	Character Toys & Collectibles, 2nd Series, Longest	$19.95
1529	Collector's Ency. of Barbie Dolls, DeWein	$19.95
2338	Collector's Ency. of Disneyana, Longest & Stern	$24.95
3441	Madame Alexander Price Guide #18, Smith	$9.95
1540	Modern Toys, 1930 - 1980, Baker	$19.95
3442	Patricia Smith's Doll Values – Antique to Modern, 9th ed	$12.95
1886	Stern's Guide to Disney	$14.95

2139	Stern's Guide to Disney, 2nd Series	$14.95
1513	Teddy Bears & Steiff Animals, Mandel	$9.95
1817	Teddy Bears & Steiff Animals, 2nd Series, Mandel	$19.95
2084	Teddy Bears, Annalees & Steiff Animals, 3rd Series, Mandel	$19.95
2028	Toys, Antique & Collectible, Longest	$14.95
1808	Wonder of Barbie, Manos	$9.95
1430	World of Barbie Dolls, Manos	$9.95

OTHER COLLECTIBLES

1457	American Oak Furniture, McNerney	$9.95
2269	Antique Brass & Copper, Gaston	$16.95
2333	Antique & Collectible Marbles, 3rd Ed., Grist	$9.95
1712	Antique & Collectible Thimbles, Mathis	$19.95
1748	Antique Purses, Holiner	$19.95
1868	Antique Tools, Our American Heritage, McNerney	$9.95
1426	Arrowheads & Projectile Points, Hothem	$7.95
1278	Art Nouveau & Art Deco Jewelry, Baker	$9.95
1714	Black Collectibles, Gibbs	$19.95
1128	Bottle Pricing Guide, 3rd Ed., Cleveland	$7.95
1752	Christmas Ornaments, Johnston	$19.95
2132	Collector's Ency. of American Furniture, Vol. I, Swedberg	$24.95
2271	Collector's Ency. of American Furniture, Vol. II, Swedberg	$24.95
2018	Collector's Ency. of Granite Ware, Greguire	$24.95
3430	Coll. Ency. of Granite Ware, Book 2, Greguire	$24.95
2083	Collector's Ency. of Russel Wright Designs, Kerr	$19.95
2337	Collector's Guide to Decoys, Book II, Huxford	$16.95
2340	Collector's Guide to Easter Collectibles, Burnett	$16.95
1441	Collector's Guide to Post Cards, Wood	$9.95
2276	Decoys, Kangas	$24.95
1629	Doorstops – Id. & Values, Bertoia	$9.95
1716	Fifty Years of Fashion Jewelry, Baker	$19.95
3316	Flea Market Trader, 8th Ed., Huxford	$9.95
3317	Florence's Standard Baseball Card Price Gd., 5th Ed.	$9.95
1755	Furniture of the Depression Era, Swedberg	$19.95
3436	Grist's Big Book of Marbles, Everett Grist	$19.95
2278	Grist's Machine Made & Contemporary Marbles	$9.95
1424	Hatpins & Hatpin Holders, Baker	$9.95
3319	Huxford's Collectible Advertising – Id. & Value Gd.	$17.95
3439	Huxford's Old Book Value Guide, 5th Ed.	$19.95
1181	100 Years of Collectible Jewelry, Baker	$9.95
2023	Keen Kutter Collectibles, 2nd Ed., Heuring	$14.95
2216	Kitchen Antiques – 1790 - 1940, McNerney	$14.95
3320	Modern Guns – Id. & Val. Gd., 9th Ed., Quertermous	$12.95
1965	Pine Furniture, Our American Heritage, McNerney	$14.95
3321	Ornamental & Figural Nutcrackers, Rittenhouse	$16.95
2026	Railroad Collectibles, 4th Ed., Baker	$14.95
1632	Salt & Pepper Shakers, Guarnaccia	$9.95
1888	Salt & Pepper Shakers II, Guarnaccia	$14.95
2220	Salt & Pepper Shakers III, Guarnaccia	$14.95
3443	Salt & Pepper Shakers IV, Guarnaccia	$18.95
3737	Schroeder's Antiques Price Guide, 12th Ed.	$12.95
2096	Silverplated Flatware, 4th Ed., Hagan	$14.95
3325	Standard Knife Collector's Guide, 2nd Ed., Stewart	$12.95
2348	20th Century Fashionable Plastic Jewelry, Baker	$19.95
3444	Wanted To Buy, 4th Ed.	$9.95

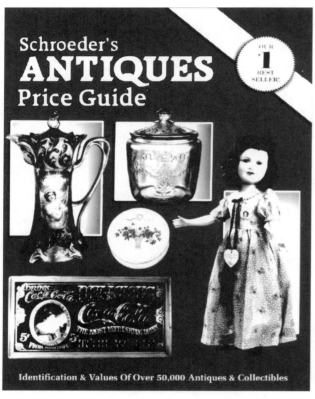